REPUBLIC
IN
CRISIS

REPUBLIC IN CRISIS

Congress Against the Executive Force

by ALFRED de GRAZIA

Professor of Social Theory in Government
New York University

Federal Legal Publications, Inc.

For information, address:

Federal Legal Publications, Inc.
95 Morton Street
New York, N. Y. 10014

DESIGNED BY BERNARD SCHLEIFER

Printed in the United States of America

Library of Congress Catalog Card No. 65-28094

353.0372
D321

*The assistance of the American Enterprise Insti-
tute for Public Policy Research and New York
University in providing leave and facilities to work
on this study in 1963 is gratefully acknowledged.*

Mais si, sans se laisser charmer,
Ton oeil sait plonger dans les gouffres,
Lis-moi, pour apprendre a m'aimer.

But if, escaping the surface lure,
Your eye can plumb to the depths,
Then read and learn to love me sure.

BAUDELAIRE
Epigraph for a Condemned Book

FOREWORD

FREEDOM AND ORDER are famous, if abstract, antagonists of history. No philosopher has yet settled what proportions of them would perfect the person and fashion a perfect society. So individuals and collectivities struggle along with now too much of one and with now again an excess of the other.

Who can say that America has been preserved from the conflict? Here the problem is, if anything, worse than elsewhere. More than most people, Americans are determined to achieve both discipline and liberty. The conflict is quite apparent in the institutions of government, and especially in the relations between the congressional and executive branches.

Our thesis is that the executive of the national government represents and leads the national movement towards a society of order. Congress, by contrast, expresses the national urge to liberty. The Executive Force is winning and a new American society is in the making. The congressional or Republican Force, in its present and historical form, is weakening.

Only a theoretical reconstruction of the nature of the executive and the legislature in the contemporary world can open the mind to the disadvantages of the situation. Only a reorganization of the legislative way of life can promote a representative government fitted to the society of the future. Public debate and extensive research are needed, if reforms are to occur. We try here, therefore, to reopen the rusty gates leading to the classical arena of democratic theory.

ALFRED DE GRAZIA

Washington Square, New York
June, 1965

CONTENTS

CONTENTS

REPUBLIC
IN
CRISIS

Chapter One

THE CONGRESSIONAL SYSTEM

> *Speech has helped us attain practically all of the things we have devised. For it is speech that has made laws about justice and injustice and honor and disgrace, without which provisions we should not be able to live together. . . . By speech we educate the ignorant and inform the wise. . . . With speech we contest our disputes and investigate the unknown.*
>
> Isocrates in *Nicocles*
> (372 B.C.)

THE WORLD'S GREATEST assembly is a busy place. What it *creates* is the *final* question, but the sheer business of Congress is at least statistically impressive. Four hundred and thirty-five men and women sit in the House of Representatives and one hundred in the Senate. The Senate of the 88th Congress was in session for 2,395 hours and 8 minutes on 375 days between January of 1963 and October, 1964. It passed 1,691 measures, an average of one every 1.4 session-hour. The House met on 334 days, for half the hours, and passed even more measures. In all, 866 public laws and 360 private laws were passed.

The measures passed by the Senate included 542 that were Senate bills and 725 that had originated in the House. There were 31 joint resolutions of the Senate, and 43 of the House. Thirty-nine Senate and 54 House concurrent resolutions were passed. The Senate governed itself and expressed itself alone in 257 simple resolutions. A similar

1

record would describe the House's work. Nine bills were vetoed by the President. The Senate confirmed 122,201 appointments to federal government posts.

Major legislation occurred in many areas of life. The mind has to hop like a rabbit to think of all the interests involved.

The new laws included the Civil Rights Act of 1964, a major tax cut, a program to attack poverty, a federal pay bill, a foreign aid bill, an authorization for a new $375 million mass transit development program, a permanent food stamp program, new assistance to cotton and wheat producing groups, and an interest equalization tax to help solve the U.S. balance of payments problem in foreign trade. Congress also voted construction funds to colleges, and a major extension and expansion of the National Defense Education Act. It provided for land and wilderness conservation and passed a bill to provide legal aid to the poor. Many expiring laws, including the Hill-Burton hospital aid legislation, were broadened and extended. A treaty to ban nuclear tests was approved.

Behind the completed framework of bills passed, stood the 19,236 measures that were introduced, each representing at least an iota of energy and some of them a great deal of individual effort. But the congressmen's work did not begin or end with introducing and passing bills. They and their staffs had over a million individual contacts with the government on the individual concerns of their constituents, an average of two thousand per congressman a year. (The total obviously begins to affect some considerable part of the population of the country.) Some 46,000,000 pieces of mail came into the House post office in one two-year period, 1961 and 1962. Senate mail is also heavy.

During 1963 alone the congressmen added 32,000 pages of speeches and papers to the *Congressional Record*. They held hundreds of committee and subcommittee meetings. Half of them travelled altogether half a million miles around the world learning about international conditions, and all travelled incessantly in the United States, mending their political fences in their districts and states, giving speeches, inspecting facilities and attending conferences.

They read a great deal. The committees provided them with 3,841 recommendations and reports on legislation in 1963 and 1964. Government documents of many types pressed for their attention. They usually had to read several newspapers a day. They dipped into the vast periodical literature, and some even read books regularly.

They rarely suffer from loneliness; hundreds of constituents will stop by in the course of the year at their Washington office, while, when home, life is an unending round of visiting at their office and everywhere else in the district. Congressmen generally seek the company of their colleagues too, for from them they get thousands of helpful cues on how to act in the constantly varying legislative situations. They have to make up their minds how to vote on scores of roll calls, hundreds of voice votes, and the many occasions when unanimous consent is asked to approve some matter.

Commonly nearly a hundred Representatives will be in their first term and a dozen Senators in their first two years of office, at any given time. So the tensions of entering a new job and anticipating yet another new job prey upon the minds of many. The pay and emoluments of the congressman do not permit financial ease, and vocational concerns occupy some time and energy of a large part of the membership. The eighty-hour week is not uncommon, a sixty-hour week average. For all of his busyness, the congressman is not afforded a social shelter. He has neither the protective cordon of the President nor the anonymity of the official. He is open to personal abuse and ridicule. By comparison with the average middle-level business executive, he is harder-working, worse-paid, and less secure in his job. The conditions of work are less fancy. Good staff is harder to find. The product is uncertain.

There is where the legislative process boggles—at the uncertainty of the product. Who is to say whether these thousand laws of a session and the million favors done and the interminable haranguing of colleagues and constituents add up to the best way of governing the most burgeoning land in the world? History gives cold comfort. At best its advice is ambiguous. Faith is a better guide, and a courage that can march against bad omens.

THE UNCERTAIN DECISION OF HISTORY

> *Surely the race is not to the swift,*
> *nor the battle to the strong,*
> *neither yet bread to the wise,*
> *nor yet riches to men of understanding,*
> *nor yet favour to men of skill,*
> *but time and chance happenth to them all.*

Some optimism is possible. The half thousand members of the Congress of the United States offer a contradiction to this century of concentrated executive power. They stand amid swirling currents of dictatorship and bureaucratic centralism, yet have not been swept away by them. Even should all of their defenses now dissolve, their collective record would mark emphatically the history of the last two centuries. For only rarely in history has a great power of the world long subsisted in the form of government by assembly. Athens, Florence, Genoa, Switzerland, and other more recent European and Asiatic cases have lacked longevity or great power. Name the Roman Republic, the Venetian Republic, the English parliamentary kingdom, and the French republics since the revolution of 1789, and the roster is probably complete.

If governments by assembly were not so prominent, so interesting in themselves, and so productive of cultural and institutional leadership in the world, one might be tempted to dismiss them as deviations from the natural path of development and dissolution of states. There at one end of the path stand tribalism, feudalism, or localism, and at the other end grand consolidations of empires and centralized bureaucracies. But the several governments by assembly have been so remarkable as to inspire most of the literature of political science, to invite widespread imitation in their times and worlds, and to shake the foundations of scores of absolutely organized nations.

A truth is in their story, a truth that does not offer itself readily to view. The generations that succeed the experience can never be sure of what its potential was. Could the Rome of Cicero forever have escaped Caesarism? A Venetian historian once asked why the Venetian Republic seemed destined to last so much longer than the Roman Republic and attributed the difference to the constructive trade policies of his country. English writers have often ascribed their parliamentarianism to a vaguely defined love of liberty. Comparing the dictators and the parliaments of the French nation since 1789, which is the normal and which the past being shaken off?

The question of the durability of government by assembly has not been answered by history. It has not been answered for America. In the larger sense, it is unanswerable save by the actuality of the long future. But in the present, lessons may be drawn and a logic of legislative rule purveyed. The goal here then is, by analysis of its key institution, Congress, to declare what makes the American republic strong and what makes it weak. It is to say how the republic may prosper, and also how an opposing principle may defeat it. We are far from our goal, however. Just how far will become plain when we pose the seemingly simply query: "What is Congress?"

WHAT IS CONGRESS?

> *A crowd is an inorganic gathering, momentary and occasional, whose only bond is impulse, some common passion. But all legislatures are stable unions, organic bodies, whose members are known and esteemed, in which exists an established hierarchy of competence and influence. The actions of assemblies are almost never determined by gusts of passion, but rather by interests and intellectual currents, both of which have sturdy roots in the country.*
>
> Gaetano Mosca, *Intorno al Parlamentarismo* (1885)

Anyone concerned in the slightest with Congress learns very early in his experience with it that it is grossly simplified in the popular mind and yet it is even then too painfully comprehended to hold a comfortable place in thought and imagination. Who without much trouble can grasp the movements of two assemblies of 435 and 100 persons to the extent of being able to pass judgment upon them, much less attempt some control over them? It would seem from the beginning that the task must be impossible for any citizenry, and that those who devised such a system, far from being wise founders, were hopeless idealists.

If the Congress is to work, it must have an image that will appeal to the popular mind and a reason and explanation that must satisfy and motivate the active and informed person. A respected image there must be because there can be little hope of mass understanding, and yet, the power to destroy or let expire rests with the people; the rationale there must be because an institution cannot flourish without roots into the society and its political class.

A favorable popular image seemed not to be a serious problem in the early days of the republic. Lord Bryce, writing about Congress in 1888, felt that there had been no decline of congressional prestige in seventy years. The serious deterioration of the image began shortly before the turn of the century, for it depended upon a new theory of government. The new theory consisted of ideas of the positive state and of nationalism. Economic and social intervention and ideological integration composed an appealing base for popular affections that might be shifting to the executive establishment and away from the legislature.

The trend, which will be discussed more exactly later on, has continued to the present. The vast majority of Americans neither know nor care about Congress. Ignorance of Congress is especially noticeable among "the new elite," produced by the new technology, rapid mass communications and an impersonalized great society. In ignorance lies a grave weakness of the congressional system of government.

Fortunately for its survival the roots of Congress go out far and very deep. It is the center of a ring of institutions that compose the republic. These are populated by a large number of citizens, a great many of whom depend upon or are interested in Congress. These are the strength of the congressional system. They exist today as they did when the republic was founded, although many of them too are alienated from Congress by a newer philosophy of government. Still, so long as Congress can count on most of them and on the institutions in which they operate for collective support, the United States is apt to remain a republic. Furthermore, each new generation can, when it searches, find new possibilities in the old structures. This too helps to perpetuate the republic.

A republic is a system of government, one of whose main features is the participation of many citizens in the selection of officials. Up to the present moment, the principal workable method of achieving that feature is by free and competitive elections. Moreover, the life of a republic appears to be precarious when the number of elective officials is reduced to one, or even to a directorate of several. A republic is founded upon a system of electing a considerable number of key personnel of the government.

A republic without a legislature is difficult to conceive. Where the legislature is strong, there is never any doubt that the government is republican, or at least a representative government. (The two terms are practically synonymous.) There may be a king but the monarchy is weak and controlled. (An Englishman may insist that his country is a representative government, not a republic; popular usage would agree.) Where the legislature is weak, the existence of a republic is likely to be in grave doubt. The legislature is the main element, whether a king, or a president, or a committee, or a whole public exist alongside.

Whereas the legislature is the keystone of the republic, a number of other elements constitute the total system. Some are within the government—the presidency, courts, and executive establishment. Others are outside the government but directly connected with it—the constituencies, the political parties, the interest groups, and the press. Even many foreign nations and groups may be counted within the republican system, for they have come to have a variety of relations with and expectations from the system. There are moreover fifty states, several territories and many local governments involved in some manner in the operations of Congress.

Even while its external connections are numerous, Congress itself presents a complicated structure. People speak of Congress as a discrete entity, as they would a person or a tree. But like these entities and more so, Congress is only superficially a single homogeneous thing. It is an internal system of relations too. The House and the Senate are obvious. Less obvious are the leadership system and the committees. Least obvious are the hundreds of informal groups that form and unform as the legislative process moves along. The ordinary person is impressed by the anatomical charts used in medical schools with their bone, circulation, nerve and muscle systems in bewildering patterns. A group map of Congress on the inside would be at least as intricate, and quite as confusing.

In the final analysis, Congress is all the ways in which congressmen deal with one another, with the other branches of government, and with political groups. It is all the ways in which they deal with the people of the country. It is part of the nation and the nation is, in part, Congress.

The significance of such a view is that Congress cannot be treated in isolation. What happens to the principal elements of the governmental system happens to Congress. What happens within Congress reflects and affects the whole far-flung range of republican institutions. Of these points, the pages below will convey abundant examples. If one had the means and the evidence, he could show how a Supreme Court decision, for example, distributed its effects not only upon the judicial system, but upon the presidency, Congress, the executive establishment, the public, the parties, the federal system and the social interests of the country.

Each court opinion, of course, would vary in effect with more or less range and intensity. Similarly, a shift in public attitude towards lobbying will ramify its effects through the whole system. Within the Congress, a change in the Senate filibuster procedure would change the relations between the Senate and House, the Senate and courts, the Senate and presidency and indeed every other institution in the republic.

Naturally, under such circumstances, a complete study of the Congress has to include the republican system as a whole, with the effects of each element upon all being taken into account and measured, in all classes of events. In relatively few instances will there be no interacting effect. In a great many cases there will be moderate effects ranging out from the basic action that initially began the chain of causation. In some critical cases and areas, the action has to be watched closely because of their dominating influence on the whole system.

It is not out of exaggeration but from an exact concern for the critical point in the whole system of republican government that the relations of the Congress to the executive force is taken as the theme of this book. As a later chapter (Three) will disclose, the other elements in the republican system are often important in themselves, but are especially important as they lend weight one way or another to the principal points of balance—the legislature and the executive.

Chapter Two

EVALUATION OF CONGRESS

Before I built a wall I'd ask to know
What I was walling in or walling out,
And to whom I was like to give offence.

Robert Frost

By 1965 THE HIGH TIDE of protest that was running against Congress had somewhat receded. Yet perhaps never in the history of the republic have public opinion and its organs been so disgusted with the national legislature. One might, of course, go back to critical periods of congressional history for parallels. Was the mass of common people, which liked Andrew Jackson, as disaffected with the Senate that opposed him? Was the Congress that wrestled with President Lincoln for control of the management of the Civil War detested by the people? Did President Wilson carry the public with him in his struggle with the Senate over the Treaty of Versailles? Did President Roosevelt in his search for a larger Supreme Court successfully incite his large following against his congressional opposition? And was Truman favored over the 80th Congress that he campaigned against as "the worst in history"?

11

The answer is far from certain, but historians give little indication that the press and public were fundamentally alienated from the legislative principle. The recent reports have been more alarming.

IMAGE AND ALIENATION

We speak now always of 'legislatures,' of 'lawmaking' assemblies, and are very impatient of prolonged debates, and sneer at parliamentary bodies which cannot get their 'business' done. We join with laughing zest in Mr. Carlyle's bitter gibe at 'talking shops,' at parliaments which spend their days in endless discussion rather than in diligent prosecution of what they came together to 'do.'

Woodrow Wilson

A poll by the Louis Harris organization in December, 1963, found that 65% of a sample of the American people expressed themselves as disapproving of the record of the 88th Congress that had been in session for a year. As reported in *Newsweek* magazine, "the criticisms of this Congress are essentially rooted in what the people feel to be serious errors of omission—rather than commission. . . . Actually, taken as individual accomplishments, its support of the military defense program and the space program, the Senate ratification of the nuclear test-ban treaty, and the emergency railroad strike legislation all meet with high approval. But constituents think that the record of the session as a whole is simply not adequate." The same article records that "there is little in the way of public response to the time-honored claim that the legislative branch is deliberative, carefully weighs the pros and the cons, and, above all, is the guardian against excessive Executive power."

The public opinion is shared by the press. On May 22, 1963, the *Washington Post* reported that of 115 Washington journalists, 16 thought the President was doing an excellent job, only one that Congress was, whereas 50 believed that Congress was doing a poor job and only 13 that the President was.

The press can be particularly offensive towards Congress. A cheap popularity is to be had here too. Since no one in particular is to be insulted, the general body may be assailed without remorse or fear of reprisal. The severity of the attack will vary of course. On the one extreme, one may place a cartoon by the noted Herblock which depicts several named leaders of Congress in Russian uniforms blocking a road against an American truck driven by the President; this appeared in the *Washington Post* at the time of a Soviet blocking of American road connections with Berlin. (Herblock attracted fame years before for defending various Americans against innuendoes that they might be Russian sympathizers, wittingly and unwittingly.)

The typical editorial attack appears to concentrate upon allegations that Congress delays urgently required action: "Congress is beginning to look like a sit-down strike," write two influential columnists. It is allegedly ruled by Southerners whose only claim to leadership is that they have been members for many years; it is unrepresentative of the nation.

The highest form of journalistic criticism joins in. "The true function of the Congress," writes Walter Lippmann, "is to grant money, to maintain the framework of laws under which we live, to authorize administrative actions under the Constitution, to investigate the conduct of the government, and to hold the Executive accountable. It is not the function of the Congress to administer the government, to go behind the President and the heads of departments and agencies. . . . Yet there is a theory being bandied about that since Congress appropriates the money to run the government, it has the right to run the government."

The indictment follows: Congress "has been derelict in its duty to provide satisfactorily for a vacancy in the Presidency, and this has put the stability and the continuity of the country in jeopardy.

". . . Congress is using a procedure of smothering and strangling, rather than of debating and voting, which violates the basic principles of representative government.

". . . Congress is trespassing upon the constitutional prerogatives of the President in attempting to determine foreign policy by legislative injunctions and prohibitions."

Lippmann represents the bridge between high-brow journalism and the intelligentsia. The intellectual flow across the bridge is in the final analysis the work largely of the professors of the country—particularly many social scientists, humanists outside of the classics, physicists and mathematicians, and professional educators. There is a small core of objective analysis of the congressional and legislative process, most of very recent origin; but the vast bulk of writing and discussion of Congress is on a pseudo-intellectual level which finds easy expression in the magazines of the country. The great current of cocksure popular contempt reinforces the flow of belief from above; for once, the liberal intellectuals are joined readily with the populist mass, and Congress is the victim.

A recent account by Dr. Charles Clapp of the views of many members of the House of Representatives declares that the "legislators are united in believing that the public is poorly informed about Congress. They insist that the views held by the public do not do justice to elected representatives, their job, or the legislative process; ignoring the fact that they and their colleagues lacked proper perspective regarding Congress prior to election, some members severely indict the voters for the misconceptions they possess. Public disparagement of congressmen and lack of appreciation of their tasks and the way they perform them are among the most discouraging and disturbing features of the job. Yet they see no remedy for the situation."

Some congressmen in fact "run against Congress" themselves, regardless of whether or not their party controls Congress. They find they can win popular response and votes by ridiculing the character and performance of the legislature; they thereupon become heroes tilting for honor in the legislative jousts.

Allegations of election profiteering at the expense of the collective image of Congress cannot, of course, be applied to named cases without evidence. Neither Senator Clifford Case of New Jersey nor Senator Clark of Pennsylvania, one a Republican, the other a Democrat, can be accused of wishing to bring the house down upon their heads, though they are two of the most vehement advocates of congressional reform in Congress today. Let us hear several remarks of Senator Case delivered to the National Conference of the American Society for Public Administration on April 4, 1963:

> "Congress has been getting a black eye with the *general public*.
>
> In part, this is because of the misdeeds of a few members. Congress has, perhaps reluctantly, begun to do things about this and some of us would like to see a lot more done about giving the public facts about congressional *travel and expenses*, about *contacts with regulatory and contracting agencies*, about *financial interests* and sources of income and gifts. Putting things on the record is the best way to set the record straight and keep it straight.
>
> In part, the *decline of Congress* results from a growing feeling that it is not adequately responsive to the needs of our nation—and in the minds of some, *is not responsive at all*.

As many of you know, I am a strong proponent of Congressional reform. There are other members of our legislative body who share this concern, but I venture that the *man in Washington who needs Congressional reform most* and should want it most *is President Kennedy.*

He would be something less than human if he did not feel growing frustration as his messages citing urgent needs to the Congress are often met initially with indifference, delay and subsequent discard. As a man who urges that we *get the country moving,* he must feel pangs of despair as Congress twiddles and twaddles over his proposals for a tax cut, for an education bill, for medical care for the aged, for more medical schools, and a whole host of bills. A clear indication of the degree of his frustration is the fact that two of his major bills of the last Congress have not even been revived this year—the Department of Urban Affairs and the reform of unemployment compensation standards, a subject dear to him as a Senator from Massachusetts.

Virtually none of the President's current proposals have even reached a committee vote, much less a vote in the House of Representatives or the Senate. I do not suggest that these bills are the best or only answers to our problems, but I submit that the *President* of the United States, *elected by all the people,* be he Democrat or Republican, *is entitled to a vote,* up or down, on his major proposals . . .

Here we are in the fourth month of the Congressional session, approaching the Easter recess, which only a few years ago was considered the half-way mark in Congressional sessions. The new Congress has passed only one public law of any consequence—an extension of the draft. Not one of the twelve major appropriation bills has cleared either house . . .

Americans who are now suffering for lack of jobs, medical care or adequate education will suffer all the longer because Congress fails to face the issues. *Delay leaves public officials and administrators at all levels of government,* as well as private agencies, uncertain about how to prepare programs. Several have written me, for example, inquiring about the chances for action on the library construction features of the Administration's omnibus education bill. *They have plans to make and budgets to prepare and so it is understandable that they should like to know.*"

I have italicized some recurring themes of the Executive Force, as they appear in this typical tirade against Congress. The 88th Congress, during which the previous remarks were delivered and the "new low" in congressional prestige was registered, slipped in due course into history. Then, *mirabile dictu,* we discover that it was not so bad after all: "The 88th Congress," wrote Tom Wicker in the *New York Times* on October 4, 1964, "one of the most productive in history, went a long way in 1964 to stem what had been a rising tide of criticism of the legislative branch . . . Those who were charging a year ago that Congress was 'deadlocked,' 'frozen,' or 'senile'—some of the choice adjectives employed by critics—cannot prove it in the final record."

Agreed, they could not prove it. Nor could they prove it in the beginning. For they should have to assert in the first place their criteria, and they would not wish to say what these were—principally, that Congress should follow the President, and that Congress should follow their own policies.

ON MEASURES OF WORTH

> *Doing nothing,*
> *Yet there is nothing that is not done*
>
> Tao principle of inaction
Han Fei Tzu (3rd Cent. B.C.)

The allegations brought against Congress are sometimes put in the form of a statement of fact about Congress. Thus, it is alleged that Congress blocks civil rights legislation. At other times, the complaints take the form of a proposal for reform. For instance, it is said, "A question period should be introduced into congressional procedure, so that members of the executive establishment may regularly be called upon to explain their work on the floor of Congress and thereby to the public."

Both forms of statement imply a standard of evaluation. If civil rights legislation were not deemed of importance, it would be of no importance that Congress blocked or did not block it. If there were no problem of learning what the executive branch was up to, the question period would not excite interest. In both cases, we are dealing with the applied science of politics. That is, given a certain goal, what means can be taken to achieve it? In this applied science, as in all applied science, there exists first the problem of defining the goal, and secondly, the problem of the validity of the means.

Political debate commonly neglects or forgets the statement of first principles, the goals from which minor positions can be reasonably deduced. As a result people usually do not know what they want, or they want contradictory things, or they seek with enthusiasm reforms that are too minor to be consequential. They join forces with their true opposition. They fight their friends. Or more than anything else, they have little effect of any kind, but create a great wind.

There is a second tendency, at least as common, to reason falsely from the desire to the goal, to ignore or neglect or to be incompetent to establish which means are to be employed to reach the sought-for end. There is a failure of science, which is simply the application of recognized forms of logic and factual investigation in moving from a present set of conditions to a planned-for set of conditions.

It is impossible to judge Congress, therefore, without a clear idea of what is expected of it. Creating an "effective" or "better" Congress is a case of applied science, like medicine and psychiatry, or social work and business management, or steering a boat and setting up an international conference. It is probably more complicated than all of these. Without ends in mind, discussion of congressional performance must be largely meaningless, just as would be teaching navigation without regard to the directions of the compass, or arguing the installation of a computer in a business without knowing the direction which the business is to follow.

For certain reasons, this simple and fundamental lesson is lost upon many when they come to deal with Congress. Nor are the reasons mysterious. First of all, Congress is so old and complicated an institution that it does not occur to people to treat it as a perennially fresh problem. Or even as a rational problem. The weight of tradition hangs heavy, and impresses both lovers and enemies of the institution. It does not stimulate and tempt those who might make it work and save its intrinsic value.

Furthermore, political behavior is often blind, irrational behavior. Congress is a favorite arena for such. There, it is not necessary to specify anything or justify anything in logical terms, the many rules governing legislative behavior are formal; that is, they do not go to the heart of the game. And a few of the players behave rather as they please. Politics is still taught in the colleges and the law schools, and in the other media of cultural training of the country as a species of passionate display with elements of legal quibbling and play-acting added. Under the circumstances, the idea of Congress as a place where issues may be rationally presented and scientifically studied is submerged deep. Even if Congress would become miraculously rational, the country might be more enraged than happy.

Indeed, "rational" behavior may consist in profiting from the existing confusion. By covering up motives, concealing tactics, and creating illusion, victories can be won that would be otherwise difficult. A type of congressman inured to confusion and dedicated to sleight of hand develops and prospers. Changing to rationalized procedures—and exposing as a necessary consequence the principles under which the congressional struggle occurs—is resisted because it must work against such a congressman.

In addition, an exposure of the underlying directions of Congress as an institution and a clarification of the effects that Congress' structure and procedures have upon its legislation might serve to diminish the consensus upon which the institution depends for its survival and success. "Lifting the veil" is tabooed. It is not proper, for example, to advertise the constructive and stabilizing effects of lobbies. Consequently, challenges to Congress occur often in the form of passionate outbursts or they raise arguments about minor congressional procedures rather than basic ones. In either case, fundamental discussion of principles is avoided. Congress becomes something huge that is there, inexplicable, in the governmental system.

Finally, the goals of Congress are passed over because those who attack it are unconscious of the fact that in ideology they are anti-legislature. It is important to recognize that many critics of Congress lack self-consciousness and coherence of thought; they cannot see their reforms as more than particular improvements in the technique of conducting public business. Or, if they admit that to themselves, they may not wish to bear the brunt of the counter-attack when the clear meaning of their piecemeal tactics is exposed. What is at work in both cases is an ideology which in its full expression can be called the Executive Force.

THE GOALS OF CONGRESSIONAL GOVERNMENT

> *Pantheons in religion, parliaments in politics, equality before the law, even-handed justice, equality in conditions of exchange—these are symbols of conciliation that have played important parts in the cohesion of great states. . . . It is policies of this type that may safely be assumed as basic in a large scheme of national planning.*
>
> C. E. Merriam
> *The Role of Politics in Social Change*

If it is assumed that Congress, like all practical institutions, has some design for being, and if that design must be created by a set of choices, who must fashion the choices?

Much of this book is given over to those who say that the executive represents the people and must make the choice. Congress is to criticize and advise. Of course, this only moves the solution a step farther away, because the question would again have to be raised of the executive: What is his or its philosophy?

A minority of scholars, nowadays at least, are advocates of congressional supremacy, and these say, as does the clearest of their voices, Charles Hyneman, that Congress represents the people and therefore Congress should rule the executive branch. Thus, in his book, entitled *Bureaucracy in a Democracy,* Professor Hyneman, almost alone among American experts, weighed administrative behavior on congressional rather than presidential scales. "The American people have authorized nobody except their elected officials to speak for them. The administrator may have good judgment as to what most of the American people want but he does not know what most of the people want . . . We assure ourselves that the administrative branch of the government will respond to the wishes of the people by subjecting it to the elected officials of the government."

However, the executive and congressional populist theories are equally myths. Both rely upon a fictitious "people," which as we shall demonstrate, does not exist; nor can it exist. Equally correct arguments can be produced to show that the President and the Congress represent the "people" best—so long, that is, as nobody asks the embarrassing question: "What people is being talked about?" Congress represents different interests—different publics— than the executive branch and acts towards different ends as it is presently constituted. The people—or better, any given person, is represented by Congress if Congress satisfies him, by the President if satisfaction comes from that source, or by both, for that matter.

Professor Hyneman's myth will not bring us to a dogmatic acceptance of congressional supremacy any more than will the myth of executive populism which many eminent scholars such as Woodrow Wilson, Charles Merriam, and Louis Brownlow have contrived. If congressional supremacy—or better, a system of national government giving enhanced role and functions to Congress—is to be espoused, it will be because the consequences of such a system, as determined by empirical examination, are deemed to be preferable philosophically to the effects of any alternative system.

What Congress should be demands a personal credo. The question is not: "On what does everyone agree?", for even if all agreed that Congress should continue as a branch of government, it would be a vastly different Congress in various eyes. The only accord is among those who hold to a standard and persuade others by logical and nonlogical means to follow the standard. In short, what Congress should be asked to do is what "we" want it to do. There is no evading this position without evading personal responsibility.

If this logic is acceptable, then the additional point is to be made that the form we wish Congress to take depends on the kind of society we want. The ideal of legislative government depends directly upon the ideal of the society. It would hardly do to have the two in contradiction. The legislature is a social machine, whose activity should be depended upon for part of the drive towards American ideals. Both the machine and its product must be induced from the ideals.

However, there are many ways to state the ideals of a society, and we must seek the way that is most useful in the applied science of governmental organization. That is, we must seek operational ideals, the kind of ideals that can tell how a government should be set up and how its officers should behave.

Typically the first goals that come to mind when discussing the ends of government nowadays are food, shelter, clothing, health, and leisure. Other objectives are often put forth: protection, liberty, education, and so on. Certainly few would wish to dispute the high value of all such aims. The vision of everyone eating well, sleeping comfortably, and playing in good health is like a picture on the wall. It hangs there serene, satisfying, and final.

But a picture, whether it hangs on the wall or is a political vision, cannot create the conditions of its own existence. The fruits of life do not spontaneously generate from imagination and good will. Indeed, the image itself is nothing but a momentary visualization of the eternally changing process of the satisfying of wants. "Abundance," if that is the title of our picture, would have been painted differently a century ago and will be differently depicted a century hence.

The ends cannot be separated from the means to their fulfillment. The goals of food, shelter, health and leisure are so bound up with the ways in which they are sought, that they should be stated operationally, that is, according to the pattern of conduct that produces them. Value-oriented operations are the essence of government. From them come the abundant life. The basic satisfactions that a society provides are inherently defined as to quality and quantity by the instruments it employs for satisfying them.

Therefore, the ideals here prescribed for American society and government are operational. They are more abstract than food and shelter; they cannot well be painted and hung on walls. But they realize and incarnate the concrete goals as they invest and suffuse human behavior; and their product is real indeed.

These several American ideals can only be postulated now. They are premised, for they cannot be defined and argued at length here. If they are congenial, well and good, and the kind of Congress envisioned in this work will tend to produce that kind of American society. Those who object in part to the conditions of society stated here as a form of the ideal, as well as those who totally object, must find their own way of building Congress.

There is one exception. For those whose ideology and direction we call the Executive Force, a pattern of behavior and recommendations has been prepared in order to form a clear contrast with the Republican Force that we espouse.

The Republican Force represents the following goals for American society: American society should possess, it is premised, an optimal balance of possibilities for security and new experience. On the one hand, a wary eye must be kept on the inordinate growth of bureaucracy and centralism in all walks of life. On the other hand, a danger occurs in the reckless abandonment of precedent and rules; provision should be made for stabilizing values, and assuring expectations concerning what conduct should receive respect, authority, and income.

Rule of Law. Related to the desire for stability is the ideal of the rule of law. This demands that the system of legal rules in the society be clear and stable enough to permit all men to know them, and that all differences between two parties to the law, whether individuals, groups, or governments are involved, reduce towards the vanishing point in any contest before the law. Government should be by laws, not by men. All men should be equal before the law.

Equality of Opportunity. Related to the search for new experience is the ideal of equality of opportunity. The large diffusion of this ideal among the American people, its important place in the institutions and laws of the land, and its ultimate philosophical soundness place it perhaps foremost among American principles. It means essentially that a continuous and heavy preference should be given all social activity that permits the highest level of personal achievement, that higher aspirations should be promoted in all areas of life, and that the handicaps of less privileged aspirants to the values of society should be reduced to something approaching the position of the more privileged.

Freedom. Of great importance too is the ideal of group and personal freedom. To it is related the ideal of social and personal cooperativeness. Americans need to be left to their own social devices as much as possible. Wherever interests settle in, there governments of the most local kind and voluntary associations should form and rule. The larger society should be confined to developing only a limited group of interests. They should not be forcibly increased.

The fields of social and civic services, education, and business should be regulated in minimum and encouraged to run themselves.

Religiousness. The fourth and final ideal is religiousness. By religiousness is meant the cloak of God that shelters man, encourages him to humility and benevolence, even while he must be forever searching for final answers to existence. In religiousness, a man cannot hope to find final answers to ultimate questions on earth, and especially not in political terms. Such religiousness does not necessarily imply organized religion. But it correlates with those qualities of high importance to a republic: tolerance of differences, voluntarism, and spiritualism.

It may be true, as a group of civic leaders constituted by The Rockefeller Brothers Fund agreed several years ago, that "Democracy is a powerful idea because it draws much of its strength from religions that posit the sanctity of the individual and the brotherhood of man." Religion is still more vivifying because it shields the state from animistic impulses that tend to center there. Free religion actually permits a secular state to come into being. It is a "secular state" in the preferable sense of the word—neither anti-religious, nor dominated by an organized religion.

If these four ideals are not shared by all Americans, they may nevertheless be sought without deliberate and serious damage to those who do not believe in them. Similarly, within the limits of possibility and within the limits of strain upon the national system, the United States should foster their extension to humanity in general. By the same token, the United States should avoid aiding any people, directly or indirectly, to pursue a contrary set of principles.

"The national interest," "the public good," "the public interest" and similar phrases must in the last analysis refer to values of this sort. Hence, to avoid the treacherous argumentation that exploits the favorable view of these terms in most public discussion, it is well to state here and now that the "national interest" and the "public interest" have no meaning at all unless they refer to actual policies professed and defined and recommended for the use of the nation, as the policies above have been. They are the national interest. They are the public interest—they and the policies adopted or proposed in pursuit of their larger forms.

The "national interest" for example has been often employed as an American ideal by spokesmen for the military, the State Department, and other groups. It is a verbal and semantic weapon particularly of the executive establishment and the presidency. This practice must be guarded against. The national interest here can mean only the ideals already enunciated plus whatever self-protective steps are to be taken to see that the search for these ideals shall not be frustrated from outside the country. And the public interest is asserted to mean the same without concern over what is occurring outside the country. When not used in such senses, it can be suspected that they are mere synonyms for whatever the advocates of special interests are seeking from Congress.

From the social ideals of a society come its complexes of institutions, and hopefully, the awareness of which institutions are best suited to the perpetuation and promotion of the ideals; for there is an abundance of institutions in American society that not only foster but also threaten to destroy the institutions and ideals here put forward.

In American society, the institutions that grow out of historical experiencing of the four ideals and that deserve especial emphasis and support in perpetuating and perfecting those ideals are fairly prominent. One is the American system of law, courts, judicial process, and due process of law—the independent, non-political, objective and precedent-based judiciary. Another is federalism, the system of almost independent states formed into a single union, with each element retaining and exercising vigorously a judicial, taxing, protective, and legislating power of considerable weight and consequence. A third is the pluralism of churches and voluntary associations. Yet another is the relatively free system of business enterprise.

The relatively localized and citizen-supervised educational system is another important representation of the ideal. So is decentralization of all government administration. The decentralization of political parties is necessary too. And finally to be mentioned is the government of the union itself, which is government by legislature, protected by the principle of separation of powers and checks and balances. How the legislature operates is to be detailed below; for the moment, only its presence in this group of institutional complexes is to be noted. These institutions that are built around the four stated ideals, that nourish them and project them into the future can well be called the Republican Force of the nation. Those institutions that can be invented in the future and that accomplish the same purposes are also of the Republican Force. Congress is the spearhead of the Republican Force.

Chapter Three

THE PUBLICS

> *There is sufficient diversity in the state of property, in the genus, manners, and habits of the people of the different parts of the Union, to occasion a material diversity of disposition in their representatives towards the different ranks and conditions of society. And though an intimate intercourse under the same government will promote a gradual assimilation in some of these respects, yet there are causes, as well physical as moral, which may, in a greater or less degree, permanently nourish different propensities and inclinations in this respect.*
>
> Hamilton, *The Federalist*

THE OUTER WORLD of the congressional system limits and shapes Congress, but cannot govern it. The exception to this rule is the Executive Force. The outer world is otherwise composed of the people, the press, interests, and the political parties. The judiciary may also be counted among the elements.

It is incorrect to speak of the public as if it were one and alone. There are many publics in the United States. Any distinct clusters of opinion around an idea, a movement, an interest or any grouping whatsoever are publics, including all constituencies that choose public officers.

Congressmen have their eyes on four constituencies in general—four publics they might be called—and any number of sub-constituencies. The four constituencies are, first, their personal public to whom they owe their election. Then occurs the constituency of the President that affects their

relation with the presidency and reacts with their own constituency. Third, the individual constituencies of their
fellow-congressmen are of importance because these shape
the legislature to which they belong and affect the form of
what they can and cannot do in the legislature as individuals.
Finally, congressmen acquire special constituencies as a result of their committee assignments: these are usually functional groups such as the army, postal employees, or scientists. Only the first two publics, the personal and the
presidential, are treated here.

Within their own districts may exist a number of sub-
constituencies, depending upon the complexity of opinions
and interests in the district. There are of course also interest groups. To a great extent, a congressman's dealings
with his constituency amount to the sum of separate dealings
with his sub-constituencies.

THE NUCLEAR CONSTITUENCY

> *To be governed by one, is not safe ...*
> *Yet to be distracted with many is worse ...*
> *To take advice of some few friends is ever honourable.*
>
> Francis Bacon
> "Of Followers and Friends" (1625)

The most important sub-constituency is the congressman's
personal following. It is ordinarily a group of friends,
associated party officers, and dependent office-holders, reinforced by acquaintances grateful for past favors and ex-
pectant of additional ones, and admirers who are individually alert and informed on congressional politics or
leaders of favorably disposed groups. Their number may
be quite small, perhaps only forty persons, or may mount
into some hundreds. It is this *nuclear constituency* that sorts
and screens stimuli, and reacts to the congressman's behavior in a fashion that is intelligible to him so that in the

end its influence and ideas are the most important of any group in the district. If anyone can control him, the nuclear constituency can. It is in a sense a controlling *alter ego.*

The character of the nuclear constituency depends on the character of the congressman. Several types of relations are apparent. One kind of congressman uses his nuclear constituency as a public relations machine, principally in political campaigns. Another may use it as an administrative machine in and out of office. Another may use it as a council of co-managers. Still another may let himself be run by his nuclear constituency, secure in the knowledge that its members know best the constituency's wishes and have his interests at heart.

From the nuclear constituency there spread contacts with, on the one hand, a large number of interest groups and, on the other, a generalized public whose relations with politics are only incidental or sporadic. The groups generate demands and pressures whose impact upon the congressman depends upon his span of dependent interests, the strength of his nuclear constituency, and his popularity with the general public.

THE INTERESTS

> *How stand we now? Confusion in government,*
> *bemused chaos up, and conscience down,*
> > *—thou are so drunk*
> *and deep in nothing save it be merriment.*

> Duke Wu of Wei, 811-756 B.C.
> *The Confucian Odes*
> (Trans. by Ezra Pound
> Harvard U. Press, 1954)

Duke Wu of ancient China sounds like a typical denouncer of "the interests" and the "lobbyists" in modern America. Such extreme sentiments only endanger a correct attitude towards republican forms. The major interests of

the United States are well known. Labor unions, the public
works segment of industry and commerce, the major industries of the district, educators, Negro groups in a number
of constituencies—these are perhaps the most common con-
stellation of continuously active interests within the particular districts around the nation. Many others become
active on occasion and have a well-beaten traditional access
road—church groups, veterans, fraternal orders, and professional associations of doctors, social workers, and the like.

In recent years perhaps more than formerly, interest
groups have been nationalized. This means that a pressure
of a given interest will be spread among a large number of
congressmen in both the Senate and House and in their districts. The conditions under which certain congressmen become the targets of or associated with certain pressure
groups are rather complex. But they include the "avail-
ability" of a congressman, whether this occurs through con-
viction, need of support, persuasibility, presence of the
interest in sharp form in his district, or other reasons. Naturally the place occupied by the congressman in the
Senate or House hierarchy, which is discussed below, makes
him more or less attractive as the potential supporter of a
group's policies.

In recent years too, the executive branch of government
has experienced an increased pressure from organized
groups. This trend is directly connected with the larger and
more intensive delegations of power from Congress to the
bureaucracies. There is a wide variety among agencies as
to their permeability by groups from the outside. Some
agencies absorb their pressure groups and use them; other
agencies treat with them at arm's length.

On the whole, however, Congress is more congenial to
the lobbyist, that is, the spokesman for a pressure group of

an interest, than are the agencies of the executive establishment. This is not, as some might think, because Congress
is corruptible or gullible, but because the main instrument
of pressures is the vote and Congress is more persuasible by
opinions. In addition, the attitudes of the Republican Force
are more those of the lobbyists than are the attitudes of the
Executive Force; we refer to beliefs in federalism, decentralization, business independence, and the ideas of economic minorities.

Again, in recent years, as the executive establishment
has grown in functions and everyday powers, more lobbyists
have turned towards federal administrators for help. And
federal administrative forces have sought to influence pressure group policies. The more funds and maneuvers open
to them, the more the administrators can impress cooperativeness upon the pressure groups.

In increasing numbers of cases, the line between a government agency and the group being regulated is getting to
be difficult to draw. Here is a crucial area where a double-
pronged movement is developing—carrying pressure groups
into the executive orbit and filling the need of the Executive Force in its struggle with the Republican Force to have
types of allies or constituents traditionally associated with
the opposition. In one agency after another—Commerce,
Agriculture, and State, as examples—administrators are active in creating special publics resembling in most ways
congressional constituencies, though they lack an independent elective vote.

These are the major developments of interest groups in
relation to executive and Congress, not that expected or
predicted by most observers of the past, namely that pressure groups would come to dominate congressmen. Almost
to a man (and there is little reason to doubt their general

accuracy) congressmen will deny the larger influence of any interest group in their district. They will not deny contact. They believe that it is essential—and certainly it is important to outside appraisers of the situation—to distinguish between a voluminous communication with lobbyists and being intimidated or dominated by lobbyists. They are often frank to say that lobbyists provide information that otherwise would be difficult to come by, for reasons going to the fact that Congress possesses rather underdeveloped intelligence facilities, that the executive hides information, and that the most subtle and critical truths often emerge from a clash of convinced partisans.

That the American people live under some laws framed by lobbyists is indubitable. That these laws are—certainly no less than and probably more than the average law—contributions to the republican ideals and Republican Force of the country, can be asserted with some confidence. The major doubt would arise from laws favoring special interests, often emerging from lobbying, which tend to establish monopoly and other rigidities in the market place. Despite an almost congenital belief in laissez-faire, congressmen do not have enough favorable reinforcement to withstand all such pressure. Apart from this situation, the interests would not seem to threaten the paramountcy of congressional rule, nor would they seem to be contributing much to the advance of the Executive Force.

THE WHOLE PUBLIC

> *The fabric of American empire ought to rest on the solid basis of the CONSENT OF THE PEOPLE. The streams of national power ought to flow immediately from that pure, original fountain of all legitimate authority.*
>
> Hamilton, *The Federalist* (1787)

The people as a whole is another question. It has already been suggested that by the people is meant politically

a number of publics. These publics range on the score of
interest and involvement from the apathetic to the highly
involved nuclear constituency. They range in the subject
of their concern from publics that are tied up with neigh-
borhood and private matters, to those that are tied up with
national and international affairs.

But these latter do not form one public. Rather there
are regional publics, such as the Old South and the Pacific
Coast, publics that attend only to international questions
and are constituents of the United Nations as much as of
the State Department and the President. There would be
congressional constituencies, presidential constituencies,
and agency constituencies, all in the informal sense of the
term, constituency, that indicates those who attend to particular officials of the government in their search for representation.

Of these and more, the two that are of most interest
now are the congressional constituency and the presidential
one. They are commonly not separated in the mind. When
most people discuss and even write about American politics,
they tend to talk of a great undifferentiated public (which
does not exist), and pressure groups (which in many cases
are sub-constituencies). The congressional constituency,
culminating on the scale of involvement in the nuclear constituency, is a surprising and disconcerting presence to the
true presidential constituent. The presidential constituent
is one whose primary and often sole interest in politics is the
incumbent and potential competitors for the presidential
office.

To define exactly the boundary and describe the behavior of the two constituencies is not easy. There is of
course a good deal of overlapping: a citizen may attend to
both congressional and presidential politics. The impact of

these double-constituents holds together the national (and international) political process. For they are on the whole inclined to make the same demands on both congressmen and President. Many, probably most of them, are more presidentially inclined. A much smaller number would be congressionally inclined.

When we consider the two purer constituencies, again the congressional one seems the smaller. In the end, the presidential constituency is much larger than the congressional; it is likely to be, however, less persistent and less inured to the hardships of politics.

Estimates of the size of these two constituencies and their overlapping or double form would vary from district to district around America and from time to time. National opinion surveys and district polls help ascertain them. Generally, over 90% of the adults of the country might be expected to know who is President at any given time. On the average, covering all congressional districts of the country, less than half of the adults would know the name of their congressman in the House of Representatives; even fewer can name both of their Senators. Knowledge of the name is one measure of the first big leap from apathy to involvement. In the present case, it indicates too that in the gross sense, the congressional constituency is much smaller than the presidential one.

From the minimum of participation in the constituency to the maximum there occurs the full range of civic activity. From mere awareness to voting, the drop in number of participants is in the millions, but proportionately small. In the range between mere voting and expressing oneself politically along with being fairly well informed about public affairs, most members of the constituencies drop out. They are inactive. Perhaps no more than 10% of the adult population remain in the calculation, and of these constituents, by far the larger number is presidential rather than congressional. The reasons for this bifurcation are many; the main historical reasons are that the schools and press of the nation are centered upon the White House, the President is personalized to the ultimate extent, and the powers of the presidency have grown. But the phenomenon is much more complicated than that. It becomes intensely psychological and then ideological. How else can it be explained that polls of presidential popularity show the President almost always to "be doing a good job" and much more chosen than all conceivable competitors? This phenomenon occurs even after a close presidential election. It occurs even when the President is under heavy criticism, as for instance, in June 1965, when President Johnson, presumably embarrassed by the bad turns of events in Santo Domingo and Viet Nam, was said to be doing a good job by some 70% of the citizenry.

That there is a primitive attractiveness to rule by a single man appears to be a fairly well established anthropological principle. Sebastian de Grazia, Hocart, Evans-Pritchard, and Fred Greenstein are several scholars who have set up the relevant materials. That the despotic principle is connected psychologically with the authoritarian father in the family is also well-grounded theory. Furthermore, the first stages of civilization—on the edge of which modern man hovers—accentuate rather than depress the monarchical idea.

People are usually taken aback when an ancient or psychic phenomenon is brought home to their own behavior for the first time; however, one must insist upon facing the likelihood that a good deal of the popular sentiment relating to the President is nothing more nor less than the proverbial attachment of a people to its ruler, and is precisely the same sentiment that the founders of the Constitution sought as a group to diminish and confine.

To this old type of attachment which the American revolutionary generation called "the monarchical sentiment," has been joined in more recent times a rationalistic, efficiency movement that purports to see in executive integration the "one right way to do things." That there is *no* "one right way" is the thesis of some later pages. That the *belief* in such is part of the ideology that energizes the Executive Force is the relevant point here. It is part of being a believing member of the presidential constituency.

The presidential constituency acquires a great many adherents through the activity and figure of the President in foreign affairs. To most of the world America is symbolized by the incumbent President and perhaps several potential or past competitors for that post. To them, psychologically, the United States is a monarchy. America's "king" and "the crown princes" are their royal family. When the American government operates as a federal republic, or as a government by legislature, or as a free enterprise pluralistic society, the world thinks in terms of a king meeting with bootless resistance which he manfully overpowers or which saps his strength. The inevitable "liberality" of the presidency, which owes much to domestic political causes, is the generator of great and consistent enthusiasm for the presidency abroad, and in turn the foreign feeling is transmitted back to America, there to kindle like emotions.

No doubt some of the rage of American "isolationists" is due to their sensing a process that they cannot define. The process which they cannot define is in part the subtle transformation of the world into a constituency "virtually represented" (to use an antique term) by the American President and to a lesser extent by the American government as a whole. In the return cycle of this process of "virtual representation" the feelings of foreign "constituents" penetrate the American press, public opinion, and especially the members of the executive establishment (particularly the State Department and its connections throughout the academic and social structure of the land).

Thus, the presidential constituency is not only enlarged somewhat, and not only influenced by foreign ideas and desires, but it also sees its focal point, the President, as a much vaster figure, no mere man, a center for world emotional attachment.

Still the presidential constituency leaves much to be desired as a supportive group. Its members are more ideological than practical; it is concentrated, so far as its informed and active part is concerned, in the academic halls and among temporary office-holders. It is split up, most of all, into those who wish the incumbent to prosper and those who wish him ill and have one or more alternate "crown princes" in mind for an early succession.

An important result of the lack of a competent active following in the public as a whole is to send the President in search of a larger professional, paid staff. (This abets the tendency for only the rich to apply for the presidency.) He also resorts to the executive establishment, especially a larger White House staff, for more constituents, and seeks further to nationalize and integrate the political party. He appoints more often from the bureaucracy; 48% of President Johnson's first 280 major non-judicial appointments were already in government service.

His tactics, moreover, veer towards rallying mass opinion to solve problems of public affairs. Too vast to be in personal contact with its leader, the presidential constituency feels him through television, magazines, and newspaper columns. They respond to him by viewing television screens and buying newspapers, by some variation of their voting behavior, and by pushing a little against the leaders of their interest groups or congressmen.

By contrast, the congressional constituency is of smaller gross dimensions in the nation as a whole and in each state and district. But it contains the larger nuclear constituency. It numbers more persons to whom politics is a way of life and more persons with tangible local interests that are best pursued by the congressional route. It is more of a working group as it is found throughout the country. It is not so easy to excite but has a tenacious grip on the realities and techniques of politics. Its liaisons with state and local politics (except to some degree in the large metropolises) are more varied and extensive.

Small businessmen and autonomous managers of branch factories are prominent in the group, more so now that the welfare state has reduced the number of those subsisting upon the good-will of the politicians. To a considerable degree the most direct beneficiaries of national welfare policies have joined the constituency of the President.

Congressional constituencies of course are far from uniform in social composition and outlook. In a great many districts and states, the republican outlook is dominant and supplies the Congressman or Senator with heavy backing; they become independent of the executive. In other districts, the situation varies from time to time; there the representative is now a part of the congressional system, then again a part of the presidential one. Some of the districts are more or less permanent parts of the presidential system.

The competitiveness of a district contributes to a district's moving by means of its representative from congressional to presidential party and back. Ordinarily safe districts are congressional or presidential, but not both in a short period of time. In presidential election years and during national crises, the presidential force exerts its strongest psychological pull upon the public; in less excited times, the congressional force dominates the field. The long-term trend, manifesting itself in both critical and routine periods, leads towards the domination of a larger number of congressional seats by the Executive Force.

Within the individual district, this large-scale phenomenon is noticeable in the changing character of the congressman's constituency. As one or another force waxes and wanes, the constituency alters. In the majority of districts, the congressman maintains his ruling role within the constituency system. He is not forced by the executive, or interests representing the Executive Force, or by the political party, to behave contrary to his own or his nuclear constituency's ideas.

Since people as a whole are so inactive politically, and their information is inexact and scanty, the congressman typically derives a commanding position from his personal nuclear constituency—his machine, some might inexactly call it,—and his ability to make an impression—"create an image"—say the advertising professionals, on his district's voters. This image, plus the nuclear constituency, plus the general vote favorable to his party and presidential candidate, are usually sufficient to bring reelection. The images can exist in great variety because, unlike situations where candidates are picked by party machinery, as in England, the candidates in the United States can appear in whatever form may be calculated successfully to appeal to the voters in a given election campaign.

To a far greater extent than in practically any other system in the world, the American legislator creates his own constituency and shapes and amends it over time. This fact, so important in determining the character of congressmen and Congress as a whole, is often not understood. But the end product, the independent congressman, is a result of a constituency that is founded upon apathy and that is rather shapeless to begin with.

Given the same apathy and the active role of the congressional candidates in creating their own creators, the constituents, it does not appear likely that the "people" would be able to determine the policies of the congressmen as individuals or as the Congress. Rather the representatives are fairly free to put together their own winning combinations from one election time to the next.

There are still plenty of reasons why the life of Senators and congressmen may be short and not so sweet; recessions, tactical errors, a fresh image on another man, a movement of people into or out of the district, etc. None of these threaten to wreck the old constituency system. The public is not becoming better informed or more active, either, so that there is no danger of politics becoming rationalized in the business sense, with the constituents becoming a great board of directors watching every move.

There could be imagined some changes in the congressional constituency that would make it function better as an instrument of the Republican Force. The public is not large or varied enough in the typical constituency to supply workers, critics, and intelligent claques. Only several millions of Americans regularly are active in politics. These politists, who must supply the motive force for the huge engines of American democracy, can scarcely be increased in number and are readily reducible. The myth of the active mass of citizens lulls many a potential defender of the republic who should otherwise be keen on the preservation of the species. As it is, they think it does not matter to cut out a few thousands of active citizens here and there on any plausible excuse—to prevent conflicts of interest, to pursue the merit system, by invading privacy, by character assassination, by seeking disqualifications of a legal or informal kind, by the elimination of the training grounds—often grim, to be sure—of the politically active people, and so on to successive decimations of the ranks of politists.

The Executive Force does not need an active public. It requires only a passive public. As John Stuart Mill once wrote:

> A good despotism means a government in which, so far as depends on the despot, there is no positive oppression by officers of state, but in which all the collective interests of the people are managed for them, all the thinking that has relation to collective interests done for them, and in which their minds are formed by, and consenting to, this abdication of their own energies. (*Representative Government*, 1861, Everyman's Edition, pp. 204-5.)

It is thus representative government, the republic, that needs the politists. The congressional force needs new instruments to develop its theory and support in the electorate. These will have to be put forward later on in these pages.

For the past and the present offer too few resources to preserve republican government as it works by way of the constituencies. There is a continuously growing threat from the presidential constituency, as has been shown, through the more grandiose image of the President, amplified by foreign masses, and by the American press. And a sharply thrusting element of the presidential force, the political party, stands as a potential threat too.

The important question, as this chapter has shown, is not whether congressional rule will succumb to the populism

of the constituency. That will not happen. Rather the
populist constituency is in danger of being converted into
the instrument of the Executive Force and therefore the
important question is: Will the congressman fall under the
rule of the presidential constituency?

Chapter Four

THE POLITICAL PARTIES

The political party as such has its own peculiar soul, independent of the programs and rules which it possesses and the eternal principles with which it is imbued.

Roberto Michels,
Corso di Sociologia Politica (1927)

THE PRESIDENTIAL CONSTITUENCY is not able to threaten the republican system by itself. It is too unorganized and socially distant from the contact points of the political process. It is often controlled by politicians in the districts who are not themselves oriented towards the presidency. It swells with gusts of popular emotion, but it subsides with prosperity and apathy.

The presidential constituency develops to a peak when a massive crisis occurs. War and economic distress have been the only provocative crises of the past; civil conflict over race relations is not to be dismissed, however, as a possibility in the future. All three kinds of events have left their mark upon American government in the form of an enhanced presidential position, and a tradition of personal executive power. At the same time, a steady growth of the executive establishment under the traditional interpretation of the presidential powers and the old military concept of administrative management would in time produce the same effect, presidential dictatorship.

A third and final possibility is the triumph of presidential party politics. If the presidency and his constituency get the reforms necessary to unify and nationalize the party system in America, Congress will be controlled, the executive establishment tied in tightly to the presidency, and the decline of the whole republican system precipitated.

PARTIES AGAINST THE SEPARATE POWERS

> *There would be an end of everything, were the same man or the same body . . . to exercise those three powers—that of enacting laws, that of executing the public restrictions, and of trying the causes of individuals.*
>
> Montesquieu, *Spirit of the Laws*

American history shows that the political party has been from the beginning intended by its organizers either to control the choice of the presidency or to control the country by means of the presidency. State and congressional leaders have been prominent in efforts to organize the parties to control the President. Their efforts through the years have been marked with a few successes, but generally they have fought principally a rearguard action to prevent the President's party from controlling them.

The height of power of the House of Representatives probably occurred during the first generation of the nineteenth century, when the House was compact, in full exercise of its powers, and in charge of the nomination of the President in its caucuses. If this practice had continued, the particular American legislative system probably would not have developed; rather, a parliamentary system would have arisen; the Senate would have been put down; the House would have first controlled the President and then, since the executive establishment would have grown and foreign imbroglios would have occurred, the President would have turned about and controlled the House through seizure of the party apparatus, as has happened in England.

Indeed, here is the place to suggest that from a republican viewpoint, structural connections between Congress and the presidency are usually to be avoided. The inherent potential power of the presidency constantly threatens to convert a cooperative relation into a dependent one. A second example, this one hypothetical, can be advanced. Suppose, as some ardent republicans desire, a third party is formed in the United States that is able to obtain for its presidential candidate enough electoral votes to prevent one of the two other candidates from getting the majority required for election. The election would be thrown into the House of Representatives, where, each state voting as a unit, the President is chosen from the two leading candidates.

If this happened even once in this generation, and the House did not cast its vote for the most popular candidate, it is likely that a constitutional amendment to permit the "people" to elect the President directly would be passed. This step would in turn, enhance the power of the Executive Force. Supposing the improbable, that the House of Representatives would find a way of pleasing the country while retaining its power to choose the President, the ultimate result might be another form of parliamentary government. As in England, where Parliament once chose the Prime Minister and now the Prime Minister chooses the parliamentary leaders and calls the tune for the whole body, the House in its new connection with the presidency might seem first to increase its power but would then lose the gain, and more.

None of this has occurred in America. Here the political parties have been kept in a *decentralized* condition, whereby the national party does not control the state parties. The parties are also *unintegrated;* the party of Congress is not the same thing as the presidential party, and indeed, the party of Congress consists of several parties, not one alone. Finally the parties in the districts are on the average *adjutant* rather than commanding; most congressmen use the party label for what it is worth and nothing more; most party organizations give the congressmen what they can afford, which consists usually of crumbs from the state and local table, and do not ask much in return from him.

This troika of traits gives the American party its peculiar pace and gait. The party, whether Republican or Democratic is adjutant, decentralized and unintegrated. Yet, from the beginning of parties in America, particularly from the beginnings of the mass party of Jefferson, a dissatisfaction with that state of affairs has existed. From the time of Woodrow Wilson's appearance upon the political stage and the subsequent adoration of his political writings (technically the best since Calhoun though lacking the imagination and basic truths of Henry Adams), the dissatisfaction became a creed.

DOGMAS OF THE RESPONSIBLE POLITICAL PARTY

> *It is bad to be oppressed by a minority, but it is worse to be oppressed by a majority. For there is a reserve of latent power in the masses which, if it is called into play, the minority can seldom resist. But from the absolute will of an entire people there is no appeal, no redemption, no refuge but treason. The humblest and most numerous class of the Athenians united the legislative, the judicial, and, in part, the executive power.*
>
> Acton

The dogmas of the creed can be simply recited. That they are dogmas, not neutral fact-statements, needs to be emphasized. Under Wilson's inspired leadership, the dogmas used an ethical language with which everyone might agree; the underlying philosophy, controversial and disruptive of one great belief system and the basic institutions of American life—the republican, was concealed beneath the terms "responsibility," "the public interest" and "efficiency." In one form or another, these dogmas have sparked the movement of the Executive Force in this century. Their highest expression is to be found in the 1950 report of the Committee on Political Parties of the American Political Science Association, published by the Association (though with informal rather than formal sanction), and entitled *Toward a More Responsible Two-Party System.*

This widely cited report asks for a party system that is "democratic, responsible, and effective." To this end it makes a set of recommendations for National Party Councils, one for each of two parties; the Party Council will be composed of approximately equal numbers of what we would call here Executive and Republican elements, that is, presidents and presidential nominees, cabinet members, national committeemen, state committeemen, congressional leaders, governors, and others. Its 600 to 700 members would bind up the party leadership. It would carry on the ideological work of the party and present its programs and revisions thereof. The National Convention would be reformed to be under the spell of this group but at the same time under considerable influences from the electorate, through an elaborate scheme of grass roots party-program groups from the active citizenry.

Of this set of proposals, we can say the following. No practical method is suggested for accomplishing the goal, save by persuasion, which the report admits from time to time is singularly ineffective on these matters. The language and spirit of the proposal is skillful in giving it to be understood that the new party councils will be well-balanced between the executive and republican forces. Therefore, the argument would run, fear of the executive is out of place. And no doubt there were members of the committee drafting the report, who, at least at that time, accepted this and perhaps even insisted on the seeming balance. But we must insist first of all that the scheme, despite its distinguished auspices, is cockeyed rationalism. It is cut out of whole cloth. It has no means of coming into being or persisting in being. Its only possibility of coming into being would be the prior victory of the presidential party. This would set up some such council to help run the whole party.

More of the underlying meanings will be conveyed in a moment, but the set of intraparty arrangements recommended in the Report must be mentioned. First, of course, the national councils are seen as a method of disciplining the party and imposing a program. Then in addition, staff and headquarters are to be made permanent and enlarged, on the national level, and the interpretation of the party platform is put in charge of the national Party Council (working of course with the help of the permanent staff). The programs are to be binding and the National Convention is to be reformed in this respect as well as others. As was said of the Councils, these recommended "reforms" also lack sociological substructure. They are pipe dreams, with an underlying executive force ideology, uneasily contained by members of the committee who had fears of the presidency.

The pretense of standing for a balance of executive and republican forces is abandoned in the section on the party organization in Congress that follows. There, in the eagerness to strengthen and integrate party leadership in the

House and Senate, the whole structure of the legislature is laid open to domination by the presidential party. "It is necessary that there be broad consultation throughout the national leadership of a party before a party leader is elected in either house." (This would consist of the Speaker of the House, the House Majority Leader, and the Senate Majority Leader.) As for the committee chairmen, they should not be elected on seniority principles but first of all upon their devotion to the party program. Committee membership assignments should be dominated by partisan and programmatic considerations. The legislative program should be placed under majority party control. The Senate should adopt the rule of closure by majority rule, ending the filibuster.

Two clear possibilities exist in these recommendations. One is that the present kind of congressional leadership will continue to run the Congress but more strictly than ever, in the name of Party. Such cannot be the scholars' desire because it is precisely their grievance. But the only other possibility is that the leadership of Congress will be exercising someone else's will. Whose could that be? Of this there can be no doubt: it would be the President's.

Moving into the constituencies, the Report states that greater popular participation in politics will foster "responsibility as well as democratic control in the conduct of party affairs and the pursuit of party policies." Party membership will become more attractive to people if they are given a chance to participate in the making of party policy, it declares. These passages are marked by almost incredible naivete regarding who is active in politics and for what reasons. All the recommendations in the section depend upon the advent of new attitudes. But nothing is or was in sight to make the new attitudes come forth. Pious and wishful thinking, of the kind that John Dewey used to denounce, courses merrily through the pages. It is not unexpected then that a direct national presidential primary is recommended for the future and until that great day arrives, a National Convention based upon direct vote of the party rank and file is urged.

That practically nothing of this all has come about does not deprive the report of importance. In the first place, the report exhibits what hundreds of thousands of students have been taught in the last generation in American high schools and colleges. It shows furthermore why political invention has been at a low ebb in America and Congress has had no help in digging itself out of its morass; after all, the Report came near to being the gospel of a whole profession. Other approaches, except some beginnings of logical-empirical analysis, were not developed. The gap between the views and needs of the Republican Force in America and the intelligentsia of the country grew to abysmal proportions.

Most important of all is the actual ideology embodied in the report. Though not so extreme as it might have been if certain members of the Committee had not insisted upon the ultimate danger of the executive, it remains nevertheless a moderately accurate portrayal of the Executive Force formula in regard to the place and role of political parties. Its meanings become plain out of its language: "The crux of public affairs lies in the necessity for more effective formulation of general policies and programs and for better integration of all of the far-flung activities of modern government. . . . It is in terms of party programs that political leaders can attempt to consolidate public attitudes toward the work plans of government. . . . An effective party system requires, first, that the parties are able to bring forth programs to which they commit themselves and, second, that the parties possess sufficient internal cohesion to carry out these programs. . . . The opposition most conducive to responsible government is an organized party opposition. . . . The phenomenal growth of interest organizations . . . makes necessary a reinforced party system that can cope with the multiplied organized pressures. . . . A basis for party cohesion in Congress will be established as soon as the parties interest themselves sufficiently in their congressional candidates to set up strong and active campaign organizations in the constituencies. . . . Party responsibility means the responsibility of both parties to the general public, as enforced in elections. . . . (Among the basic problems of the existing system are that) the national and state party organizations are largely independent of one another . . . there is at present no central figure or organ which could claim authority to take up party problems, policies and strategy. . . . No understandings or rules or criteria exist with respect to membership in a party. . . . (Considering new world conditions, industrialism, wider governmental participation in the economy) party organization designed to deal with the increasing volume of national issues must give wider range to the national party leadership."

As kindly as possible, the Committee explains that considerable opposition can be expected from local interests, congressmen from non-competitive districts (the leaders, that is) and from state and local party leaders. But, on the other hand "greater program responsibility at the level of the political parties is likely to appeal to administrators and the career officialdom . . ." and the President who "could then expect more widespread and more consistent support from the congressional leaders of his party."

There can be little doubt that the effects of the Report, were its recommendations to be adopted, would precipitate a decline in the republican system. Once a centralized national party is created under the leadership of a group that purports to speak in the name of the people and is led by the President or presidential nominee, and once the state-local elements are weakened and the congressional elements of the party are brought into the single unified structure through a reorganization of Congress, the Executive Force will be victorious. From then on, the congressional party would be administered from the central party headquarters under orders from the White House.

Yet all of the reorganization of the American party system is justified in the name of a "program" whose mysterious nature was left for the readers to define. It is implied that this program is by and for the "people." But the "people" is an entity at least as mysterious as the "program." The interest of the Committee in the people is touching, but suspect. It is a way of closing the magic circle so that the witching rites may begin inside.

We have already looked into the nature of the constituencies of Congress, and have learned something of popular participation and information about public affairs. The Committee apparently did not have available to it much knowledge of the people if it expected that there would be a considerable public ready to back their program. They divide the public into three groups. There is first the apathetic of whom they care not at all; then come the party regulars who they believe will support any move to help carry out the view of the party majority. Third occurs the active and independent voter. The last, they feel, can possibly swing elections for candidates promising a responsible party system.

Actually the second group, they should know, is made up mostly of the congressional constituency and has little interest in the so-called majority view. These are the people who would have preferred for the most part Taft to Eisenhower, and Kennedy to Stevenson. Some of them would, however, prefer a national centralized party and would be numbered in the presidential constituency. The third group is small by comparison and they swing from one party to another not, as the Committee asserts, because of issues and program but because of images, personages, and feelings provoked by critical events affecting their impressions of the "ins" and "outs," such as wars and economic conditions.

The Committee's continuous references to the people cannot but be regarded by the unprejudiced reader as the evocation of a myth to support what will transpire behind the altars. There, benefiting from the presumed changes in rules within the parties and Congress, a national presidential party will develop and sell a program to a constituency that will be all the larger because of the presumed decline of the republican party. The "people" who will bring this about will be the presidential faction, while the true people will hear about it in time and respond to it in the only way they can, by accepting it as their own creation and joining in the new practices.

The program itself, to which end the political party has been transformed, will not of course be any more a popular program than any issues are today, except as politicians make it so by a command of the foci of news and gossip. It will be a presidential program and will contain more than a regular good measure of centralizing, socializing, bureaucratizing, and restrictive actions, all of course under the name of liberty and welfare and rationality. The Committee Report indeed lapses at one point into the view that the clear programming which they recommend "will not cause the parties to differ more fundamentally or more sharply than they have in the past." Thus we should have two parties advocating the same or similar programs. What is the gain here then? If the parties are alike, will not the reasons for one winning over another almost surely be the same kind of reasons one finds today—the affairs of a Bobby Baker or of a Sherman Adams or of a religious slight or of a general's personality or of lost jobs? Will not the whole political process agitate the same kind of issues that it does now? By contrast now the congressman can introduce more of his own product and, in supporting another product, cross party lines, which he does freely.

Where would the gain be in the presumed program? The big difference, the "gain," in program as in structure, would be that the individual congressman, regardless of party—because both parties will be doing the same thing— will be forced to support a different kind of program, a program of centralization, bureaucracy, socialization, and personal restriction. Truly the two parties will be alike, just as the Committee declared. But they will be changed, and the difference will spell the abandonment of republican principles.

PRESIDENTIAL VS. CONGRESSIONAL PARTY

Here be four hefty nags
with a flutter and flap of falcon flags
and an unendable hullabaloo,
every state government fallen thru,
nobody left wearing black hair,
jinx on the remnants everywhere,
howling and mourning and every grief
and the kingdom rotten to its last leaf.

Earl of Jui (d. 827 B.C.)

Congress, says a prominent advocate of a "responsible" party system, operates, along with the whole national government, under a four-party system. Says Professor James Burns, there operate on Capitol Hill a Presidential Republican Party, a Congressional Republican Party, a Presidential Democratic Party, and a Congressional Democratic Party. We agree. The word party does not, however, carry formal correctness. "Faction" is the superior term. For what is dealt with is a group of party leaders that operates regularly in freedom of other groups, though often cooperatively and sometimes in conflict.

There is some question as to whether the party affiliation is at all superior to the factional one. A number of Republicans and Democrats, of "conservative" persuasion, are the congressional party. A somewhat larger number of Senators and Representatives form the presidential party. How do these terms correspond to our own? Are the presidential party members part of the Executive Force and the congressional party members part of the Republican Force?

In a broad sense, they are. They may be so not on reasoned grounds, nor even out of sympathy for their faction. Many members will find at any given moment reasons for being on one or another side that do not relate directly to the larger struggle. Some are so out of opposition to an incumbent President, of their own or another party label. Others may fall into their group out of some heated issue such as racial integration.

Furthermore, Congress has numerous independent members to whom party lines and branch lines are equally unimportant. The weakness, decentralization, and unintegration of the American party is introduced in a great many cases at the constituency level. Since the member is elected without the aid of a strong party organization in many cases, he can be independent of party afterwards, whether the presidential or the congressional. The constituency does not

limit him greatly. He follows patterns of opinion or his own
constituents, especially the nuclear constituency, without
penalty and need defer to the congressional or presidential
leadership only in exceptional cases. Actually the congressional party leadership almost never assaults him in his own
constituency. The presidential party may. The latter does
so through the presidential constituency.

The congressman in such instances watches carefully
the indications of trouble from his local party too. He himself is the voice, along with his colleagues of the House and
Senate whose districts may overlap with his, of the congressional party. There remain the presidential constituency
and the local party, state and locality oriented, who can
compete with him for identification with the party label
and through that with the votes of the purely party-oriented
constituency.

For various reasons and particularly in the northern
cities, conflicts between party constituencies and congressional constituencies have occasionally taken place, usually
as the result of a "deal" between the party and presidential
agents. Ordinarily only highly organized areas amounting
perhaps to 15% of all congressional districts contain means
of continuously relating to and supervising the congressman. Only in a few states is there both a heavy concentra-
tion of population and political machine that together result
in a Senator highly responsive to party labels as defined by
others. More districts of the House of Representatives
would be of this character since the parts of states may be
more readily of appropriate demography than whole states.
However, at the same time, the political party organizations
of the old type, the machines, have been becoming scarcer.
Independent congressmen are today discoverable in cities
where once the local organization of the party insisted upon

party discipline among all candidates and officeholders. The conclusion from this would ordinarily be that the congressman was becoming freer of party. And so he is, in the narrower sense.

But in the broader sense of the presidential versus the congressional party, rather than the Democratic *versus* Republican Party, he has been subjected to new pressures to surrender his partnership position in the first for an employee's role in the second. Not the least of the factors behind this development, and typifying the pressures bearing in that direction, was the decision of the Supreme Court of the United States in the case of *Wesberry* vs. *Sanders*, handed down in February 1964. Brushing aside claims that it must avoid trespass upon the scope of policy allowed an equal branch of government, it held that the First Article of the Constitution implied that congressional districts within the states must be roughly equal in population. Apart from the dubious historicity of its reading of the Constitution, the Court followed a path that it has been taking in numerous cases in recent years, first deciding cases on increasingly novel constitutional principles, and secondly favoring directly or indirectly the executive branch in its decisions.

In the case of *Baker* vs. *Carr* in 1962, the Supreme Court declared that the equal protection of laws guaranteed in the Fourteenth Amendment to the Constitution might prevent a state from creating districts in its own legislatures that were greatly unequal in population and referred a Tennessee case back to lower courts for disposition. Shortly thereafter it could be said that half of the States of the Union had undergone some form of reapportionment influenced in some manner by the Court's opinion.

Since the legislatures are one of the staunchest pillars of federalism, are an independent political branch of government, and have never before been the target of such broad action, the *Baker* vs. *Carr* case excited much comment and controversy. One of the consequences of the case receiving the least attention, however, was the effect that the decision might well have upon the great long-term struggle between the executive and republican forces in America.

The reorganization of the basis of the state legislatures began to introduce a heavy flow of new legislators from new districts in the cities and suburbs of the nation. The new district lines also had a part to play in the political party machinery of the states, since nominations of candidates, elections of party officials, and other matters of importance to political parties follow district lines. The areas newly granted additional seats in the state legislatures were likely to have several characteristics: they would produce pro-presidential representatives and officials; they would by the same token reinforce the governor's party in the state legislature and government; they would add to the demand for stronger centralized state parties, and on the national level to the cry for stronger national parties.

A similar chain of consequences would flow from the Wesberry case. Not only Georgia, the case in point, but all except 17 states in the Union were put on notice that they were harboring an unconstitutional inequality in their congressional apportionment by having one or more districts whose population was considerably, say 15% or more, greater than the average, and whose population was presumed to be suffering therefrom and entitled to relief in the federal courts.

The response to the Supreme Court decision began almost immediately. Within several years, reapportionment

alone, apart from other social change, will probably alter
the basic social characteristics of at least fifty districts. On
one side, some rural or urban-rural districts will be merged
into districts of larger population, and on the other side a
number of new suburban districts and other metropolitan
districts will have been created.

The results for the political parties will be that more
districts will be closely contested. Most of the merged districts will have been safe districts; most of the new districts
will be cut into areas where party competition is heavy and
a candidate once elected is not likely to last long in office.
A turnover is to be expected in a higher proportion of congressional seats. Supposing a seat to be competitive when
won by 53% or less of the vote cast, there were, in 1963,
forty-nine competitive seats in the House. Instead of numbering one-tenth of the total, as at present, the competitive
seats will number perhaps a quarter.

The consequence of this may be foreseen. In Congress
the members most in need of political party guidance and
of presidential help are the freshman members and those
from close districts. In the past and at present they are the
most restless under the slow and conservative methods of
the congressional leadership. The *Congressional Quarterly's*
presidential support index may be used for illustration; this
index shows how each congressman's voting compared with
the known preferences of the President on 186 roll call votes
in 1963. Ten out of thirteen Democratic freshmen members of the House competitive districts voted consistently
higher than the average presidential support index of the
House Democratic leadership. Nine gave the President
more support than did all House Democrats on the average. Is this because they are freshmen or because they
come from competitive districts? Both causes are working,

if the separate figures are indicative. Thirty-one out of
thirty-eight Democratic freshmen voted above their leaders' average; Democrats from competitive districts exceeded
their leaders' average of presidential support votes in
twenty-one out of twenty-four cases.

Using the same presidential support index on 52 roll
calls in 1964, we discover that twelve out of fourteen Democratic freshmen members of the House competitive districts
voted more favorably to the President than the House Democratic leadership. Eleven exceeded the average of House
Democrats. Thirty-three of thirty-eight first-term Democrats voted above their leaders' average support of the
President and twenty-three of twenty-eight Democrats from
competitive districts did likewise. The situation changed
little from President Kennedy to President Johnson, one
notes.

All of this occurs despite the large pressures on freshmen and those electorally threatened to abide by their congressional leaderships for the sake of their careers within
Congress and help towards re-election that can be provided
by their leaders. Hence it is not unreasonable to believe
that the future will bring many more congressmen who are
oriented towards the President.

The Speaker and other congressional leaders are not
immune to the trend. They already show signs of having
to adapt themselves to presidential policies, partly owing
to pressures from the congressional rank and file. The
Majority Leader is constrained to follow the President in
fundamental issues; thus Barkley resigned as Majority
Leader when he felt that he lacked the confidence of Franklin D. Roosevelt on an important question before the government. Similarly Knowland, when Republican Majority
Leader of the Senate in the Eisenhower administration, as-

serted that he would have to resign his post too if he could not go along with the President in espousing an issue in the Senate that the President believed in firmly and unequivocally.

The increase in the number of competitively positioned congressmen will bring more pressures upon the leadership. For the party holding the White House the pressure will enhance the President's power and leadership. For the party in the opposition, the tendency will be to seek more popular congressional leaders; these leaders in turn will probably have greater incentive to make a national party record, but a popular record as opposition leaders, not an "obstructionist" record.

Seniority will not count so much in the selection of party leaders as it does now. More and more the committee chairmen will have to come from districts that share the perspectives of the presidential parties. This has already been seen to be the case whenever members from large city centers achieve seniority. Now these same men will be advanced in seniority as the rural members are weeded out, and also the new members will come from the suburbs, which are oriented towards the Executive rather than the Republican Force. The suburban population looks naturally to Washington rather than to the state capital, and to the executive rather than to the legislature. The papers that the suburbanite reads, the offices he works in, the colleges he comes from—all place emphasis upon the executive and the national in his mind.

Nor can an appraisal of the future of the party system as it will affect Congress be complete without taking the matter of racial voting into account. The Negro vote in the North is heavily Democratic and relatively unchangeable in that regard. Even in the South it will probably end up

Democratic. In both cases, it must be appreciated that the degree Democratic may range from 60% to 95%, so that the Negro vote is important to both parties in the presidential races. Yet the areas of heavy Negro residence are bound to send a bloc of Negro members to each Congress. Because of the orientation of their electorate, which is strongly presidential, and their natural tendency to pull the President to the liberal side of racial issues, this bloc, which will increase in size, can be counted on to reinforce the Executive.

It seems almost superfluous to add that the issues of welfare, business regulation, home rule, and party politics will find the Negro leadership solidly behind executive solutions. The fact that Negroes as individuals may be at bottom individualistic and anti-bureaucratic means little in the face of the large and uncomprehended forces that move toward collectivism.

By "non-rational" rather than "rational" reasons, then, the desire for a centralized programmatic party system may be finally satisfied. Quite without the rationality that they may display, the scholars' wishes for the party system may come about. The transformation would occur through the inherent and acquired weaknesses of Congress, and by way of events whose consequences are scarcely foreseen by those who initiated them. By this fact, too, it is unlikely that the resulting system will behave rationally. There will be a straight loss of power from republican institutions to the executive without any increase in intelligence of the politicians—congressmen or others; nor will the new system bring more rational planning and programming of politics.

The question of what is a responsible party system will remain quite unanswered even when the fondest dreams of the advocates of the presidential party are realized. Unless, that is, the crazy logic is accepted that whatever the party may produce goes to prove it is a responsible party, the only requirement being that the members of the party are to be controlled and disciplined in a centralized and integrated way, from the top down.

THE FUNCTIONS OF PARTIES IN A REPUBLIC

> *The common man has neither the distinction of property nor that of expertness or any of the distinctions on the ground of which a person belongs to the upper class; he will be crushed unless the constitution of society attaches some power to the only distinction that he certainly possesses, viz., that of having numbers on his side.*
>
> Yves Simon, *Philosophy of Democratic Government* (1951)

It would be better from the republican position, given all of the foregoing, to resist all movements to make the party "responsible." This does not deprive the party of its utility. The political party in America performs several functions that are not only compatible with the Republican Force but also useful to the democratic political process.

One is that the party presents candidates. It digs them up when they are hard to find, and sorts them out when they are too numerous.

It fosters mobility and contributes to free enterprise and freedoms of other types in American life. It gives the poor and the less privileged a means of rising rapidly in material and other goods of life.

It greases the skids of American political practices. It promotes cooperative behavior in some respects while diminishing its possibilities in others.

It is a convenient handle for manipulating procedures and rules in Congress and other areas of politics; without party, opposition would have to be sporadically organized and would be less controlled, regularized, routinized, and predictable. Party is a tramp steamer into which practically

any kind of cargo can be tossed that cannot be carried by
regular vessels. Professor Schattschneider has lately
written:

> The parties organize the electorate by reducing their alter-
> natives to the extreme limit of simplification. This is the
> great act of organization. Since there are only two parties
> and both of them are very old, the veterans of a century
> of conflict, it is not difficult for people to find their places
> in the system. (*The Semi-Sovereign People,* p. 59.)

Moreover the party, artificially—but no less usefully for
that reason—promotes controversy and discussion of public
affairs. That the sides are impossibly drawn for the purposes of debate means that the effects of argument are more
conducive to self-expression and self-instruction than to legislative action.

In the Congress itself, party is a handy instrument, for
the above reasons to be sure, but also for justifying unin-
telligent voting, much of which has to occur. It is more
satisfying, both to the congressman and to his constituents,
for him to be able to say that he voted a certain way because that was the Republican way or the Democratic
way.

And as it is a cloak for ignorance, it is also a cloak for
wishes going against his constituency on occasion. Just as
independence from the party can be claimed conveniently
on occasion, when party loyalty and discipline are not necessary or called for on a roll call, so also dependence upon
the party and party pressures can be claimed for other votes
that are independently favored by the congressman, but not
by his constituency.

When one considers the great danger that the political
party will be the means by which the government is converted from a republic into an executive bureaucracy, it is

tempting to seek a way out of party politics entirely. If the party were kept as it has been in the past, the problem would not be acute. But, as has been made clear, with a rationale of responsible and efficient government supplied by intellectuals on the one hand, and shifts in the nature of the constituencies on the other hand, a growing centralization, bureaucratization, strengthening, and integrating of the party is perceptible.

In any event, under the conditions of universal suffrage and a democratized society, the political party appears to be indispensable. So long as half the people do not know the rudiments of government but yet vote, they require a myth by which they can vote confidently and with a sense of achievement. This the party label provides. It is a flag to which the voters can give loose and relatively meaningless allegiance. Without the party label on the ballot, half the electorate would act like wild cargo crashing from one side of the ship to the other.

A consistent theory of the place of party in the republic is needed to counter the executive theory which is all too well contrived. It would have to define a limited role for the party much like that held by parties in the past in America. It would give up the search for party responsibility and the idea that such responsibility would bring rationality in government. Party is not now, if it has ever been, the best or the most rational means of bringing together will and intelligence. If congressmen seek those twin virtues through the party system, they will end up automatons carrying out the will and intelligence of the presidency and executive establishment.

Chapter Five

THE MYTH OF THE PRESIDENT

For you they call, the swaying mass,
their eager faces turning,
Here Captain! dear father!

Walt Whitman

"IMAGINE, IF YOU WILL, an official body provided for by
the Constitution and set up in Washington. It is composed
of several hundred men who come from all over the United
States. They have large powers. Although they are disciplined by some leadership, particularly expressed in one
man, and must direct themselves therefore at certain given
national ideals, most of them have their own jobs to think
about and are reaching for their own way in life. Though
sometimes they act in unseemly haste, they usually take a
long time to resolve an issue. They are not necessarily responsive to the 'popular will,' though they swear by it
frequently. Individuals among them have often very little
information of what others are up to; even the most powerful and best informed among them may be unaware of what
is happening either in the group or in the government and
outer world. Such is the presidency of the United States."

Such also is the Congress of the United States. The paragraph begins to make two important points about American government: the presidency is a collective organ of the government; the President is part man and part myth.

By myth is meant that a number of qualities are given to every President that are either quite fictitious or large exaggerations of the real man. The myth is not alone the property of the untutored mind, but of academicians, scientists, newspapermen, and even congressmen.

In fact, much of the difficulty with the institution of the presidency is the overlay of myth and magic on the President. The fatal need for personification of society, animation of ideals, and worship of heroes introduces continuous disorder into the matter-of-fact problems of running a country.

Be it as it may, the Constitution has provided a single chief of state who is both the ceremonial and expressive monarch and the active executive head; the democracy has provided that he be elected by direct popular vote; and it is up to each generation to contain him.

THE PRESIDENT AS EXECUTIVE

In some commonwealths where the legislative is not always in being, and the executive is vested in a single person who has also a share in the legislative, there that single person, in a very tolerable sense, may also be called supreme.

John Locke, *Of Civil Government* (1690)

In a hundred places the President-at-work is described. The description usually contains a listing of his duties and powers. The implication is that he takes care of these matters personally. Actually, the President does almost nothing by himself. He is surrounded by staff. The Executive Office numbers over 1500 persons, of which a third pertain to the

White House, and another third to the Bureau of the Budget, the rest falling in various special agencies such as the Council of Economic Advisers, the National Security Council, and others.

The Central Intelligence Agency is usually included in the Executive Office of the President and numbers some thousands of employees. But then also the heads of agencies and just about anyone else in the executive establishment and a number of outside consultants are at the beck and call of the President. Thus the decision-making of the President can take on the aspects of crowd behavior, or, when organized, the conciliar decision-making of Congress.

On a normal issue that comes before the "President" some dozens of persons are involved. It might be presumptuous to say that more of a collectivity is engaged than when the same type of issue would come before the Congress; but it would be equally presumptuous to say that *fewer* persons were taken up with the matter. Stephen Horn shows, for instance, how dozens of executive officials became involved in the development of a White House position with respect to Senator Kefauver's bill to set up a question period in Congress. All the while, World War II was going on, but the President and cabinet officers became seriously involved too.

To take another example, despite the gross haste with which it was actually designed, the anti-poverty bill of 1964 was proudly described by Sargent Shriver, introducing it in congressional committee hearings, as the product of dozens of informed opinions in the executive agencies.

On the whole, probably *more* persons occupy themselves with the executive's policy than with the legislature's and for longer periods of time. But the character of their involvement differs greatly. The executives file politely aboard; the congressmen sometimes swamp the boat of policy in launching it.

It would perhaps be permitted to say that the President has a determinative voice on the normal issue that the presidency takes up whereas the top oligarchs of the Congress pay more courtesy to one another's determinativeness. (Yet President Truman *did* say: "One word from me, and everyone does as he pleases!")

It might also be permissible to say that the President is the step-up transformer for more initiatives than any one of the congressional oligarchs; that is, one can say a little more accurately "to get a new national policy, get the President's support" than "to get a new national policy, get the Speaker's support" or "to get a new national policy, get the support of the Speaker and the Majority Floor Leader." Still, no matter how carefully these ideas may be phrased, they are bound to appear incredible to the vast majority of people in America and the world outside. The President is an image of power to get things done, the Congress is not.

The President is a Congress with a skin thrown over him. Let us suppose that we have a gymnast executing various movements that end in a good round of applause. As he appears to the naked eye, he seems well-coordinated, graceful, smooth, tireless, and properly directed. But let the eye of the watcher perceive the true action of the muscles, the organ, and the mind beneath the skin, and he will observe all the near-misses, the strains, the compensated inadequacies, and the poisons formed, gathered, and discharged through the system under exercise. The hesitancies of muscle and mind that must accompany even the best performance will be visible. Should he be harsher in his judgment of the athlete exposed than the athlete covered? The President is the athlete covered; even the presidency, the collectivity, is the athlete covered because it operates under all the fictions of the single person. The Congress is of course the athlete exposed.

Presidents can come from private life, from Congress, and from governorships. If they are mediocre before they become President, they immediately lose that quality and become heroes. It is doubtful that the average President is of greater education, oratorical ability, IQ, experience in governmental affairs or physical beauty than the average Congressman. In fact, Lord Bryce, the well-known commentator upon American institutions at the end of the last century, thought fit to write an answer to the question: why great men are not chosen Presidents. Perhaps he begged the question. It can be argued far into the night that Presidents are no less "able" than Prime Ministers of England, French Premiers, and Russian Czars and dictators. Since such arguments would be more than likely on a completely confused plane, it would be best to eschew them. The only point of consequence here is that the office makes the man, very much as in the slogan that "clothes make the man."

And the President plays to the office. His first term is filled with reelection politics: he is primarily creating a personal image that might dwarf any potential opponent in the reelection campaign to come. Congress responds with resentment, and the build-up of paranoia in the legislative branch commences, so that the business of government can never be conducted in a matter-of-fact way. Each branch must fortify itself and perceive in the other not the normally cooperative or conflicting humans, but a spiteful menace.

The President, one personalized being, has the advantage with the mass media and the general public. Under the tutelage of journalists and historians, they speak of him as the author of the years of government in which he serves—

the Administration of Jefferson, of Jackson, of Buchanan, of F. D. Roosevelt. It would not only be psychologically more healthful, given republican premises, to reduce American national history to congressional periods rather than presidential ones, but it would be scientifically more accurate in that the more regular changing of Congress each two years produces greater effects typically, even given the same presidential incumbent, than the change of Presidents. That this is so little done, except precisely among those expert in government, is indicative of the connection between personification and reputation for power.

The myth of the President is thus wrapped up in the fictions of a single heroic leader, which defies the truth of the normalcy of the typical President and the collectivity of his behavior. Many more myths are related to the central one and derived from it, creating a veritable fairyland.

One myth begins with the Constitution. It has it that the President is responsible for seeing that the laws shall be faithfully executed. We do not speak here of the growth in the legislative power of the President. It is well known that every last opportunity for leverage in the constitutional powers of the President has been used to increase his powers. This is no myth; the Constitution has simply been stretched and interpreted to accommodate the development. We speak rather of the fiction that the President executes the laws. He cannot do so personally, of course. Once he might, today he cannot. The President in a real sense is no longer the President.

There is a grand irony. The more powers that are put to the President to swallow, the less of a constitutional President he can be in reality. But not in fiction. The law of agency is a marvelous and mysterious creation of the human mind over many centuries from its birth in the great

Roman legal system. By its operations, people are said to do things that they not only do *not* do but that are actually not known to them as having been done by anybody else. The trouble caused by this situation is not so much that it occurs, because indeed it must occur out of the plethora of business, but that it is believed *not* to occur and therefore people act in terms of its "truth" rather than in terms of its utility.

In part the President is an office, the presidency, whose head knows what is going on in government and has something to say about it. Secondly the President is an office whose head knows what is going on but has nothing to say about it. Thirdly, the President is an office whose head does not know what is going on and has nothing to say about it. There is a little of the first in the presidency, a good deal of the second, and a great amount of the third. It is well to understand this fact. The Constitution provided for the President; it did not provide explicitly for the presidency; nor could it provide for an all-seeing all-doing executive. The President should be seen as a person furnished with a license to capture as much as he can, and as Congress will let him, of the flora and fauna of a gigantic reservation. He should not be regarded as a highly efficient omniscient commander of a vast country.

MAJORITY (MINORITY) CHAMPION

> The artistic ability of Thrasymachus seems to me to have gained him victory in the field of pathetic expressions on old age and poverty. Really, he has acquired ability to stir a whole crowd of people at one and the same time to frenzy and then to charm them out of it by magic, as he said. He has become very good, too, at attacking or answering allegations on almost any basis.
>
> Plato, *Phaedrus*

Many feel regretful that the President cannot oversee and do everything. The President is the only true representative of the people, they believe. If he does not command the apparatus of the government and society, he should. So says for example, Theodore Roosevelt. Woodrow Wilson from whom the theory of the omnipotent President sprang full-blown puts the case appealingly:

> His is the only national voice in affairs. Let him once win the admiration and confidence of the country, and no other single force can withstand him, no combination of forces will easily overpower him. . . . If he rightly interpret the national thought and boldly insist upon it, he is irresistible; and the country never feels the zest of action so much as when its President is of such insight and calibre. Its instinct is for unified action, and it craves a single leader. . . . A President whom it trusts can not only lead it, but form it to his own views. . . . If he lead the nation, his party can hardly resist him. His office is anything he has the sagacity and force to make it. (*Constitutional Government in the United States,* 1907, pp. 67-9.)

Wilson rightly placed the President as potential popular idol, and declared that even the political party would bow before the people's anointed. Ordinary reasoning and logical behavior are useless before the rush of public emotions. The President represents by his personality and by a free choice of issues to place before the country. Unlike Congress, he can conceal his doubts in his inner office and behind seeming action. For so powerful is the amplification of the press behind the President that his expressions are taken for action itself and an expressed will to save the country from Disaster X is taken in the absence of vivid proof to the contrary to *actually* saving the country.

Despite all of this force, on many occasions the President cannot be said to represent the nation but is asserted to do so by those who command the written word. Such occurrences are common when the nation is well-off and the attention given politics is small or an issue is abstract or principled and discourages mass participation. Examples would be found in Truman's efforts to repeal the Taft-Hartley Act, and Roosevelt's attempt to increase the Supreme Court's membership. Strenuous presidential efforts could not raise a great favorable public. Yet since the President is "liberal" by the nature of his office and the character of his constituency, and since the writers about politics and government are largely liberal, the President is alleged to have a pipeline to the great people that he in fact does not have.

In a literal sense, in fact, no American President has been the proven choice of a majority of the people. Suffrage restrictions, indirect election of the President, apathy among potential voters are only several reasons why this is true. On a dozen occasions, among them Lincoln in 1860 and Wilson in 1912 and 1916, the winning presidential candidate received less than a majority of votes cast. But what begins non-logically cannot be destroyed by logic. Where a majority cannot be found, a plurality will do, or in the end just a bigger crowd.

If the President represents the whole people, he would not so often represent the minorities; yet the latter is the reputation that he also bears. The President does represent some minorities, like everyone else, but underrepresents other minorities. He may have felt a majority pulse in going into the first World War, but he did not feel the pulse of the German-American minority who saw the war as a conflict of self-interested European powers, with America as a dupe of England. He may have supported the aspirations of Negro minorities a generation later in civil rights matters but could not be said to express the views of other urban minorities who wished to check the liberties of Ne-

groes. All of this is said without need to mention the many
sectional minorities that have been represented or not represented by the presidency in history, such as the South.

One must conclude that far from representing the majority or the minorities, or for that matter the "little people"
who through the ages have always looked to remote ruling
figures for succor, the President represents now one and
now another and then again both at the same time. He is
the champion of the minority when the minority is angry,
critically positioned, and uses its votes (perhaps for lack of
other weapons of social justice). He is the champion of the
majority when the majority is alert and demanding. He is
the representative of the "little people" in any case, and of
the minority and majority in all cases except the above, too,
whenever he engages in the thousands of acts and expressions of daily life that show the head of state to be not only
ordinarily human but more so.

ADVOCATE OF THE PUBLIC INTEREST

> *Of the three forms of government, the democratic form, in the real
> meaning of the word, is necessarily a despotism, because it establishes
> an executive power; for the "all" which is not really all decides con-
> cerning, and sometimes against, the one who has not participated in
> the decision. The general will is a contradiction to itself and to
> freedom.*
>
> I. Kant

Stemming no doubt from his image as representative of
the whole people is the prevalent myth that the President's
views constitute the public interest or the national interest.
We have already given grounds for believing that the idea
of a national interest is approximately the same as that of
the public interest with the national security element added,
and that the public interest is whatever one asserts to be
good for the country and is agreed with by others. The

others, of course, can be few, many, or practically every-body. To say that the President is custodian of the public interest or of the national interest is presumptuous. The President is custodian of *a* public interest, his own, and that may be popular or not, shared by Congress or not. In short, he is no better off than any other citizen in supplying a public philosophy, except that he has more power to implement his views.

Actually, if anything is meant by the slippery expression, it is that, because of how he is chosen and because of his role in the system, the President will emphasize certain policies and propound certain ideas. It appears, for example, that it is very difficult for a federalist, "voluntarist," decentralizing, "isolationist" politician to be elected President, or if elected President to espouse such policies. Neither Robert Taft nor Dwight D. Eisenhower could move ahead at the presidential level with his original notions.

On the other hand, it is perfectly possible for a man to rise to eminence in Congress with such views. Robert Taft, Howard Smith, Styles Bridges, and William Knowland are several of many cases that could be offered in proof.

At the same time, opponents of such views may likewise lead Congress: one thinks of Rayburn, Humphrey, McCormack, or Lucas. Does that mean that Congress lacks the key to the public interest that the President has? Not at all. It means that congressional leadership may be coming up with an alternative conception of the public interest, which may be accepted or rejected by citizens as they please. Was President Jackson acting in the public interest when he wrecked the United States Bank? Should Grant have annexed Santo Domingo? The secret service policy of Theodore Roosevelt, the cabinet appointments of Hayes, the denial of access to public papers by Cleveland—in these and many other cases Congress and the President clashed vehemently.

Take the Cleveland incident. Congress must have a relatively unrestricted access to public agency information if it must legislate. Cleveland dismissed over 600 officials without cause and by denying Congress access to the papers on their dismissals prevented it from judging the adequacy or even the legality of the dismissals. The aware public apparently supported Cleveland. One might reasonably argue that the public interest was on the side of Congress.

All of which should be obvious, save that people (and scholars) are usually shortsighted and uninterested in indirect consequences. Few of the many dozens of books written about Congress and the President suggest that the Congress may be as amply expressive of the public interest as the President. This becomes indeed a great hurdle in achieving a permanent balance of power between the executive and legislative.

Professor Lawrence Chamberlain not so long ago prepared an analysis of leading legislation over a fifty-year period, in an endeavor to see what were the origins of the laws. They are listed below as they were found by him to have originated in the Congress, in the office of the President, in both equally, or through the efforts of lobbyists. We shall comment upon the origins of the laws later. The important conclusion to be suggested here is that only the most presumptuous of partisans would be able to see in the list of laws a correlation between the presidency (or the Congress for that matter) and laws in the public interest.

An asterisk indicates that one or more bills dealing with this subject had been introduced without administration support and had received substantial consideration of Congress before the administration took a definite position.

PRESIDENTIAL INFLUENCE PREPONDERANT

Agriculture	1	Agricultural Adjustment Act of 1933.*
Banking	3	Silver Purchase Repeal Act of 1893; Emergency Banking Act of 1933; Gold Reserve Act of 1934.*
Business	3	Securities Act of 1933;* Securities and Exchange Act of 1934;* Public Utilities Holding Company Act of 1935.*
Credit	3	War Finance Corporation Act of 1918; Reconstruction Finance Corporation Act of 1932; Home Owners' Loan Corporation Act of 1933.*
Immigration	0	
Labor	1	Second Employers' Liability Act of 1908.*
National Defense	6	Militia Act of 1903; General Staff Act of 1903; Selective Service Act of 1917; Naval Construction Acts of 1901-1905; Naval Construction Act of 1916; Navy Act of 1938.*
Natural Resources	0	
Railroads	0	
Tariff	2	Underwood Act of 1913; Reciprocal Trade Agreements Act of 1934.*
	—	
	19	

CONGRESSIONAL INFLUENCE PREPONDERANT

Agriculture	2	Capper-Volstead Act of 1922;* McNary-Haugen bills, 1924-1928.*
Banking	6	Currency Acts of 1873;* 1878;* 1890;* 1900;* 1908;* Glass-Steagall Act of 1933.*
Business	1	Sherman Act of 1890.*
Credit	3	Federal Farm Loan Act of 1916;* War Finance Corporation Revival Act of 1921;* Agricultural Credits Act of 1923.*
Immigration	9	Chinese Exclusion Act of 1882;* Chinese Exclusion Act of 1892;* General Immigration Acts of 1882;* 1903;* 1907;* 1913;* 1917;* 1921;* 1924.*
Labor	3	Department of Labor Act of 1913;* Second Child Labor Act of 1919;* Norris-LaGuardia Act of 1932.*
National Defense	4	National Defense Act of 1916; National Defense Act of 1920; Selective Service Act of 1940;* Naval Disarmament Act of 1920-21.*
Natural Resources	2	Carey Act of 1894;* Act of 1897.*

Railroads	3	Interstate Commerce Act of 1887;* Valuation Act of 1913;* Transportation Act of 1920.*
Tariff	2	Wilson Act of 1894;* Payne-Aldrich Act of 1909.*
	35	

JOINT PRESIDENTIAL-CONGRESSIONAL INFLUENCE

Agriculture	3	Agricultural Marketing Act of 1929;* Soil Conservation Act of 1936; Agricultural Adjustment Act of 1938.*
Banking	4	Federal Reserve Act of 1913;* Thomas Silver Amendment of 1933;* Silver Purchase Act of 1934;* Banking Act of 1935.*
Business	2	Clayton Act of 1914;* National Industrial Recovery Act of 1933.*
Credit	2	Federal Home Loan Bank Act of 1932;* Emergency Farm Mortgage Act of 1933.*
Labor	4	First Employers' Liability Act of 1906;* First Child Labor Act of 1916;* National Labor Relations Act of 1935;* Wages and Hours Acts of 1938.*
National Defense	3	Army Act of 1901;* Naval Construction Act of 1929;* Naval Construction Act of 1934.*
Natural Resources	7	General Revision Act of 1891;* Newlands Act of 1902;* Weeks Act of 1911;* Migratory Bird Act of 1913;* Migratory Bird Treaty Act of 1918;* Migratory Bird Refuge Act of 1929;* Taylor Grazing Act of 1934.*
Railroads	4	Hepburn Act of 1906;* Mann-Elkins Act of 1910; Emergency Railroad Transportation Act of 1933; Transportation Act of 1940.*
Tariff	0	
	29	

PRESSURE GROUP INFLUENCE PREPONDERANT

Labor	1	Railway Labor Disputes Act of 1926.*
Natural Resources	1	Clarke-McNary Act of 1924.*
Railroads	1	Elkins Act of 1903.
Tariff	4	McKinley Tariff Act of 1890;* Dingley Tariff Act of 1897;* Fordney-McCumber Tariff Act of 1922;* Hawley-Smoot Tariff Act of 1930.
	7	

Of the ninety major laws studied, approximately twenty per cent fall to the credit of the President; roughly forty per cent were chiefly the product of Congress; about thirty per cent fall into the joint presidential-congressional category; and slightly less than ten per cent are identified as primarily the handiwork of external pressure groups.

Two among various reasons for the continued adherence of the notion of public interest to the presidency may be suggested. One is that Congress passes a great number of private bills and bills affecting localities. It constantly rises, too, in support of individuals being abused. This gives the impression of localism, and partialism. The fact that the executive branch of government from day to day engages in hundreds of thousands of similar actions, as part of its obligation, does not reflect back upon the President. The congressman cannot turn down even some dubious cases and must fight for many an unromantic petitioner; the President can confine his special acts to giving medals to heroes, a hero by definition being a person already certified to be in the public interest.

At the other end of the spectrum of actions, the President derives identification with the public interest from the fact that he is concerned with foreign affairs and military security. Naturally, here in a vast area where there are no constituents, the national interest appears plain, and the President is its custodian. This image seeps back into the domestic areas of policy and lends a convincing quality to presidential pretenses in this area as well.

Furthermore, the government, the public, and the nation are tied up together semantically; as words they hang together and permit any one of five million federal employees to impress a private citizen with the allegation that only the nation, that is, the national employee, can define what the national interest is, and only the public, that is, the public servant, may define the public interest. These distortions of meaning are none the less effective for being childish; the vast presidential constituency is not the best educated constituency to be found. It operates on a rather low level of political awareness, information, and skill.

RESPONSIBILITY AND INITIATIVE

> *Shell game. A sleight-of-hand swindling game in which a small pellet, the size of a pea, three walnut shells are used, and the victim bets as to which shell conceals the object; hence, any game in which the victim has no chance to win.*
>
> Webster's New International Dictionary

If the President lacks a monopoly of the national interest, may he not still be the center of responsible government? "The Buck Stops Here," said the little sign by President Truman's desk; no matter who may "pass the buck" to someone else in an evasion of responsibility, the President —luckily for the nation—cannot evade final responsibility.

This is another myth. What are election campaigns but at least large-scale efforts at claiming credit, that is responsibility, and disclaiming blame, that is "passing the buck"? And on a smaller scale, the campaigning goes on all the time. The President, it is true, is charged with signing certain documents, cutting various ribbons, and even with the giving of an indubitable (momentarily) order to fire a great missile volley upon an enemy. But only the veritable acts in themselves are inescapably his. Everything else about them may be passed off, concealed, distorted, parcelled off, and denied. An equally true little sign could read "If it's bad for us, kick it around until it gets lost."

In days of old, it was both a childlike belief and a formal myth of the law that "the king can do no wrong." All mistakes were ascribed to officials and outsiders. One must not imagine of course that the king always escaped political blame. The myth had its limits of acceptance, depending upon conditions, and so with the President. Indeed, the President, though better situated to receive the benefits of this myth than anyone in the country and far more its beneficiary than anyone likes to admit, is more readily blamed than many a chief officer of American business corporations

such as the General Electric Company, or benevolent associations such as the Ford Foundation. Yet blame is not
lightly ascribed to the President: it is rare indeed that a
public opinion poll of the nation will show a majority who
will not say: "The President is doing a good job."

Devotees of the presidency are fond of the phrase
"strengthening the responsibility of the President," by which
they mean usually "making the President more powerful."
If the idea is that of trying to gather together all of the
mistakes that several million federal employees can make
all over the world and laying them upon the presidential
doorstep, it is mad. If the idea is one of making the
presidency so strong that it can suppress and control the
evidences of malfeasance and neglect from all over, the
idea has possibilities.

If the idea is to make the President "who is responsible
to the people by election" now "responsible in fact for all
that the people elect him for," we must ask what in fact the
people do make him responsible for. The "people's mandate" is a term that may satisfy newspaper editors and even
many congressmen, but rarely a careful scholar or expert
upon opinion. When the people's mandate is boiled down,
what remains is "get in" or "get out." And in the case of
Presidents, no matter what they have done in their first term,
it usually says "stay in." Such general expressions are
scarcely calculated to assist the President in being "responsible."

It is probable that the more sophisticated advocates of
"placing greater responsibility" upon the President and
"making the government responsible to the President" are
actually urging a greater coordination and integration of
government—in the departments, the separate independent
commissions, the Congress, and the state governments.

Again the President is to be given greater powers. He is pictured as the Great Coordinator and Integrator.

Yet the President is already charged with so many responsibilities that he has enlarged his staff by several hundred times in the last century. If he is to be given even more extensive powers of making determinations for the agencies, for the Congress, and for the country as a whole, it stands to reason that he will not make the determinations himself but will turn them over (if he ever receives them personally at all) to subordinates. These are not and would not really be "subordinates"; they make the final determinations in a great many important cases and only by fiction and by courtesy are called "subordinates."

If we are to confine our analysis only to the present, we do not see in the operations of the presidency a degree of coordination and integration of work that is higher than that to be observed in Congress. Nor do we discuss the larger executive establishment here. Confining oneself to the thousand-man Congress-cum-assistants body and the thousand-man President-cum-staff-and-associates, that is, the presidency—which body functions in a more integrated, coordinated, and efficient way? To answer such a question, it must be asked, what are the veritable measures of such performance? These are not impossible to devise.

Comparing Congress and the presidency:

1. Which body's members know more about what their co-members are doing?

2. Whose members know more about what the other body is doing?

3. Whose members know more about what the bureaucracy is doing?

4. Whose members know more about what is going on in the country?

5. In which body does an idea have the greatest chance of being born, and once born, of achieving some consideration?

6. In which body does an idea that is to be ultimately adopted pursue a path that a group of outside scientists and experts on logic, intelligence operations, and administrative procedure would say bring to bear the more powerful interests and instruments of intelligence?

7. In which group does an order by the top leadership obtain the quickest response throughout the group?

8. Which group's ordinances obtain the quickest response in the country and in the executive establishment at large?

9. In which group is a policy originated and processed into final form most quickly?

10. Which group can give the most ready and thorough response to problems arising out of the operations of the executive establishment?

Here are ten criteria of coordination, integration, and efficiency, three terms that are almost useless and certainly dangerous unless they are qualified. To every one of these ten questions, the general answer may very well be: "Congress." And if such is the answer, then a serious indictment may be read to the numerous contingents of experts upon government who over many years have played upon these supposedly neutral and scientific terms to transform the nature of American society and government from a republican form to an executive system.

It is untrue that congressional work is generally undertaken in confusion, without expert knowledge and planning, and without consideration of all points of view. Sometimes when this happens, as with the "War on Poverty" Bill of 1964, the faults lie with the President. It is a myth that the presidency embodies more discipline, foreknowledge and expertness.

The scientific planning, technocracy, and scientific management movements in America have in this century produced an image which, transferred to the presidency, has provoked this myth. Rational foresight, long-range planning, and full and deliberate consideration of alternatives are supposed to be features of the top executive. If they are not already, they would be, save for an obstructionist attitude on the part of old-fashioned congressmen. In a fat work which is good on details but short on general order and intelligence, Professor Holcombe has written, "The experience of the generations under the Constitution has taught that only Presidents, and candidates for the presidency, can conveniently produce plans for the effective use of the legislative powers of Congress."

Holcombe himself gives examples of the contrary and there is no firm basis for his conclusion. In fact, both the presidency and the Congress plan for the most part unscientifically. Their capacity to use applied social science—economics, sociology, and administration—is untutored and inadequate. Yet that Congress is worse in this regard is doubtful. Holcombe might more accurately have said that "the teachers of the constitution have lately taught that only Presidents . . . etc."

So far as sheer knowledge is concerned (and knowledge is after all *one* concern of good planning), Congress is superior to the presidency. So much is admitted by writers who may be in the course of appealing for more permanence in the high offices of the executive branch. As the Second Hoover Commission reported: ". . . Men of long experience just change places in the Congress in taking over the important committee posts. The Congress continues to have men of experience in its important positions, and a large pool from which to draw these people, while the executive branch tends to get a group of limited political experience in the highest political positions of secretary, under secretary, and assistant secretary." *

The President himself and his immediate staff may or may not have extensive governmental and political experience. Still there are and will always be a group of congressmen who know more about any single agency than does the Chief Executive. They are the only people, these congressmen, who know any considerable amount about the agency outside of the civil servants running the agency. Their potential great value must be admitted, even if their realization of it for the national good be doubted.

But is knowledge used for planning? Individual congressmen may be experts, but does the whole Congress have a program? The answer must be first a question: "What is a plan?" And what are the limits of planning? So that we have four questions from one. Congress has only a very limited notion of planning and programming. The noblest effort in that direction in recent history, and perhaps since the Radical Republicans of the reconstruction period, was that of Senator Robert Taft in the Eightieth Congress, 1946-48. He had several proposals, inter-related and consistent generally with his philosophy. But this was not

---

* Commission on Organization of the Executive Branch of the Government, *Personnel and Civil Service* (1955), p. 220.

treated too well by his colleagues and only part of it was enacted.

Holcombe records that "only two congresses, the Fifty-first (1889-1891), which was Republican, and the Fifty-third (1893-1895), which was Democratic, were able to execute comprehensive party programs. Both of these programs the voters promptly repudiated at the polls." (p. 210) It cannot be ventured that a certain way to political success is a program, even a successful one.

In consequence, it is not surprising that Presidents, too, lack comprehensive programs in the valid sense of the term. A program, or plan, is ordinarily defined as a group of proposals connected by a set of consistent underlying principles. If this is too strict a definition, it may at least be said that a program cannot be whatever the President may wish at any given moment. But that in fact is the way in which the word is used by the presidential party and to a large extent adopted by the press and Congress. The President's program is more a smorgasbord than a diet, but whatever he wants is called part of his program.

It is actually his calendar, that is, those matters that he hopes at any given moment to get congressional action on before the next time he revises the calendar. Thus in 1962-64, a strong Civil Rights bill was part of the President's "program"; it was accelerated or decelerated with changing conditions, and at times was bypassed by other bills such as agricultural support bills.

When the President, as has been the practice for the past several terms, presents to the country at the beginning of each year in his State of the Union message, a long list of goals, he again does not present a program and certainly not a plan, at least not by our terms. For his program is a stringing-together of a great many things that he would like to do for the country—a few of which are concrete enough to be legislative proposals and fewer still of which would be enacted into law. Therefore, one would not be doing the presidential system an injustice to say that the President's program is another myth of the presidency.

It is even doubtful whether the President should be conceded to have more initiative than the Congress, although the impressive sort of listing of goals that was just referred to would seem to clinch the title of the Great Legislator for him.

It has become the pattern in the last generation for Presidents to have rousing, if childish, slogans. "The New Deal," "The Fair Deal," "The Great Crusade," "The New Frontier," "The War Against Poverty" and "The Great Society" help create the impression that the President has creative ideas, energy, and a program. Sober reality testifies to the contrary. Becoming President is too much a merry-go-round to fix a program in mind. Staying President is too dizzying to remedy the lack.

Neither Congress nor the presidency produces programs in the logical long-range sense. Individual laws are another matter.

Lawrence Chamberlain's documented survey of the origins of major legislation shows, for example, that the Congress was the source of many more important laws over a period of half a century than the presidency. (See above, pages 81-82.) A large group of laws was, to be sure, attributed to the joint efforts of both congressmen and presidency. Perhaps the situation has changed to give the President more of the initiative in the past few years. This is doubtful, however, once the cobwebs of myth are wafted away from the hard facts.

Between 1953 and 1963 less than 50% of the legislation proposed by the President were enacted into law. Those enacted were only one-third of all laws enacted. These were the findings of a Congressional Quarterly survey. For instance, in 1959 Congress approved 93 of the 228 proposals submitted by President Eisenhower; in 1963 it passed 109 of the 401 proposals of President Kennedy. Still these are only surface indications: the President often proposes hopeless bills; further, his ideas often come from congressmen originally. The Peace Corps, for example, would be remembered by most people as President Kennedy's creation. Actually its creator might better be said to be Congressman Reuss of Wisconsin.

The story of Congress, though that of a marvellously organized machine from one perspective, is, from an equally valid perspective, a set of biographies of legislative heroes, men who have by themselves or a couple of colleagues worked strenuously and brilliantly to originate, research, develop, and enact into law through the tortuous mazes and disheartening obstacles of the legislative and executive processes some vision of a better arrangement of human relations in society.

TIME, SPEED, AND CRISIS

> *Banded together as they are—working a system which, like all systems, necessarily proceeds in great measure by fixed rules—the official body are under the constant temptation of sinking into indolent routine, or, if they now and then desert that mill-horse round, of rushing into some half-examined crudity which has struck the fancy of some leading member of the corps.*
>
> J. S. Mill, *On Liberty*

It is also a myth that more time is wasted in Congress than in the presidency. The President's time is "wasted" in many ways, some of them impossible of reform, as the time he must spend with numerous minor potentates, and signing a great many letters and documents as Head of State. Other time he may choose to spend on petty matters, taking a day to name a boat, or three days to appoint a postmaster of Pittsfield, to use examples from the schedule of John Kennedy. Actually it may be offered for consideration that the President is so much needed for the petty ceremonials of government that he cannot possibly be an executive and should not be given the more serious tasks of running the great agencies and studying the processes of legislation on numerous substantive questions.

Since the President's time is so occupied, it is likely to be a myth also that "speed and dispatch are the characteristics of the presidency" in contrast to Congress. A new idea born in a bureau will normally take several years to grow to acceptable maturity in a budget message of the President. Another year for the test of the legislative process is required for final acceptance. If the Congress were eliminated from the process, the idea would simply move more slowly through the executive offices. An idea born in congressional circles often shortcuts or speeds through several bureaucratic echelons. What passes for "speed and dispatch" in the presidency is usually emergency action— referred to variously as "fire-fighting," "trouble-shooting," "crash programs," "disaster relief," etc. And of course there are the prompt responses to foreign aggression against American interests, which the presidency has the power to make, with or without simultaneous consultation with congressional leaders. This species of emergency action, civil and military, has produced an unwarranted reputation for speed and dispatch on affairs in general.

To expand the domain of the presidency further, the whole area of governmental powers has been opened up by the doctrine of the age of crisis. The "age of crisis," the "permanent crisis," the "cold war," the "critical times" —all demand mobilization of the country for decisiveness, speed and dispatch. Again occurs the premise that these abilities are incorporated in the presidency, which is quite doubtful. But the other premise is doubtful too. The problems of today are perhaps grave and critical, but none of them are likely to be solved by collapsing the decision-making process by some months to save time. The French had a decade to save the whole of Indochina from the Communists; the United States had another decade to save South Viet Nam. Never during this period could it be said that the executives of either government revealed some intrinsic advantage over the legislature, or were compelled to act urgently and without recourse to deliberative councils.

Almost invariably "time saved" is time wasted: important decisions are badly made, consequences are not foreseen, opposing views are not taken in account, and remedial measures are sooner called for. The attempt in 1961, directed by the presidency, to unseat the Cuban government of Fidel Castro resulted in the Bay of Pigs invasion, which one authority, T. Draper, wrote is generally considered to be "one of those rare politico-military events—a perfect failure."

Crisis is where one seeks it. It is everywhere, if one feels it. The age of anxiety is itself a potent cause of the age of crisis. The presidency is in this sense much more excitable than Congress. It is by the same token the focus of the anxious crowd of the age.

The story of how real crisis has in the past brought power to the presidency—power that was not to be relinquished thereafter—has been often told. The presidency rides tall in the saddle with every American military adventure. The bigger the war, the larger the shift of power from Congress to the presidency, and the longer the period required for partial recovery. Laws and practices of World War II inimical to the Republican Force still rule the country, even some that are poorly translated into civilian terms.

The largest reason why the presidency grows in wartime is psychological, not administrative. The conduct of war by the presidency is not impressively efficient by comparison with war conducted by Congress. History is biased as it is read on this point. The Continental Congress gave General Washington no more trouble than Lincoln and his cabinet gave his generals, or Truman and his advisors his. The confusion in the presidency during World War II was as astonishing as any in the history of the country; by contrast, except for its initial over-enthusiasm, the conduct of Congress was decorous, matter-of-fact, and effective.

Congress was too modest in fact. This has been a constant trouble in times of emergency. Congressmen, being only human, are themselves subject to the man-on-horseback hallucinations. The releasing of powers in generous and vague terms to President Johnson in 1965 to deal as he saw fit with the Viet Nam conflict was typical; congressmen were stuck between their feelings of patriotism and their rational role as initiator and critic of policy, and surrendered completely to the former. And they are pushed by many of their constituents. Any remedy for presidential aggrandizement during military emergencies has to circumvent the psychological paramountcy of the President; this cannot be challenged directly without further exciting popular demands for dictatorship. The procedure in wartime must be coolness and careful constitutionalism; when peace comes it must be prompt and complete reversion. When war and peace are undistinguishable, both procedures must be continuously undertaken.

In this age, which as well as being an age of anxiety and an age of crisis is an age of applied social science, it is a growing practice to create crises. And at creating crises the presidency has no peer. It has the instruments. It can stir up the press, call White House conferences, begin "crash programs," point with alarm to underprivileged people of different sorts, and altogether discover innumerable pockets of crisis in the world.

Each crisis can mean a new program and increased functions for the government, that is, the executive establishment. The crises of today are the programs of tomorrow. The presidency is almost always then a permanent beneficiary of crises that it may discover at home or abroad, for from them it achieves powers and personnel in abundance.

The crisis myth lends support and substantiation to the myth of the lonely and overworked President. A European writer, Roberto Michels, long ago pointed out that the complete picture of the "duce" required the alternation of periods of frenzied sociability with periods of equally intense loneliness. The American President is rarely alone but it is said that he is lonely, made so presumably by "the terrible weight of decisions only he can make."

Apart from the fact that the President *need* take no decision himself, there is the question of how many presidents have made up their minds alone how many times, and whether when such occurred a feeling of loneliness was imparted. One might submit that every man and woman, unless deficient in normal mental qualities, makes decisions of equal relative and subjective weight in life, and often feels misunderstood and afraid, which gives rise to a feeling of aloneness.

With a million-dollar income, in cash and kind, and a huge staff and retinue, the President need be neither lonely nor hardworking. If he wishes to drive himself into a state of fatigue and desperation from working, he may of course do so. But he has less excuse for so doing than, let us say, the small businessman, the writer, the newspaper editor, or the congressman, all of whom lack the bolstering environment the President inherits and the luxurious resources for easy decision-making that he has. Every busy person has to protect himself from pestering and self-pity. It is probable that in this recurring legend of the President lies an attempt to aggrandize the person and office; in it lies a risk of making him nervous at the thought of overwork and fearful of appearing indecisive to himself.

The latter would be bad, for, goes the myth, good Presidents are strong. Said Woodrow Wilson in 1898, "Other Executives lead; our Executive obeys." But he did his best to change this lamented condition. So the "good" Presidents manipulate Congress, bulldoze Congress, set the people upon Congress and achieve their ends. *Ipso facto* this is the public interest—and really the writings of Wilson, Binkley, Lippmann, and other authorities on the President say no more than this. On the other hand, when congressional groups overpower the President or frustrate his demands, Congress is said to be recalcitrant, obstructive, and incompetent.

Actually, can it not be said that a "weak" President is good when inaction, cooperation, etc., is desired, and a "strong" President is good under other circumstances? Presidents are of many types, and even if weak and strong were used objectively, they would be terms far too simple for the reality of presidential-congressional relations.

There are passive Presidents, such as Eisenhower, Coolidge and Hoover, who usually let Congress alone and hope for the best. There are positively principled Presidents such as Wilson and Truman, who believe and act on the idea that they should present a large legislative program to the Congress for enactment, but exert pressure from a fair distance. Some Presidents see Congress as a body to be dominated and exploited, as the two Roosevelts. Jefferson and Kennedy worked to win over Congress to their proposals by party intervention and continuous liaison. These categories and others can be distinguished. They are useful principally to underline how varied the sets of relations between Presidents and Congresses can be.

The background of Presidents is far from uniform and leaves little hope of generalities. No one type has a monopoly of "better relations" (a meaningless phrase in itself) with Congress. The presidency has sometimes been a means for outside forces to push through into the top policy levels of the federal government against the will of the professionalized, long-tenure congressional oligarchy. The cases of Eisenhower, Grant, and other generals, not to mention unsuccessful candidates such as John W. Davis and Wendell Willkie, come to mind. A military man is ideal for the spearhead of such a movement to reorganize a party against its regular congressional faction or to get a new contingent of managers at the top in Washington. Yet success does not necessarily attend such efforts. Congress usually finds that a general, perhaps because of his West Point education and his eternal concern over funds in his military experience, is deferential to it.

The development of the institution of state governor as the proving ground for presidential candidates in a way accomplishes the same purpose. In the last two generations, Wilson and Franklin Roosevelt exemplified the supposed trend, which, it must be admitted, is scarcely detectable since Roosevelt, except among potential and actual candidates for the President's office. Whether it be military men or governors under consideration, it is not at all sure that any dominating influence over Congress and congressional government must be met facing outward. Congress itself has its own complement of men who would gladly "reform" it drastically.

REPUBLICANISM OF THE PRESIDENTS

I happen, temporarily, to occupy this White House.

Abraham Lincoln

Given the numerous types that occupy the presidency, is it not possible to have a long-term cyclical balance that will produce eternal equilibrium? A strong President and a complaisant Congress would be followed by a weak President and a domineering Congress, and so on indefinitely. And occasional lapses from this situation would be more than made up for by the untidiness of historical waves, so that the very uncertainty of events would prevent any stabilizing of a new order of executive supremacy or dictatorship.

This might be the case if it were not for the growth of the executive establishment. As in the Roman Empire and the French Republic, the bureaucracy provided all the background cushioning that was needed to accommodate the weak executive chiefs who happened along. We are getting ahead of our story here, but it is well to appreciate how dictatorial revolutions happen and what they signify.

It seems absurd to the average American to contemplate a presidential dictator. It seems absurd for three reasons.

He thinks of the genial past incumbents. He has had a deficit of experience with a government that challenges his root ideas. And he dreams that a dictatorship is a government that is disliked by the people (and by himself who identifies with the people). When a foreign authority like Dennis Brogan calls the President "an elective emperor," the American smiles; he knows better.

Concerning the geniality of presidents, the "average American" can be logically refuted, though actually he cannot be changed. From a small schoolboy, he has been taught to respect the President, particularly the dead Presidents, and the text writers have taken to heart as nobody else the ancient injunction, *de mortuis nil nisi bonum.* The harsh, violent Jackson becomes a thoughtful liberal, at the hands of a liberal modern historian. So no matter how reviled the live politician, the dead President is revered.

As Professor Charles Beard pointed out once, the authors of the Constitution and most early Americans were not so sure of the automatic virtue of the President. Wrote Hamilton in Number 22 of *The Federalist,* "In republics, persons elevated from the mass of the community, by the suffrages of their fellow-citizens, to great stations of preeminence and power, may find compensations for betraying their trust. . . . Hence it is that history furnishes us with so many mortifying examples of the prevalency of foreign corruption in republican government."

Indeed, when it came time to explain why the President was not given complete power to make treaties with foreign powers, Hamilton wrote, in Number 75 of *The Federalist,* "The history of human conduct does not warrant that exalted opinion of human virtue which would make it wise in a nation to commit interests of so delicate and momentous a kind, as those which concern its intercourse with the rest of the world, to the sole disposal of a magistrate created and circumstanced as would be the President of the United States."

But we need not rest with theoretical writings, no matter how sound. Just before the Civil War, it might have occurred that a President was elected who had confederate sympathies and who might in a subsequent conflict have joined his interests with the seceding states against a presumed majority; who would have been the traitor, who the would-be dictator if the secession had been made unnecessary by his partisanship with the confederate cause?

Franklin D. Roosevelt would probably have gone on as President for so long as he lived, a kind of American Salazar as the ideas of the New Deal receded in originality and importance in the new America.

Under the peculiar circumstances of American foreign policy just after World War II, there were the circumstances of the candidacies of Henry Wallace, first for Vice-President whence he would have been President and later as candidate of the Progressive Party for President.

And then there was Aaron Burr. His name rings ominously in American ears. They must remember who he was. He was a man of "impeccable" background, intelligent, well-educated, son of a University President and minister, handsome, adroit in human relations, admired by men for his virility, courage and skill, and by women for his courtliness and sweetness of disposition.

He tied Jefferson in the vote for President of the United States, and was eliminated only after unprincipled bargaining that might have elected as well as defeated him. He thereafter seems to have engaged in a conspiracy to seize the western territories of the United States and to form a new nation with himself as President. Tried by the Supreme Court for treason he was acquitted for lack of two witnesses to the overt act. The founding fathers, in their anxiety to protect the rights of individuals at the bar made it difficult to accomplish full protection against treasonable officials, even though they may have perceived such possibilities.

Thus, the average American, thinking of past Presidents, exercises a selective memory. With historians to help him, he represses unfavorable experiences. Not so much the Southerner, who has had them in unerasable abundance. It is simple to educate a Southerner to the dangers of presidential tyranny because he believes that his ancestors were suppressed under Lincoln, and to a lesser degree under other Northern Presidents.

Most Northerners, of course, will dismiss this illustration as wrong. What they may ignore, in their haste to dismiss, is that dictatorship has to do with loss of freedoms and it is illogical to dismiss another man's view of freedom as inconsequential when seeking to determine whether a dictatorship exists. They further conceive that a "good" man cannot be a source of despotism. They finally forget, in their enthusiasm over Lincoln for having saved the Union, that a number of serious blows were directed at republican institutions during the course of the war. If they wish in fact to venerate Lincoln, they might most fittingly do so because, in Charles Beard's words "his violations of the Constitution, if such they were in fact, were trivial in comparison with his fidelity to the mandates imposed on him by the supreme law of the land." (*The Republic,* p. 62.)

"THE FREEDOM BOSS"

> *It is impossible to make great largesses to the people without great*
> *extortion: and to compass this, the state must be subverted. The*
> *greater the advantages they seem to derive from their liberty, the*
> *nearer they approach towards the critical moment of losing it. Petty*
> *tyrants arise who have all the vices of a single tyrant. The small*
> *remains of liberty soon becomes insupportable; a single tyrant starts*
> *up, and the people are stripped of everything, even of the profits of*
> *their corruption.*
>
> de Montesquieu, *Spirit of the Laws*, Bk. VIII, ch. 2

Again and again in discussions of dictatorship it appears that people reject its possibility because of their notion that despots must be evil men. They are quite wrong. The opposite is the case. Despots are usually well loved. And to say that the American people cannot love a despot shows little knowledge of American history, the American character, and the nature of despotism. The American states and cities have had a goodly number of bosses. Characters such as Huey Long of Louisiana, Stephenson the Ku Klux Klan Governor of Indiana, Boss Hague of Jersey City and Talmadge the Elder of Georgia.

Imagine, then, the "freedom boss," as he can be called. He becomes dictator by giving people freedom. He gives to 30,000,000 old people greater security by national welfare schemes, and "security is freedom." He champions Negro rights and ingratiates himself to 12,000,000 Americans to whom "rights are liberties." To the intelligentsia—writers, artists, architects, and performing artists—go grants and subsidies and understanding; another million people who believe this to be in support of "free expression" will admire him.

A million scientists too will pocket their subsidies, enjoy their new laboratories and approve, in the form of a quietly reasoned dogmatism, his "understanding of science" that enables the free world to grow great in knowledge. Large grants to educators from the federal treasury and cordial "acknowledgment of their important role in American life" through a multitude of well-financed conferences, fellowships, and research projects will bring applause and support from 5,000,000 more who need these "tools of freedom."

Such activities give ample scope to the ambitions of a great many bureaucrats; society will now award them greater respect, and to the bureaucrat "respect is freedom to do a useful job with dignity." To 2,000,000 civil servants are added three millions of the armed forces whose energies are needed (respect again) and freed for many missions throughout the world. There remains but one more necessary ingredient and here the presidential dictator must make a choice. He may decide on the one hand to give to unions "freedom of association" (the Peron formula). On the other hand he can give employers "freedom of management" and "every worker's right to a job" (the Mussolini formula). In the first case he will gain 30 millions and in the latter 20 million adherents.

Some 74 to 84 millions of adults are included in the previous calculations out of a total adult population in the United States of about 110,000,000 persons. Thus about two-thirds of the American people are caught in the net of "the Freedom Boss." A great many ideological opponents, cynics, sceptics, apathetics, and hostile interests can be eliminated from these larger groupings, and from the remainder of the population, and still there would be an ample basis for a popular dictatorship in the name of freedom. In a country of "nice guys" a dictator should be a "nice guy" too; but that quality is easy to find and, if not found, to create.

An advantage of our speculative analysis is that the interweaving of the executive establishment with the presidency is to be perceived. The problem of dictatorship in

America is linked up with an administrative revolution. Unless we are treating of a "banana republic," it is the bureaucracy that finally creates the conditions of dictatorship in a land—not economic conditions, wars, corruption, "bad leadership," popular apathy, or lunatic fringes.

That is, there must be the essential conditions of centralization, integration, a monolithic concept of the public interest, a welfare or socialist state, and a prepared uniformity of opinion, if a President is to become dictator. The congressional and Republican Force will tend to resign and disintegrate under the steady wearing power of the great state. And there is a dictator only because the bureaucratic state must have a face. It wants a personality to supply blood and guts to the form of rule. It needs the President as the frozen pond needs a skater to make a winter scene perfectly human.

"TRUSTEE OF THE NATION"

> *This natural royal law is conceived under this natural formula of eternal usefulness: since in free commonwealths all look out for their own private interests, into the service of which they press their public arms at the risk of ruin to their nations. To preserve the latter from destruction a single man must arise, as did Augustus in Rome, and take all public concerns by force of arms into his own hands, leaving his subjects free to look after their private affairs, and after just so much public business and of just such kinds, as the monarch may entrust to them.*
>
> Giambattista Vico, *The New Science* (1725)

The last sticking point of the person who will not believe that we have a permanent problem of dictatorship by the Executive Force in America is in the precise imagining of the machinery of transition. That is because he personalizes the process excessively—vaguely but excessively. The transition is accomplished in a hundred guises that in the end amount to a complete set of transfers from old institutions to newer ones, from republican to bureaucratic ones. The personality element is minor; whether the Head is hated or loved is relatively unimportant. The institutional change is major. That institutional change is well on its way too; at least two-thirds of the necessary transformations have been accomplished. They need to be routinized and expanded.

As to the physical achievement of a permanent head of the Executive Force, along, say, Soviet lines, where indefinite tenure is the rule, this may come through an elected President, or in the line of succession to a resigned President (forced by a presidential-executive party in Congress allied with elements of the executive branch). The transition might even be accomplished by a person who has been called in or elevated in position to act as arbitrator of a deadlock between the President and Congress. A military man of courage and prestige, such as the late General MacArthur, would be the type sought out for such a role. He would then maintain his position as "Trustee of the Nation" afterwards, for the "duration of the crisis."

That the Constitution might not carry such a title and give it powers is not an insurmountable barrier. If only that which the Constitution prescribed were in being, half the apparatus of government would have to disappear. The President himself is mostly a non-Constitutional creation. If George Washington had decided to become Speaker of the House instead of President under the new Constitutional government, the whole history of the institution of the presidency and Congress would probably have been changed. In any event, amendments to the Constitution are no longer thought to be as difficult to bring about as they once were. They will be much easier for the presidential party after the reorganization of the state legislatures and Congress brought about by the Supreme Court in the decisions of *Baker* vs. *Carr* and *Wesberry* vs. *Sanders.* And finally, even if an amendment to repeal the 22nd Amendment and permit a President to succeed himself were desired rather than one creating the Trustee of the Nation, but were politically impossible to bring about, the law of the Constitution might not interfere with an incumbent President from remaining on and on in office.

For the Supreme Court as constituted and as it has laid down that law, has shown a capacity for admitting interpretations of the Constitution far at variance with the language of the document but in accord with the existing pattern of political power. If the President ran for re-election, only the Supreme Court could deny him the right under the Constitution, and the Court would have to take up the case in the first place, and then, if it did so, might well decide the question was too political to handle (for it *has* but it also *has not* denied itself that luxury in recent months) and the 22nd Amendment itself might be found in conflict with other powers granted the presidency under the Constitution and therefore declared invalid or strictly limited.

There is little use to further conjecture on how the Amendment might be repealed, cancelled, or ignored. It is not difficult to reason how, with or without the Constitution, a determined and powerful move to keep a President or Trustee in the highest position of power indefinitely can succeed. The more critical problem is how the Executive Force manages to triumph over the Republican Force. This is the salient question of sociological history, retrospective and prospective. The other, a minor sociological problem, descends into petty legalisms and personalities and neither protects a nation from disaster nor prepares it for glory.

Chapter Six

THE EXECUTIVE FORCE

> *Bureaucratic authority in the modern world has, wherever it has developed in large-scale associations such as nations or metropolises, led always to the weakening of the role of collegiality in effective control. Collegiality unavoidably obstructs the promptness of decision, the consistency of policy, the clear responsibility of the individual, and ruthlessness towards outsiders in combination with the maintenance of discipline within the group. Hence, for these and certain other economic and technical reasons, in all large states that are involved in world politics, where collegiality has been retained at all, it has been weakened in favour of the prominent position of the political leader, such as the prime minister.*
>
> Max Weber,
> *Wirtschaft und Gesellschaft*

A SOCIETY THAT is being peacefully subverted, rather than conquered by violence, is disarmed because the new force is not composed of "bad men" nor is it a "conspiracy." Lacking the threats that excite resistance, it cannot be mobilized for defense. "Men born to freedom," wrote Justice Brandeis once, "are naturally alert to repel invasion of their liberty by evil-minded rulers. The greatest dangers to liberty lurk in insidious encroachment by men of zeal, well-meaning, but without understanding."

The presidency, we have said, is the spearhead of the Executive Force in society. The President is not ordinarily an unpleasant person; he certainly does not incarnate evil.

Left to himself he would usually make a mark like that of the Speaker of the House. But he embodies the nation in the popular mind; and all those things that go to heighten that embodiment are anti-republican. In the second place, through the presidency and the executive branch of the government, he is compelled to front for the Executive Force. He supplies symmetry to the government, makes of a trunk a neat pyramid.

Through him it can be said that "the people rule," and every government today must have a way of "proving" that the people rule. So long as Congress is powerful and competes with the President along lines set forth in the Constitution or along lines that may be newly developed in the future, the dangers of executive usurpation of the republic are controllable. Congress not only fights the President; it shores him up in a fundamental way. For, as Congress weakens, the President becomes less republican and more executive. He builds upon unrepublican elements; he derives his public, his councillors, his initiatives, his influence, his missions differently. He comes to get them from the executive branch, the career service, what could be conveniently called the bureaucracy but had better, since the word lacks objectivity in popular speech, be called the civil service.

THE DIMENSIONS OF LEVIATHAN

> *"When social habits decay they must be met by new laws, nor is this an intentional departure from the Ancients, but in order to correct mistakes and arrest decline. Administration must adjust itself to society, and currency changes with the generation."*
>
> Sang Hung-Yang, Lord Grand Secretary
> Huan K'uan, *Discourses on Salt and Iron*
> (81 B.C.), trans. Esson M. Gale, 1931, p. 27

The civil service, as the great engine of the Executive Force, molds the President more than he shapes it. If the executive revolution is finally consummated, the President will be of the new image much more than in the old; he will resemble the Executive Force infinitely more than the force will resemble him as he is and has been. That is, his mode of address, associates, traits, functions, mode of work, will be derived from the executive branch. He will come into office not in the boots of Andy Jackson, but in the haberdashery of Harry Truman. He will be neither rural nor urban, but suburban, for there is where the executive suite is fashioned.

Ambassadors have been transformed in the name of all that is holy to the Executive Force—namely efficiency, control, expertness, integrity, and permanence, from politicians and businessmen into career civil servants. The cabinets of Presidents have been transformed in membership from politicians into business managers. The environment of the presidency has become more formal, carefully guarded, and rooted into the civil service. All of this has occurred however, with careful attention to the "personality" of the President.

This cannot be left to accident. There is not only a political investment in his image. There is a governmental one. The government image is over time the more important by far, because it is the only exciting edge of the executive front. The Executive Force can accomplish everything except personification. For this it needs the President.

Cannot the Executive Force become supreme by way of and behind the banner of Congress? It could only do so if Congress could free itself from its present foundations. But this is almost impossible. Congress, as we have given reason to believe, is an institution deeply imbedded in federalism, the free enterprise system, and decentralization of society and politics. It represents basically these values.

It can only represent the Executive Force by means of the President and nationalized politics. In part it has come to do so and ultimately, of course, when the Executive Force does triumph, the President's party will win in Congress and the Republican Force in Congress will wither away and be replaced by a weak but "satisfactory" representation of the Executive Force.

But it should be made clear at this early stage of discussion that the Executive Force can conquer either without violence or with it; it needs the personality of the President but not any particular President; it is not a conspiracy; and it is never subject to approval (or disapproval) by a single vote of Congress or the people, though its many parts may be involved in hundreds of elections and votes.

In order for the Executive Force or any other force in a society to accomplish a revolution it must possess certain attributes. We have said that the Executive Force has such a possibility in America; therefore it must possess those attributes. These qualities include in the first place *size:* enough people, activities, money, and weight must be commanded by the new force to give it momentum. All of these the Executive Force has.

In the matter of numbers of persons involved, first of all, the Executive Force is ample enough to recast the society. At the present time, civil and military government employees on the municipal, state and federal levels constitute about eleven million persons. These form over one-seventh of all employed Americans. In addition, many millions of employed Americans are tied directly to the governmental occupations by contract and other forms of direct dependency.

Directly involved in the federal government are five million persons, half in the armed forces and half civilian. Governmental civilian employment is rising on all levels, both absolutely and relatively to non-governmental employment. It is risky to project rates of growth, but between 1940 and 1964, federal civilian employment grew by one and a half millions, by 150% over 1940; the same growth by 1984, twenty years from now, would more than double the present number and would then give over twelve millions. The projection of the military would give an even more fantastic total. Projection of governmental employment in the states and localities would produce somewhat the same effect.

We say that these are fantastic conclusions and under ordinary circumstances they are probably so. It should be noted, however, that governments do not have to employ people in order to rule them. Rule can be accomplished by spending, by taxes, and by regulations. In this connection, the gross figures are not comforting to the anti-executive forces. As Roger Freeman has pointed out in *The Conservative Papers,* it took 160 years, from 1789 to 1948, for federal spending for civilian purposes to reach seven billions of dollars in the year. It required only another sixteen years—from 1948 to 1964—to boost spending to $46 billion. "If this rate of progression were to continue for another twenty years, virtually all income and product in the United States would be channelled through and distributed by the government." Again a fantastic conclusion. In Fiscal Year 1964, federal government payments to the public totalled about $122.5 billions.

Taxes, it could be said, followed the same pattern but in 1964 income taxes and in 1965 excise taxes were actually reduced. However, these reductions of taxes were in the face of irregularly but generally occurring deficits in the federal budget, generally increasing state taxes, and generally increasing state, local and federal debt. No matter how this combination of events is explained, it cannot spell out a diminution of governmental activity. On the contrary, the prevailing attitude of the elements composing the Executive Force at this time, including the President and the departments of government and the presidential party in Congress was that not enough was being spent by governments on the civil infrastructure of the economy and it was being "starved" in the midst of private affluence.

Actually the number of federal activities has been increasing. If the localities and states were not enlarging the qualitative scope of the specific activities they were undertaking, it was because they have already many years before, and unknown to most citizens, become involved in just about every known kind of occupation, skill, and industry, including slaughterhouses and electric plants; now they were deepening their penetration. The federal government is meanwhile actively enlarging its scope. No old activities are dropped; new ones are undertaken.

For example, only a close examination of the 1963 Budget as submitted to Congress could reveal the presence of expanded and new activities.

1. Projects start little, which must grow big. For example:

> "Appropriations of $16 million are requested for 1964 to enable the Corps of Engineers to initiate construction of 32 projects with an estimated total Federal [note other governments implicated] cost of $348 million." (*Budget*, 1963, p. 82)

"Appropriations of $8 million are included for the Bureau of Reclamation to start eight new projects estimated to cost $285 million in total."

2. New programs slip in, often as research projects:

The Department of Commerce is to initiate a program "to encourage more extensive and imaginative use of technological developments to increase productivity," (p. 88) and will also begin a new comprehensive transportation research program (pp. 89-90). Studies are progressing on feasibility of developing a supersonic air transport (p. 90).

Such appear as requests for New Obligational Authority, funds sought for activities previously approved by Congress. There are dozens of new activities born annually under such NOA.

In addition, the Budget for Fiscal '63 contained the not unusually large number of 29 proposals for legislation authorizing new activities (pp. 69-110). Examples of the new legislation sought would show, in the field of international affairs, requests for a National Academy of Foreign Affairs, office and housing construction, and removal of the ceiling on Arms Control and Disarmament Agency spending. These were, of course, only a small portion of all new proposed activities; strictly speaking (that is, by the theory of budgeting usually espoused by the Executive Force), they should be separately submitted as bills, and their funding provided for separately or in a supplementary budget.

The arguments employed in achieving new activities or in obtaining budget increases for the old are similar in form:

1. A new need has been discovered, felt, defined. Public opinion exerts pressures, it is said; statistical indices are brought forward in a typically muddled and ambiguous

form; and White House Conferences and other stimulating devices are organized to form the very attitudes they are alleged to measure.

2. Rising costs are claimed in regard to existing activities. The rising costs are usually attributable to other governmental activities and to economic and wage policies of the government.

3. The example of other agencies, other governments, and non-governmental groups are brought forward to show that "everyone is doing it" and the petitioner should not be made to be shamefully exceptional.

4. The agency or activity has not had a raise in budget in years, it is pointed out.

5. The materials, construction, or system employed for doing the job are "old," "outmoded," "inefficient."

6. The agency was not given enough funds to do the job in the first place; it has done the best with what it was given, though. A variation of this theme is that the activity was proven successful in a pilot project but needs more funds if it is to accomplish what was originally expected of it.

Thus goes the routine argument of expanding activities and budgets in the executive establishment of government. Once the premise underlying each argument is accepted, surrender to the requests becomes fairly inevitable. The process sweeps up not only the Executive Force elements, but many congressmen as well, the latter seeing to it that a rough proportion of all spending is maintained on projects strengthening their local preserves and their administrative and political allies—the famous "pork barrel" projects. It is unfortunate that a scientist has not produced a Political Logic and Accounting System Analysis of total government effort to go along with the conventional Fiscal Accounting analysis, which is philosophically blind and politically helpless.

It should be emphasized that actual expansion of activities, with and without much new spending, and greater spending, do not alone promote the movement toward the executive state. The merging of activities of all levels of government in the guise of cooperation and the operational presence of federal agencies in the activities and livelihoods of many millions of Americans through the contracting process are trends of great importance too. The aircraft industry is almost totally dependent on federal contracts (for instance 95% of all complete aircraft); 39% of all shipbuilding and repair, 38% of all scientific instrument deliveries, 30% of all rice mill products and 27% of all radio and TV equipment are paid for by the federal government.

Furthermore, it matters what *quality* of activity is affected by the government. The educational system, the press, the police, the arts and sciences—these are areas whose mark upon the culture is much heavier than their economic weight and numbers of personnel would indicate. Also the quality of activity affected has to do not only with those types of activities that are *directly* covered by new rules, but also with activities that are altered and often discouraged by the competition of government, such as private schools, religious groups, welfare associations, some insurance schemes, foreign trade concerns, publishing houses, and others.

Besides, government advantages cause disproportionate growth in certain sectors of the culture—as in certain kinds of sciences and arts, or in non-profit and tax-exempt (and therefore regulated and regulable) organizations such as foundations. The Executive Force moves into these areas. The dollar-trends of budgets and the number-trends of personnel do not accurately reflect these major cultural trends produced by one kind of government—that of the Executive Force—moving against another kind—that of the Republican Force.

A survey by Charles A. Reich in the *Yale Law Journal* (v. 73, p. 733, 1964) establishes the great weight of the "new property" in American society. The *new property* consists of the various forms and amounts of wealth created by government.

Income and benefits are placed at $58 billions as of 1961 on the national, state, and local levels. Such would be social security benefits, unemployment compensation, aid to dependent children, veterans' benefits, and state and local welfare.

Jobs are a second form of New Property, nine million persons (we say 11) work for a government, and three to four millions labor in defense industries. To them must be added their families. All have a kind of property interest in government, says Mr. Reich.

More plausibly—and impressively—are listed occupational licenses (ranging from longshoremen to medical practitioners), franchises (as in taxicab medallions), contracts ($50 billions in defense alone), subsidies, the right to use public resources (as with television licenses, oil land, grazing lands, river facilities, buildings, docks, etc.), and services (postal, insurance, technical information, education, and others). The fact that government expenditures amounted to $165 billions in 1961 while personal income exceeded $416 billions would perhaps give pause—the proportion is rising—but the governments of the country give, under conditions that are extremely varied, a vast intangible wealth in the new property that must by now total many billions of dollars. There can be no doubt that practically all Americans—whether possessed of the oldest, the recent, or the new forms of property—are closely associated with the governments in their use and disposition of property.

Dr. Murray Weidenbaum of the Stanford Research Institute has pointed out that in 1960 in seven states—Kansas, California, Washington, New Mexico, Connecticut, Arizona, and Utah—defense work accounted for 20 to 30 percent of the total manufacturing employment. Considering the huge federal landholdings in the Western States and Alaska, and their dependence upon irrigation in many areas, as well as the presence in their midst of federally supported industry, and then the usual range of federal and other governmental activities, it would be too much to expect strong opposition to rising budgets and ever new activities in these areas.

Therefore, considering indirect impacts as well as conscious, direct forces, there can be said to exist an aggregate of similarly positioned and active manpower sufficient to define the shape and form of American society and culture. Computing out from a nucleus in the Presidency and career service of many thousands of well-placed officials into a mass of several million dependent employees and retainers, and from there into many millions of related and sympathetic quasi-dependents, and finally into many millions of a favorable constituent public, we arrive at a figure of perhaps one-third to one-half of the population. To all of these people, federal help means something; it is more than a word which might evoke simple mental images. It is an interest.

THE OFFICIAL PERSONALITY

Shake yourself free from the manikin you create out of a false im-
pression of what you do and what you feel, and you'll at once see that
the manikin you make yourself is nothing at all like what you really
are or what you can really be.

Luigi Pirandello, *Each in His Own Way*

Again, to repeat, this interest which moves the Executive Force is not a conspiracy. Its members wear no uniform. Most of them would be completely innocent of
participating in anything beyond everyday Americanism.
This becomes quite clear when we survey their background.
It would be hard to distinguish them from other Americans
of similar status except that the largest body of them work
for the federal government. Professors Warner, Van Riper,
Martin and Collins have questioned thirteen thousand of
them at length to learn what kinds of people they are. Completed, lengthy questionnaires were received from about
7600 career civil servants, 1300 foreign service officers, and
1900 political appointees—from the moderately high level
of GS 14 up to Cabinet level—and 2100 officers of the armed
forces, on every level from Colonel and Naval Captain
upwards.

Higher civil servants and military officers come from
all over the country, are more educated than the American
people generally and come more from families of the higher
occupations. True, the same general pattern characterizes
most persons who belong to occupations of higher skill and
higher pay ranks of the society. If one wishes to discover
whether bureaucrats and officers are different in ways that
might affect their participation in, and the product ex-
pectable from, the Executive Force, he would have to make
finer comparisons. He would especially have to compare
them with the leadership of the other elements of the gen-

eral elite such as business leaders and educational leaders, and with the republican elite—congressmen, state legislators, party officials.

To a certain extent Warner and his associates have done so. They show that federal civilian executives come from large cities in a ratio of 1.8 to 1 over expectancy, that is, over the way the population of the country was distributed in their infancy. Fewer came from small towns than would be expected (the ratio was .64 to 1). Women were few in the group as in the civil service as a whole: there were 459 high level women executives out of 476,448 women in the great, general class of civil service (G5).

The group was highly educated, 95% having at least some college education and one in ten carrying the PhD degree. Their fathers were often professional men (19%) or businessmen (17%), sometimes owners of businesses with gross annual earnings under $50,000 (14%). Some 14% of the fathers were farm tenants or owners, another 21% skilled or unskilled laborers.

The federal executives tended to come a little more from New England, the West North Central States and the Mountain States than could be expected by the population of those areas where they were born; and they came a little less from the East South Central and West South Central states than the population of those areas would warrant (but this would be a deceptive figure, since the Negro population, largely concentrated here in 1930, was not active, meaning that the whites were "overproportionate" in top executive posts in the federal civil service). The executives entered the service at an average of 27 years of age and stayed. Most of them were working in a region of the United States differing from the region of their birth, or abroad.

It would appear from a study of backgrounds that the higher civil servant has more of a head start in life, achieves a better education, and moves a good deal farther from his birthplace than the average American. In these characteristics, he is only typical of every other element of the American elite, business leaders, congressmen, educators, military leaders, and even labor leaders.

A few more significant differences reveal themselves when compared with the other leading elements, however. In comparison with leaders of big business, the executive leaders of big government are much more educated formally and are more professional in their education, with many more higher degrees. They have moved around a great deal more geographically; if moving abroad or to another region of the country is termed being "nationalized," 77% of federal civilian executives are nationalized in comparison with 45% of the big business leaders surveyed in a similar study. But they have stayed with the same business (the federal government) much longer. They come somewhat oftener from the Plains States and the South. We see, therefore, a few hints of cleavage of background, but these are surprisingly small.

So it is with the military leadership who resemble closely the civil servants and do not differ remarkably from the business leaders. Educators present another case. The top educators are, of course, the most educated. They are loaded with degrees. They are also the most mobile, and come on the average from the highest echelons of society. They are deviants to one side of the elite.

Congressmen are deviants to the other side. They are educated well above the norm for the population but not to the level of civil servants, the big business leaders, or the educators. If all the special schools and institutes that the military conduct are counted, they are less educated formally than the military too.

Furthermore, congressmen are less mobile. They rest where they began, in most cases, except that they know Washington, D. C., well. They have the highest occupational mobility, that is, have experienced more different kinds of jobs. Their social antecedents, though again of the more skilled, educated, and well-to-do groupings in the general population, are more mixed and proportioned to the population profile than any other elite element here discussed.

One would have to introduce the small businessman, the farm owner, the high school teacher, the small professional man, the real estate agent and the foreman in order to get the background and social bearings of the congressman. And of course the budding image—the "Junior Congressman" in the political machinery of the country—the state legislator, the country judge, the county clerk and town mayor, the state committeeman and city boss.

Then the realization comes. The congressman relates to a different America than the higher civil servant. Than the military man and big business leader too. And especially is he at poles from the educator.

Better than statistics on birthplace and education would be reports of personality studies of those who constitute the elite. There are remarkably few of these, or at least few that can be construed to sample validly the diversity of types bound to exist in large groupings of men. Warner and his associates administered prolonged personality interviews to 257 civilian federal executives and the results were of interest to our thesis about the Executive Force. Stating

that on the whole the personality profiles discovered were
similar, the researchers went on to declare:

> In general, the career civil service executive possesses
> psychological characteristics that may be described thus:
> he possesses lofty aspirations, the majority of which stem
> from external influences, from heroic figures or models, and
> from demands made upon him by the system and by his
> role as a career man.
>
> Achievement orientation is strong. For the most part he
> achieves in a good way by direct action and mobilization
> of inner resources, . . . Yet the career civil service executive
> frequently experiences feelings of inadequacy and lack of
> insight into the means to be used to realize his lofty
> ambitions. . . .
>
> Intimately part of a large and complex system of affili-
> ation and connection, he is entangled in the dilemma of
> striving for independence and severing ties of affiliation
> and dependency, yet retaining such ties and support.

It is obviously not easy to portray a collective character.
There is some ground for asserting as do the authors that
the civil servant becomes "too tied" to the need for guidance from the organization and tends to initiate only rarely
and then as a group member.

The upper civil service thinks of itself as an elite, a socially superior and select group, according to the Warner
survey. But "in spite of this conception of themselves as
an 'elite' they feel that perhaps others in society do not
share this belief and instead hold to the popular stereotype
of the civil servant as a bureaucrat. . . . These 'people outside' are materialistic, less educated, and less intelligent;
they sell their souls. Because of this, their views count for
little."

The researchers move ever closer to the thesis of the
Executive Force in describing the psychological world of
of the civilian executive:

To most federal executives, the external world looms strong, formidable, rigidly structured, and relatively intractable. There is little room for free play of the imagination, of independent and unilateral action, for going it alone without fear of consequence. To these people a world closely bounded by rule and regulation, by situational demands, and by structural imperatives is a real world which must be coped with at all times and in all ways. . . .

The civil servants are not aware often that they labor under restrictive conditions:

(Still) a significant group of executives simply would not understand our delineation of the tight controls existing in the federal world. It is not that these men would not agree; they would not understand. To them the organizational interconnections are not restrictions but represent a vast expansion of possibilities and opportunities. Such men move through the intricate interlockings of bureaucracy easily and skillfully, pursuing their own ends and fulfilling their own purposes.

Passivity and dependence are common traits among the federal executives:

Even when the system is formidable and threatening, to the executive it appears the source of help and nurture. He is dependent upon it, and this dependency tends to pervade his thinking. . . . For many of these executives the dependency has become symbolic and represents unresolved dependency problems experienced in earlier years and carried over to the federal executive situation. In fact, there is evidence from the material that movement into these positions is in part determined by a need for escape from the more vulnerable situations in the 'free' professions. . . .

One tends to approach problems with care not to upset the state of affairs, nor to call too much attention to oneself, not to push issues to the crisis stage. To do so may cause a retraction of the supportive and nurturing aspects of the system and a frightening pushing forward of its domineer-

ing side. In the coping mechanisms of most of these men,
there is a strong element of system-deference. . . .

In general, the sort of person who finds innovation in
itself rewarding and stimulating cannot well fit the role.
It is for this reason that federal executives in their interviews and TAT protocols appear by comparison reacting
rather than activating. . . .

They are, in vast majority, idealists. . . . (But) this
overweening idealism does not contradict the dependency
leanings and the subservience to authority.

To put the case brought by these scholarly authorities
simply, then, the major cluster of psychological traits discoverable in the Executive Force is as follows: a dependency upon a great organization to supply his motives and
needs and happiness; a strong respect for authority; a small
need for innovation; a large idealism and serving of a cause
in work; an insulated and restricted environment which
yet seems free to those in it; a caution and a persistence
and honesty in work.

To perhaps a somewhat lesser extent or perhaps only
differing in shadings, the other major executive elements
are similar: the military, and the foreign service. Considering that the United States civil service, in its large-scale
form, is only a generation old, we may expect a hardening
of these traits as time goes on and recruitment becomes increasingly selective. Even as experienced now, they are
hardly the traits one would choose to emphasize in a system
aimed at promoting republicanism.

The cluster of traits typifying the Republican Force is
markedly different. The grouping itself is spread out over
far more elements of the population. This makes it even
more difficult to speak of it as having a cluster of traits. We
depend on a variety of studies less focussed in this regard
than the Warner associates study of the bureaucracy. Some

indications of what congressional character is like can be found in a set of conversations carried on and reported as editor by Charles Clapp. Matthews and Hyneman have analyzed the background of legislators. A work on the Legislative System by Professors Wahlke, Eulau, Buchanan, and Ferguson goes into the motivation of four sets of state legislators. A study by Lewis Dexter captures congressmen at work puzzling through a set of issues. McConaughy studied South Carolina lawmakers and T. V. Smith wrote of Illinois legislators and congressmen. And so on; the materials are not full or systematic.

Yet there is little doubt of the direction that the differences take. Congressmen are strikingly different from the upper civil servants. They diverge early in life. They have different characters. They serve different interests. And they lead different modes of life. Even if only one of these four conditions were present, the two groups would contrast in character and behavior.

They like politics earlier and believe in it as a way of life. The need for immediate response from others is more felt among politicians. They sense that they must please people here and now. Many more congressmen are lawyers, raised and educated to controversy. They often visualize the party system and all of politics as a kind of litigation where the presence of two parties to the contest is more important than whether there is a one right side. By contrast, the bureaucrat sees in the administrative process a means of finding the one and single truth and views interventions from the outside as interferences with the achievement of the true way, the "scientific" way.

The congressmen come from more turbulent and changing environments. They are influenced by a great many interests that can never intrude into the administrative

establishment. A Nevada Senator cannot be ignorant of
gambling, a New York Senator of Puerto Rican affairs, a
Texas Representative of cotton farming. Their knowledge
of these affairs comes as a part of a whole experience with
their constituency. Administrators of the federal government must also concern themselves with these fields, but
as specialists devoted to them alone, as Internal Revenue
officers, as social welfare professionals or as soil conserva-
tion officials. Not until the top of the federal government
hierarchy is reached does one get the complete "holistic"
representation of the social forces that the congressman
has to build into his personality in the primary geographi-
cal constituency, district or state. For this and other reasons, their personalities are more varied, their motives more
complex. A civil servant, it can be appreciated, is not well-
equipped to judge a congressman.

Much of the difference between the legislators and the
executives is summed up in the fact that the legislators
have many roles to play, the executives essentially one.
The executive may have to face many situations; but even
then he is permitted to use the same face. The congressman has to identify much more deeply in his numerous
roles and his character shows the effects.

IDEOLOGY OF BUREAUCRACY

> *Of course we're all supposed to belong to the Castle, there's supposed
> to be no gulf between us, and nothing to be bridged over, and that
> may be true enough on ordinary occasions, but we've had grim evi-
> dence that it's not true when anything really important crops up.*
>
> F. Kafka, *The Castle*

From the differences of character and conduct come naturally differences of ideology, and by interaction in its
turn the ideology adds to the differences. The ideology of

the executive branch of government accepts the myth of the President, because, as we have indicated, it needs it for new increments of power and for personified defense. It shares the myths of responsibility, coordination and integration with the President, and adds depth and power to them. It presents the notion of a representative bureaucracy to compete with the once exclusive character of Congress as representative of the people. And it surrounds its work with the pall of sovereignty that moves from one activity to another. Ultimately in the exuberance of authority, a mother who does not diaper her baby properly becomes in a sense of the same stripe as the soldier who deserts in time of war. All these beliefs form the ideology of administration. Every day of the year, they look out upon the hulking and the contrasting way of life of the republican.

Let us look first to the meaning of administration to the bureaucracy. We have already shown how the notions of responsibility and integration help accrue power for the presidency without necessarily bringing what would universally be termed benefits to society. The administration of course participates in the accrual of presidential power. The flank of the struggle for integration that is carried forward principally by the executive branch is that charged with getting Congress out of the business of administration.

"Let Congress play politics. Let executives administer!" So goes the slogan of officialdom and the text writers. Actually, the notion that there is something substantial belonging to administration and only to administration is not tenable. Administration in reality is the tasks that a person who determines his own work-load wishes to assign to others. He keeps to himself "policies." There is no objective standard for telling him otherwise. The Emperor Nero fiddled while Rome burned. A mad thing for the Chief Executive to do in a moment of grave crisis! But Nero loved the arts, and left the "details" of governing to others. Most executives cannot play the violin and the paths of their definitions are devious. Would counting the hams in the White House kitchen, as President Coolidge used to do, or reading ten thousand lines of fine print in the Federal Budget be the tasks of the Chief Executive?

What happens to lend a species of "objectivity" is that a large group of people will objectify their own preferences, call these "policies," call all other behaviors "administration," try to keep in their own hands the first and entrust the other activities to others. Manuals accepting and describing the last process are textbooks of administration.

If there is no "objective" distinction between politics and administration, the setting of the distinction must itself be a political question. And of course it is. But here has occurred a paradox—all the more strange if it were happening now for the first time in history: Deprived of the power to make the distinction because Congress was first to make it and empowered to continue its definitions over time, the administrators turned their badge of shame into a shield of virtue. With the help of professors and political reformers, they could claim that there was an objective science of administration, that this was a glorious science, that it was directed straight toward truth, efficiency, and the public interest except for the intrusion of politics. But once politics were removed from the scene, all would be well-administered. Administration was given an expanding definition. Wherever a public activity might be criticized, there was politics: the universal remedy—objective, efficient administration. Lowly housekeeping became a great mys-

terious science; from the leavings of the political tables was
fashioned a great cuisine.

There is a dictum of Roman Law, actually of all legal
systems, that "for every case, a law can be found." Administrative theorists are quite as unabashed. "For every decision, there is a principle of administration." Under the
circumstances, then, any power over bureacracy that Congress may have can, depending upon the circumstances of
the moment, be denounced as an intrusion upon what is
the natural province of administration, and in extreme cases,
of the Chief Executive. Congress could adjourn forever
and never be missed.

* * * * *

The everlasting bureaucracy is the military. Revolutions, whether English, American, French, Italian, German,
Russian, Indian, Indonesian, or Chinese, may destroy the
civil administration but it will be born again from the military engines of revolt. Always ready to give examples
stand the military and always ready to heed example are
young regimes and old.

The most skillful and courageous men of history have
been those who dared to tell a people that it might live
without armies or free of military control. And of all constitutions the American must be numbered among the bold-
est for the distance it went in subjecting government of
the military to the legislature, letting militias to the states,
and allowing arms to the citizenry.

Withal the military has presented continual problems
to American democracy. It has at the same time been the
means to the preservation of the republic from external
enemies, and from disruptive civil influences; it has been
a training ground in some respects for democracy among
an otherwise too undisciplined population. These consid-

erations must be borne in mind when criticizing the role of armed forces in a democracy. The military presents problems fundamentally of hierarchical authority, of psychological aggressiveness in the human mind and soul, and of secrecy. These traits of military affairs tend to be emulated by civil administration in other sectors of society. They also create a frame of mind in the population as a whole that is anti-republican.

Thus "unity of command," the "one right way," "decisiveness," and other slogans of the old military machine are conveyed into civil organizations and ordinary affairs. The personality types favored in the military schools of old lend models to civil recruitment and official behavior. The object of military "administration" is an enemy, yet the aggressiveness that must be taught, maintained, and exercised with regard to enemies becomes often a part of the learning of civil administration and is maintained and practiced upon one's fellow-citizens. Further, the administered population—no matter how independent in education and spirit—will contain a great many people who will read into the presence of any governmental agent the authority and force of the soldier.

Three methods of suppressing this problem and three alone have ever worked. One is impossible in the near future: that is to abolish the armed forces and disarm the police. A second is to civilize the military. The third is to reduce to a minimum the participation of government in activities that extend domination to other fields of life. To the credit of Congress, but even more to the credit of the armed forces themselves, the American military is the most civilized in the world. Its officers are democratically recruited and its men are representative of the country. The indoctrination experienced within the forces as to the nature of leadership, the limits of discipline, respect for civil authorities, care for other human beings, and co-operative work relations—far from being an abrupt unfortunate departure from civil standards—is on the whole superior to the training given in civilian society.

Still, when it comes to the question of bureaucracy versus legislature, the military bureaucracy is said by all authoritative students of the subject to have the upper hand. New weapon systems, new forms of organization, increases in budget, and foreign areas operations occur more at the will of the military oligarchy than of the committees on the armed forces and appropriations. Nor are the military administrators stopped short of their reasoned demands by the presidency, except on rare occasions. The most important recent instance of a curb upon military power, Section 412b of the Military Construction Authorization Act for Fiscal 1960, which in effect made military procurement annually reviewable by congressional committees, was the work of the House oligarchy, not the President. Professor Raymond Dawson analyzed the case and emphasized its importance as precedent.

There is room for much more innovation in control of the military, extending to basic theories concerning the nature of military activity in modern society. "What is military and what is not?" is a simple question that has not been posed since the eighteenth century, though it is generally admitted that the conditions of military operations have drastically altered in this century. One opinion, widely held among political scientists, has maintained that a continuous crisis in world and domestic affairs gives birth to a "garrison state," the antithesis of legislative supremacy. In every single advanced country of the world—in Western

Europe, the Soviet Union, Japan, and the United States—
this event has not occurred. Permanent crisis has not
brought the military to the fore.

It must be concluded that other factors—self-confident
civil leadership, general prosperity, skill in handling the
psychological problems of military relations, and the in-
timidating atomic bomb—have kept militarism at bay. The
underdeveloped countries, on the other hand, have been
going through a period of aggravated militarism, quite in
line with their general determination to commit all the
historical errors of the West in catching up.

The bad example provided by the military of the West
then is no longer an immediate threat but an indirect and
long-range one. The military is and has been, despite the
best recruitment and governing policies, a socialistic influence over society. In the second place, the military sets
a bad example on spending. A continuous justification of
civil government activity is heavy *military* activity. It is
almost impossible to persuade congressmen, officials, and
citizens to restrain their demands for new programs and
increased spending so long as they see how much is voted
for defense items. To take one case of many, how can
scientists be expected to stand on principle in rejecting
federal research aid of many kinds, when billions of dollars
go annually into military research? Especially is this true
when what they wish is only a small fraction of the sum of
military research. A similar logic prevails throughout the
fields of welfare, business regulation, agriculture, and urban
affairs. There may be only two solutions in general: to
civilianize military activities and subject them to ordinary
standards, so far as possible; and to stimulate by means

short of nationalized administration the growth of civilian activity, such as research and development. Congress is not organized well for these purposes. It could be, and proposals to that end are to be made later on.

The financial aspect of the military example is paralleled by its secrecy side. A critical element in the core of military operations is the maintenance of security against potential enemy intelligence. The grotesque ramifications of this militarily essential task in times both remote and recent are well known. The germ of secrecy is in all militarized and thence bureaucratized groups. Just as agencies will fall into free spending, if not continuously controlled, they will fall into the vice of secrecy.

At the end of February, 1964, President Johnson announced to a pleased nation, specially called to order by the massive apparatus of presidential publicity, that a new military aircraft, the A11, had been developed, with a speed of 2,000 miles an hour. This plane would now be converted into a civilian transport. The *New York Times* carried the story on the front page. On March 2, the *Times,* now delving into the background, stated that the secret of the plane had been leaking out through aviation industry channels, and the presidency had then decided to take over the public announcement in a dramatic fashion.

A few days later, a brief dispatch, buried in an inner page dominated by advertising, reported that Senator Allot, a member of the Senate Appropriations Committee, which is supposed to pass on details of the defense program, knew nothing of the costly aircraft project. The Senator asserted he had followed all available details for four years and "not one word was said about" the new plane that may have cost a hundred million dollars or more.

On July 2, the newspaper carried a report that economic and technical problems would perhaps delay the introduction of a supersonic airliner until 1980.

Who gained by this sequence of stories, that occurs time and time again? First the President, who was glorified; second the military, who were credited with a creative triumph. Who lost? First the Congress, which was ignored, and possibly duped; second the public, which was flattered and fooled. The press worked in its usual way, to worsen the problems being discussed.

Only Congress can be the hero of the dramatic unending struggle against secrecy. Rarely in American history has the presidency worked well on problems of free information. The same is true of the executive establishment throughout, including the military. This is not to say that conditions have always been bad or that republican policies have not been pursued by a great many appointive officials. More precisely, it states that the descryable tendency of bureaucracy and executive leadership in the United States and everywhere else in time and space is to increase the scope and number of its actions that are hidden from the world outside the agency.

The reasons why the output of information in the American bureaucracy is restricted are several. A certain item of information might benefit a potential enemy. An item of information, say about a plan to sell government gold on the open market, might jeopardize a public policy. An item might alert criminals to modes of detection or an impending police action. Another might be damaging to a person's privacy or reputation, as could be the exposure of his income or his background. Still another might, if released, implicate the agency's or another agency's personnel in illegal, improper, or embarrassing behavior. Information may be withheld simply because an agency's personnel is secretive by character, or possessive, or arbitrary, lazy, or stupid. It may be withheld because nobody has ever queried it, or because no means of releasing it have been devised. Information may be concealed too in the campaign for new programs, more funds, and more personnel as part of the tactics of promoting such things. Secrecy, finally, is often practiced as a ritual, to keep everyone in an agency in line and to give them stronger morale.

Whatever the reasons during a particular episode, the effects of secrecy on the conduct of a republic are deleterious. Secrecy in a free state is a powerful weapon against the state. In a closed state, the danger is less, for secrecy is the weapon of all against all. No matter how difficult, arrangements must be devised whereby Congress or its agents may discover at any time all information in the hands of the executive branch. No file should be locked against it. In turn, sanctions against the mishandling of such information, whether the injured party is society, a group, or an individual, should be arranged and the victims "made whole." Congress itself should bear the protective machinery against abuse, perhaps in the form of a special officer or committee to whom agencies or citizens might appeal. It should be remembered that the Senate, not the executive, was the final disciplinarian of Senator Joseph McCarthy.

In the past generation, the rise of a serious competitor to the military and functional bureaucracy has been experienced in the growth of science in government. A sizable portion of the hundred billions of annual federal expenditures is under the direct control of persons holding advanced academic degrees, speaking the jargon of a specialized science—be it social welfare or astrophysics—and receiving their moral and civic training principally in conventional administrative theory and the mental habits of a small narrow discipline. The scientific establishment is to the intelligentsia as the military is to the manual working class: It is the source of models, inspiration, folklore, and jobs. (There are as many college professors in America as there are coal miners.)

The touchword of ancient administration was the will of the monarch. That sufficed to let bureaucracy dominate a realm. The modern age—set up in revolutionary revulsion against traditional monarchies—has been partly overcome by bureaucracy in a new rational guise, preaching efficiency, integration, and responsibility. Now science, itself trained in the latter-day doctrines and *par excellence* bureaucratic in its habits, comes upon the political scene and allies itself with, as it is welcomed by, the administrative establishment. At all salient points of the threat of the Executive Force— in organizational theory, spending policies, secrecy, recruitment, education and training, attitudes toward republican habits and practices—the scientific establishment reinforces the trend.

United with ordinary bureaucrats, they are a formidable adversary to congressmen. United with military men, their position is practically dictatorial. The defense against them cannot be the traditional lawyer's palaver or the politician's guile. Neither patriotism, nor experience, nor humaneness. Nor an ever-commanding majority in the precincts. Only counter-intelligence can be a viable defense: the employment of the best of scientists in the country in the service of the legislative branch.

The armament of the Executive Force is not completely described until recent developments in the concept of responsibility are reported. To bolster itself against charges that, whatever else it may be, it is not responsive to the people, the administrative establishment has been moving toward the idea of "representative bureaucracy." By representative bureaucracy is meant an administrative establishment whose leaders express and behave in accordance with the people's desires.

Conventional theory of political science has argued that the people elect congressmen and the President to represent them; the President and Congress enforce popular desires upon the administration; and the bureaucracy behaves responsibly, that is, representatively. How little this theory accords with the facts is apparent to all, and has been described already in this book. Representation is a complicated set of relations among many groupings of constituents and a great many officers. Every person can be said to be represented to a different degree in different areas of interest with regards to different officers; he has an elective relation directly with some of the officers; with others he has an indirect, even highly remote relation, as for instance a voter of Chicago with a Committee Chairman from Florida; or a 1/100,000th relation to a congressman in Nevada and a 1/200,000,000th relation to the President.

Bearing such considerations in mind, what can be offered as a theory for comparing the quality of representation offered by the civil service with that offered by Congress? Of necessity, under any form of government, decision-making is diffused through vast reaches of officialdom and associated non-governmental agencies. Even under the most ingenious kind of representative arrangements, only a minor fraction of the multitude of persons will possess formal representative responsibility in the old sense, that is, with elections as the governor of their relations with their constituents.

In the great majority of cases, elective representation may exist but only via assumed authority, not by formal grant through the constitutional authority. (For example, the labor union leader or corporate president may be an elected official, but is not chosen by a formal constituency authorized by the United States Constitution.) In addition, a great many officials and agents who make important decisions governing other people's lives are appointed by functional associations, chosen by examinations, or named by other officials both elective and non-elective. It is clear that modern society is governed in every sense more by non-elective than by elective officials.

It would be therefore naive to expect not only that all of these might be subjected to election (which was once the solution actually posed by direct democrats and even now is a powerful fantasy-wish of the same type of person), but that a handful of properly-positioned elected representatives could ensure the representativeness of this multitude of decision-makers.

Can any device ensure their representativeness then? Probably so. Five suggestions can be advanced here:

1) Increasing the tactical skills and controls of those who are formally representative of the constitutionally approved interests of the country will have some effect. Strengthening legislatures and local councils everywhere is indicated.

2) Fostering imitation representative governments on a large scale in other areas and echelons of government can be recommended. This is of course what "representative bureaucracy" is.

3) Introduction into the recruitment examinations and applications of persons vested with a public character of

questions designed to eliminate persons psychologically un-
suited to the ideology of republican government.

4) Propaganda within the government offices to promote
appropriate attitudes among minor officials.

5) Strengthening the prevalence of republican attitudes
in the social system as a whole.

Representation, it has to be emphasized, is not a neutral
quality. It must be always representation of some interests
more than others. It can be the subject of education, however, if only in the very beginning the question of what
shall be represented is clarified. For this purpose, that is,
for establishing the basis of the five listed and desired conditions, a "Republican Consensus" can be made the condition of membership in the government in any capacity except election to Congress or the presidency.

Unless this is done no one can dispute anyone else's
claim to being representative of the people. The official
can compare himself with the congressman and say: "I
know my clientele, my constituents. I consult them; in
fact, I engage one committee after another composed of
representatives chosen by the interests that I deal with,
and our agency never acts without awareness, responsibility, and representation. Our policies are as democratic
as any coming from the Congress, and we furthermore act
in the name of the popularly elected President."

We can applaud the ways in which the modern administrator seeks to understand and work with the public;
we cannot go further than that. First, the constitutional
grounds, the rules we play by, do not recognize the priority
of larger claims to representativeness. Secondly, the representation provided by congressmen is more extensive because the congressman is a specialist in representation; he

spends his life attuning himself to problems of representation; he lives by its definition and holds office tenuously because of changes in the constituency. The congressman is a fulltime representative, the official only parttime on the job.

Thirdly, merely on the question of representing samples of the American people, Congress emerges as a fairer mirror of the land and people. Few congressmen come from constituencies as narrow as the typical constituency of the official. Compare, for example, a Senator from Georgia with a bureau chief in the Department of State or a member of the Securities Exchange Commission. The Senator represents large cities and rural areas, clerks, workers, farm tenants, owners and professionals, teachers, soldiers and sailors, all religious groups, and a variety of political jurisdictions numbering into the hundreds. Even the most varied administrative constituency cannot stand comparison with such. Even if the official called in every interest and element of the public relevant to his task he would not approximate the varied constituency of the whole State of Georgia, and Georgia is only average in complications.

Fourth, the branches of the politician's representation go on and on into the public, whereas those of the official come to dead ends of opinion. The nuclear constituency of a congressman, which we have described earlier, has strings that go out and down into the district and state. By contrast the department head and agency chiefs have a retinue that carries far down into the career service until it contains the anonymous clerks and workers with a job, not a constituency. (If they have constituencies—as rangers, extension agents, purchasing officers, revenue agents, and others do, they are of the narrow, specialized kind detailed in the example above, and therefore open to criticism as being segmental, non-national, and non-public.)

Some of these arguments appear to be supported by a recent study of Dr. John Corson, who, in an intensive survey of one-fourth of all top civil servants (8600) concluded that:

1) Only about one-third of the top executives are responsible for many-sided programs.

2) The top men are specialists on their subject-matter, not generalists, and their subordinates are specialists too.

3) Less than one-half spend much time formulating the plans and major policies of their agencies.

4) Two-thirds of the super-grade civil servants have spent their careers in one or two agencies.

These facts along with much of the other material of this chapter should make the advocates of "representative bureaucracy" ponder their position. The combination of power with narrowness and of narrowness with policy passivity can be stultifying.

In the final analysis, moreover, so rooted in the Congress and so much concocted out of well-wishing and meagre powers is the administrative representation, that should congressional power and representation disappear, administrative representation would precipitously decline. It is a moon made luminous by the sun. It has not gained the strength to exist and flourish by itself.

It could conceivably do so. It simply has not. If it did, it would grow over a long time or by revolution. Then there might be a real question for republican theory—that is, whether a better republic might be formed through a host of little legislatures connected functionally with the myriad agencies of government and culminating in a grand Congress or legislature, which would be quite different as to its constitution and procedures from the present Congress.

But that time is not now or immediately foreseeable. Should the present Congress decline and become a vestige, as did the Roman Senate, the French Estates General, and at times the English Parliament, the effective cause would be the Executive Force operating through the presidency. What would ensue might have a panoply of new representative devices, but almost nothing of the true processes and effects of republican government.

Chapter Seven

CONGRESSIONAL SELF-GOVERNMENT

> *Those who blame the quarrels of the Senate
> and the people of Rome condemn that which
> was the very origin of liberty. They were
> probably more impressed by the cries and
> noise which these disturbances occasioned
> in public places, than by the good effect
> which they produced . . . From the time
> of the Tarquins to that of the Gracchi, that
> is to say, within the space of over three
> hundred years, the differences between these
> parties caused but very few exiles, and cost
> still less blood . . . only 8 or 10 of its citi-
> zens sent into exile, and but a very small
> number put to death and even but a few con-
> demned to pecuniary fines.*
>
> Machiavelli, *the Discourses*

CONGRESS SEEMS NOT at all as well-behaved and orderly
as the Supreme Soviet of the Soviet Union. So the naive
may imagine it to be in the throes of self-destruction. They
forget an ironic lesson of history: The most lively and
powerful of institutions are in constant turmoil and struggle. Someday there may be discovered a way to govern
well without squabbling, but history will contribute few
precedents.

The Athenian democracy was turbulent, yet immensely
productive and militarily strong. The Roman aristocracy
was fratricidal but produced time after time the necessary
contingents to destroy foreign opposition. The English
nobles exiled, slew, and dispossessed one another without

145

halting the steady rise of England as an international power in the 15th, 16th and 17th centuries. Congress can be a forceful and creative institution even though politiking, filibustering, conniving, compromising, "wheeling and dealing" are its everyday processes.

Here we discover, as in other parts of American government, that the gap between the stories told to schoolchildren and the true story causes unnecessary hardship to the republic. Congress must not only survive, but it must carry too great a burden of myth.

So valuable and scarce a commodity as political power is rarely earned and spent in tranquillity. Despotisms, we know too well, may lend an impression of quiet dominion, but, through the telescope, show the most intense struggles occurring around the central points of power. And, from time to time, revolutionary explosions shake the peaks of society and reverberate through the plains below.

It needs repeating: Congress is the most exposed branch of government. Its operations are evident. Its audience may be fooled but is not thereby to be made reverent. Thus emerges a great difference between Congress and the President and Civil Service. The misconstruals of Congress work against it; the myths of the executives work *for* their greater power.

What can be a more important and destructive misunderstanding than the view, repeatedly attacked in these pages, that Congress has surrendered its powers? Congress has surrendered its *image* of power, not its powers. And that loss, together with accruals of strength in the presidency and civil service, bid to sink the foundations of republican government. To put the matter another way for devotees of game theory, "Congress *vs.* the Executive" is not a zero-sum game; each set of elements is fed or deprived by other sets of elements in the society and from creative institutional changes.

THE POWERS OF CONGRESS

> *Legislation is, as William James suggested of democracy as such, a business in which you do something, then wait to see who hollers, and then relieve the hollering as best you can to see who else hollers.*
>
> T. V. Smith, *The Legislative Way of Life*

Whereas in earlier pages Congress was shown to be an active, indeed the principal, source of legislation in modern times, here Congress, when compared with its successive embodiments through time, can be shown to be of undiminished strength.

Suppose, for example, that a recent Congress, the 87th, say, be contrasted with an ancient one, the 4th, say. A comparison of the titles of laws passed by the two gatherings might suggest an answer.

THE IMPORTANCE OF CONGRESS THEN AND NOW

A comparison of the work of the 4th and 87th Congresses for indications of the scope, domain, and intensity of powers exercised in major actions taken by each. (Both lists are partial)

TYPE OF LAW	4TH CONGRESS (1795-6)	87TH CONGRESS (1961-2)
I. Government Organization	1. Pay of Congress and other officials	1. Enlargement of Rules Committee
	2. Pension Act	2. New Federal Judgeships created
	3. Altering Circuit Court Sessions	3. Vs. Poll Tax as Vote Qualifier
	4. Mint Operations Regulated	4. Adding Original Jurisdiction to District Courts
	5. Admission of Tennessee	5. Appropriations for operating the government

TYPE OF LAW	4TH CONGRESS (1795-6)	87TH CONGRESS (1961-2)
	6. Compensation of jurors, etc.	6. Changes of conflict of interests and bribery laws
	7. Appropriations for operating the government	
	8. Accounting system for contractors and others	
II. Armed Forces	1. Appropriations for the military establishment	1. Appropriations for the military establishment
	2. Payment for horses killed in battle	2. Funds for military aid to foreign countries
	3. Changes in the military establishment	3. Regulation of reserves on active duty
III. Internal Improvements	1. Lighthouse Construction	1. Loans for mass transit facilities
	2. Buoys in Boston Harbor	2. Public works (airports, water pollution control)
	3. Acts for sales of public lands	3. Communications satellites act
		4. Space exploration
IV. Welfare	1. Act on quarantine	1. Raise in minimum wage
	2. Act on relief and protection of seamen	2. Loans and grants to depressed areas; also public works
	3. Act for relief of persons imprisoned for debt	3. Housing loans
	4. Land grants to missionary societies	4. Unemployment pay period lengthened
	5. Emergency relief to owners of stills	5. Manpower retraining
	6. Licensing and regulating the coasting trade	6. Sundry benefits for disabled veterans, blind, deaf and other groups
	7. Pensions for disabled veterans	7. Drug industry regulation
		8. Agricultural subsidies
V. Foreign Affairs	1. Act to regulate trade and intercourse with Indians and preserve peace on frontiers	1. Increased mutual security aid

TYPE OF LAW	4TH CONGRESS (1795-6)	87TH CONGRESS (1961-2)
	2. Affirmation of legislation regulating U. S. foreign affairs machinery	2. Peace Corps and Alliance for Progress formed
	3. Passports for U. S. ships	3. Arms Control and Disarmament Agency created
	4. Special appropriations for President to deal with Algerian diplomacy	4. U. S. to cooperate wtih OECD
	5. Adjustment of claims from war damages	5. President authorized to lend to UN
	6. Setting up trading posts for Indian trade	
VI. Taxes and Revenue	1. Extension of time for debt assumption	1. Tariff adjustments
	2. Loan to Washington, D.C.	2. Tax Credits for machinery investment
	3. Reorganization of customs collections	
	4. Duties on passenger conveyances	

The general nature of the changes over five generations is fairly apparent. Three broad similarities reveal themselves:

1. The scope of intervention and activity into various areas of society and individual lives seems equally broad at both times. Spending to find agreement with the Bey of Algiers is not less radical than the Alliance for Progress.

2. The proportion of the population affected and the extent to which it is affected seems alike. The domain and intensity of power have not changed much. Rescuing distillers from economic troubles is as sharp an intervention as assisting a depressed area. The Indian trade affected as large a proportion of Americans as foreign trade does now.

3. The complexity of decision, given the available means, appears not to have changed much over time. It

is unlikely that the average congressman of the 4th Congress could do a better job locating and building a lighthouse off Cape Cod than one today could do on a space satellite. Both would hasten to hire the "know-how." The general public is awed and frightened by complexity; Congress could once run an army of a million loosely disciplined troops and govern a country bursting in all directions, but is mistrusted with a missile base or skirmish in Viet Nam. Yet they give a boy a hundred times as many horsepower to ride as his grandfather had. Is there behind this, not logic, but a failure of nerve?

The differences between then and now are nevertheless important.

1. Government assumes more human risks nowadays. Housing, unemployment, depressed areas, and manpower retraining are examples. These are details of scope. They are critical details because they are at tension points of greater involvement of personal hopes and fears.

2. A greater assumption of continuing administrative activity is indicated in new programs and carried over from old. Foreign aid programs and all the other projects just cited are examples, together with the built-in programs such as agricultural subsidies and social security. This means enlarged possibilities for the continuous accretion of personnel and activity.

One conclusion may be that Congress is no less capable of handling the nation's business today than it has ever been. Another may be that the rooting in government offices of hopes concerning personal problems is a prime cause of favorably changed public attitudes toward an administrative establishment. Still another might be that only formidable machinery can prevail against nonrational accretions of powers in the administration, machinery which is not part of the classical equipment of Congress.

The powers of Congress, it is plain, are numerous and capable of expansion and contraction within broad limits even in the short run. In the long run, they can grow still broader and larger. At the same time, they can be exercised at the initiative increasingly of the executive branch and in a jungle of powers already exercised and under administration.

The limits today are broader than they were originally. Politicians of 175 years ago would have been shocked at the license Congress has acquired and the courts permitted. And each licensed area is only barely occupied to this time. Much more could be legislated in each area, extending the scope, weight and domain of congressional and governmental influence on American life. Here are some of the things that Congress could do within its present powers if it wished:

It could transform the Supreme Court and federal court system.

It could materially affect the existence of political parties.

It could greatly restrain the President.

It could enlarge the civil service greatly or cut it back greatly.

It could make America a socialist country.

It could force organized religion to live a precarious life.

It could militarize the people.

It could restore the earlier and independent kind of federalism.

It could give up numerous rights to foreign powers and international organizations.

It could level the income of the American population to a very narrow range of differences.

It has all of these powers and more. Yet it is generally conservative, moving with reluctance into all of these fields. For it is under severe self-restraint, more so than the presidency. The President uses his powers to the hilt; Congress uses only a fraction of its powers. And when Congress uses its powers, it tends more and more to use them in a way that promotes the growth and power of the administrative establishment and thus to further limit the possible directions of new legislation in the future.

Congress is caught up in the great world-wide tide of centralization and collectivism, despite what amounts sometimes to an hysterical resistance to the tide. In 1796 and thereabouts, when Congress was legislating at a not much different pace and with no more force than today, the powers not used and the powers not possessed were exercised by the local governments and non-governmental associations and individuals. They were scattered over the country. They did not enter the vaults of the bureaucracy. Since governmental power, no matter how rarely employed, is nearly always stronger than non-governmental power, congressional supremacy could not be said to have been threatened by the broadest and fastest grants and sales of political rights and obligations.

Once, however, that the created powers began to lodge in the halls of government, every new creation added to the competitive power of the administration. Unlike corporations, local governments, voluntary associations, and individuals, the administrative establishment contains by nature the magic of sovereignty and the majesty of the law.

OLIGARCHY AND SENIORITY

> *Strong prejudices of any kind; obstinate adherence to old habits; positive defects of national character, or mere ignorance, and deficiency of mental cultivation, if prevalent in a people, will be in general faithfully reflected in their representative assemblies: and should it happen that the executive administration, the direct management of public affairs, is in the hands of persons comparatively free from these defects, more good would frequently be done by them when not hampered by the necessity of carrying with them the voluntary assent of such bodies . . . [yet] It would be absurd to construct institutions for the mere purpose of taking advantage of such possibilities.*

J. S. Mill, *Representative Government*

Far from being a simple thing, the supreme legislature of the United States is a structure connecting hundreds of groups, both formal and informal. Piled one upon another are blocs, parties, committees, sub-committees, cliques, state delegations, friendship groups, breakfast clubs, and sports groups. Groupings are based further on religion, region, occupations and ideology. All lace out to connect hundreds of staff members and into the executive establishment and all over the country.

With a myriad of groups in the legislative system and a set of great powers, exercised far below capacity, one may suspect that there exists within the whole a divergency of views and interests. Such is, of course, the case. Only by great exertions can Congress develop a program of its own. Only by assiduous work can any group within it achieve a success. It is no place for the casually dropped idea that is picked up because of intrinsic merit and adopted. "I don't believe" said one respected strategist, "there is any man in the House who can do a really effective legislative job on more than two bills in a year." * But then there are few places for facile reform in the institutional world

* Clapp, *op. cit.*, p. 107.

anywhere; the social ground is fertilized with ideas in abundance.

The main shaft of congressional movement occurs through the oligarchy. Let us call it the "leadership" to be polite. This group would include the Speaker, floor leaders, and committee chairmen in the House and a looser establishment in the Senate. The partisan organization of the two chambers excludes one or the other party all the time, but minority party leaders might as well be included in the definition; they would, after all, be officially leaders but for the grace of a few votes here and there, and next year they may well be in authority. Perhaps the chairmen of sub-committees on appropriations should be included. Actually, at any given time, a better way of determining leadership is by asking a sample of third-term congressmen and four-year-plus Senators. Summing up their nominations, like counting election results, would give a fairly accurate listing of the oligarchy. The results of this so-called sociometric test would relate closely but not perfectly to the purely formal test used here.

Both chambers are run rather more democratically now than fifty or a hundred years ago. Both the oligarchy of the two houses and the Speaker are less in command. Writers ordinarily applaud Woodrow Wilson's emphasis upon the power of committees in running the work of Congress. This he bespoke in his *Congressional Government*, published in 1885. He discovered a phenomenon that had been present in varying degree for a half century. Before then, the committees had much less force. Congress was small enough to permit more informal government and fewer sub-groups. It spent less, and permitted itself then as always the luxury of many individual contacts with the bureaucracy.

During and after the Civil War, with an extension of the powers of government and the presidency, committees multiplied and the congressional leadership of chairmen began to formalize. Yet the Speaker was a prime beneficiary of power increments, until finally he was toppled in the famous palace revolution of 1910. When he was overthrown, the victory did not go to the mass of members. As usually occurs in revolutions, both small and big, the redistributed powers went to another group of the elite, this time the committee chairmen.

The new committee system then was regarded as something of a reform of congressional government. If this is borne in mind, some degree of reasonableness can be injected into the discussion of congressional government, which is often and unfortunately posed as a struggle between oligarchy and democracy. We do not beg the question whether the reform is now itself in need of reform. We say only that until the question of the oligarchy is discussed as one of how may Congress function well rather than one of a usurpation of power, we shall not be able to understand or reform Congress. Or, put more bluntly, it is a question of whose oligarchy shall run Congress.

Oligarchy is the *sine qua non* of all action groups. Some members must have more to say than others. Who says leadership says oligarchy. The House of Representatives is an oligarchy, certainly. It can be pictured as a pyramid in which a few men hold large powers, a large number considerable powers, and a great number small powers. To credit this point, it is necessary only to ask any and all congressmen whether this is so. Though there may be some differences of view as to how much power is concentrated in how many hands, the major thesis will be accepted.

Indeed, if one were only to consider the last resort of the principle of equality in the House, which is the fact that each congressman has only one vote to cast on every issue coming before the House, he would find that this surmise too vanishes into oligarchy. On some occasions, votes are rounded up, corralled, branded and tallied by and for the leadership. When this process does not occur, it is sometimes because it is unnecessary; the members ask the informed leaders how to vote. Or a revolt may be taking place, a not infrequent occurrence. Or because a member exercises his ultimate right to be a maverick. Or because the personal district problems of a member excuse him from the collective discipline. This is the usual case, since the Congress is committed by its present leadership and history to much more of a consensual policy than the oligarchical nature of the Congress would lead one to believe.

Time after time, members will assert that they are rarely pressured. They are in no sense forced except in a rare emergency, the frequency of which is not known but would perhaps average once a session. Since perforce congressmen vote in groups, the group act is misconstrued to be a proof of the oligarchy at work. Actually the forces of consensus operate independently of the ultimate weapons of the oligarchy. One cannot doubt that the great measure of freedom allowed the member of Congress in his voting both explains and determines the quantity and quality of legislation.

Legislation that some group, perhaps the presidential group, wants in an anguished way, as "a key part of the President's program" flounders about, is nipped at and altered, and may or may not emerge into law, and if so, rarely on schedule. The fault may not be in the oligarchy, for this happens often when the oligarchy is committed. But the oligarchy may be committed to the single piece of legislation, not to the destruction of the belief-system of Congress. It may favor a bill of the presidency but not the imposition of oligarchy beyond the normal level of pressure, usually expressed in words such as "we'd like you to go along with this if you can see your way clear."

A close-up of the oligarchy will give some impression of their divergence from the average of Congress, and the other elements of the elite that we have discussed. The leadership of Congress, the total number of which, defined as above, is ninety-two, averaged about 61 years of age in 1964, compared with an average age of 53 for all congressmen. Does eight years of difference in average ages produce some critical difference in ability and views? Perhaps in special cases. It certainly causes some discontent among the young, but then the old may not tolerate youth well either. Congressional leaders are older than business leaders, on average, and older than bureaucratic and especially military leaders. The average age of the President in the years 1900-1965 has been 57.3 years. But again these are facts without much meaning. The dream of youthful leadership will always remain a dream, at least statistically, and of those youths who are plucked from the ranks to live the dream, some will succeed and others will fail. Half the adult population is below 29.5 years old; they must abide the older half, which possesses power and dignity.

The leadership of Congress is chosen by a process usually summed up in an expression hateful to rationalists—the seniority system. But recent studies have gone far beyond the early descriptions of the seniority system in Congress. Whereas at one time it was purveyed and believed that the progression of members to the highest places occurred through automatic ascription by the criterion of length of unbroken tenure of a seat in the chamber, it is presently affirmed that seniority is only the major criterion in a relatively flexible system for filling posts of leadership. Nicholas Masters tells us from his studies of the House that both Democratic and Republican committee assignments are handled by

> small groups composed of senior members appointed and greatly influenced by the party leaders. . . . Party leaders, working in conjunction with their committees-on-committees, use assignments to major committees to bargain with the leaders of party groups and factions, in order to preserve and fortify their leadership positions and conciliate potential rivals, as well as to reward members who have cooperated. Assignment to the major committees is restricted, with some exceptions, to members who have served two or more terms, who are 'responsible' legislators, and who represent districts which do not require them to take inflexible positions on controversial issues. . . . Although a number of factors enter into committee assignments— geography, group support, professional background, etc. —the most important consideration—unless it can be taken for granted—is to provide each member with an assignment that will help to insure his re-election.

To this analysis, other experts on the committee process, such as David Truman and George Goodwin, would probably agree.

No enduring institution in history operates on other than a seniority system: this fact seems to have been forgotten in the clamor to reform the congressional seniority system. To put it another way, almost without exception, whether in the fifth century before Christ in Greece and China, or in China and the United States today, whether in churches or armies, labor unions or universities, factories or newspaper plants, leaders have been members longer on the

average than followers. Since being members longer implies chronological aging, leaders are usually older than
followers too. Leadership therefore is almost always visited
by the infirmities of age more than the followership, and by
the same token the followership is plagued by the vices of
youth. Whether one is worse than the other depends again
on what one wants to come out of the group process he is
considering, in this case the legislative process.

The employment of seniority in Congress is actually congenial to the functioning and purposes of the institution. It
places the institution as far away from the reach of the
presidency and partisan politics as possible. It prevents
ignoramuses from being charged each two years with the
running of an intricate machine. It makes the control of
the vast executive branch of government a possibility instead of a macabre joke, for some semblance of continuity
and expertness in this most difficult set of tasks is maintained.

It ensures the exercise of influence on the part of minorities of various kinds. Minorities occur in safe districts—
whether the minorities are dwelling in the southern hills
or in northern Negro neighborhoods, farming beets or raising oysters. But the case would better be put as follows:
America is composed of minorities; this is no rhetorical concept; it is a highly complex and diversified country in
nearly every imaginable sense, ethnically, religiously, economically, climatically, ideologically, characterologically, socially, occupationally, and so forth; every one of these
interests has some public voice by means of one or more
congressmen.

If we had command of a variety of statistics unfortunately denied us, we might venture to say how many voices
would be muffled by a substitution of a "merit" system or
popularity system for the seniority system. Perhaps half of

the variety of interests voiced in Congress would be eliminated by the destruction of the seniority system. The theoretical mechanics are clear: popularity would introduce the
President's men, for who can be more popular in Congress
than someone embraced in the public light by the President? The President's men would present the President's
"program"; the President's "program" consists of those measures calculated to favor those interests clustered in his
national plurality plus not fully assured groups. This collection even when broad, is far from achieving the diversity
of the Congress under the seniority "safe seat" plus modify-
ing factors system.

As for merit, any "merit" test that does not reduce to a
popularity, or a bread-and-butter, or a seniority test is unknown to political systematics: it can be conceived, but its
realization is an impossibility in government; where merit
will enter, it is the sporadic effect of whoever, under whatever the existing system may be, has both power to influence
appointments and uses it for the "public good." The only
place the merit system can be exercised as such is in the
first grade of grammar school.

The seniority system then is many things plus a correlation with years in office. Since this system lacks another
name, it may as well be called the seniority system. And
since the delicate instrument that could create the whole
desired combination of traits in the leadership has not been
invented, the seniority system, often a blunt instrument to
be sure, is employed.

It would be wrong to think that the old rulers of Congress do not possess the respect and even loyalty of their
less influential colleagues. Even among politicians, to whom
loyalty is a costly virtue, there is a considerable devotion to
the oligarchy. This shows in interviews among congress-

men, as contrasted with, say, interviews among junior executives in business firms, or professors in relation to university presidents and deans. The loyalty in part comes from the respect held for the seniors, which in turn reflects first the deference and respect which are given the less influential colleagues by the experienced members and the skills possessed by the leaders.

A gulf yawns between the general public's estimates of various congressional leaders and the estimates of them made by other congressmen. Whereas mass media are judging a man by his colorfulness *a la mode* and his advocacy of popular ideas, the congressmen are judging by internal civic merit and skillfulness in the legislative process. Not that lofty qualities of humaneness and philosophy are ignored by the one or the other, but the emphasis in each case is different.

The congressional leadership is almost indistinguishable in educational background from the rank and file. Most have a college degree. One-fifth of Congress calls itself Methodist; over one-fourth of the oligarchy is the same. Baptists are not so overproportionately present. Catholics are slightly underproportioned in the whole and among the leaders, being 13 out of 92 and 99 out of 533. Jews are now scarcely underproportioned in either membership or leadership. Some of the Methodist and Baptist members will be reapportioned out soon.

What part of the religious designation is typically translated into public policy is not clear. Merest speculation might suggest that, should the Catholic members increase, an increase in earthly pessimism, a drive for security, and a somewhat greater respect for organized voluntary associations will perhaps be noted. The effects of an increased

Jewish affiliation would go almost entirely to polishing up Congress' "mirror image" of the nation.

At the same time, we can say that religiousness is mostly a verbal confession of congressmen. No one should speculate on such internal matters as spiritualism, perhaps, but it is obvious that questionnaires will not answer the question whether Congress is a religious body. It is probably somewhat less religious, on the average, than the population as a whole. But this religious weakness is not perceived, because it is on all fours with the secularism of political science, American social theory, and the American intellectual tradition. It is correct, in the sense of good social manners, to be restrictive of the role and activities of religion in society. Only some of the Catholic members seem to feel that their religion provides an alternative world-view to the conventional majoritarian beliefs. Secularism will continue to grow under present and expected conditions. The antireligious interpretation of the First Amendment grows stricter as other clauses of the Constitution, such as the Fourteenth Amendment, become devoid of fixed meaning, all at the hands of the same Supreme Court.

Disproportion is clearly manifested in occupations. The fact that so many congressmen are lawyers is too well known to dwell upon. Little change is promised here. The number of scientists—natural and social—is gradually increasing and is perhaps proportionate to the number in the population. The oligarchy is not extraordinary in these regards. Actually the oligarchy may be more urban than the Presidents, six of the last eight of whom have had rural origins; perhaps those who make so much of "rural backgrounds" statistics can make something of this. There is not much disproportion of leaders who come from districts of heavy farm population. The proportion of farmers and farm managers found in House leaders' districts is a fifth higher than in the country's population as a whole and a little higher than the proportion found in the districts of the rank and file.

If the urban composition of the states of the Senate leadership is examined, it appears to be considerably less than that for the country as a whole, 60% versus 70%. The House leadership, however, shows the largest difference from the House as a whole and the population. Over half of them come from rural districts, 58%. Fourteen percent come from suburban districts and 28% from urban ones. The proverbial rural bosses of the United States seem to be tracked to their lair at last, in the House leadership!

It is not easy to specify the effects of the disproportionate rural cast of the leadership. Certainly farmers get benevolent attention, more perhaps than they would otherwise receive. Also, the leaders of Congress appear to be somewhat untypical of the American people, in this rural quality, statistically speaking. But, of course, no leadership group is typical. Labor union leaders, priests, and other elites are by no means mirrors of their constituents.

Moreover the substitution of urban for rural legislators may result in the selection of more urban representatives, who would turn out to be less typical of either the whole or their own population than were the displaced rural legislators. That can readily happen when a legislator comes from a minority within his district, such as a labor movement, a church group, a real estate group, and so forth. Or some lawyers of limited interests.

A twenty percent difference, to conclude, is statistically significant but behaviorally may convey few important effects. Certainly the quality of the individuals who leave or enter the congressional club is a much more important factor in the production of results. So is the way in which the members—whether rural or urban—are organized to get work done.

THE SYSTEM OF SUCCESSIVE MAJORITIES

The means by which a majority comes to be a majority is the more important thing.

Samuel J. Tilden

From *who* legislates to *how* they legislate is an easy step. Many people take the step backwards: Considering *how* they legislate, the legislators must be a strange and poor lot! The process of making laws appears to be unspeakably complicated.

But the reader is already conditioned against this error. He knows that the presidency and bureaucracy are typically as slow and tortuous in their formulation and determining of policy as Congress. Their operations, however, are concealed beneath the skin of a single personality, the President, who because he is one, seems active against the dim huge backdrop of big government.

What is to be newly established here is the meaning of congressional procedure in all its complexity. It may be stated as follows: *Congress operates principally through the decision system of successive majorities.* For governing a society and for representing a society this method is superior to both the traditional method of the executive and the populist representation of the President. The method is more modern than the others. Ultimately, in a thousand years, if not in ten, it will prevail.

The meandering careers of bills should be examined in this light. Seemingly no greater condemnation can be visited upon congressional procedures than the limited representativeness of a particular committee, say, the Rules

Committee of the House. To think that a single chairman can block the national will is intolerable (we pause to remind ourselves that the chairman is only a single man in the sense that the President is a single man and the national will is a term that can only begin an endless argument over who represents what). Moreover, to see this fate of the legendary wandering Jew visited upon one's favorite bill seems to prove that congressional procedure is only a form of persecution; from one committee to another, from one hopper to another; first here and then there on the legislative calendar, and when it passes one house, it must go to another, and when it passes both it must go into a conference committee of both houses to adjust the differences and alter the whole, and even so the activity may now be merely authorized, because to get money the idea must risk another set of committees and individuals. How can all of this be justified?

It cannot if it is viewed as just stated. But in a constructive sense, which begins when we consider that reasonable men have created this system over centuries of time, a rational quality can be imparted to the system that may not only be understandable but that may prove to be superior to that found in competing methods of processing important decisions in society. The very procedure of moving from one man to another, from one hopper to another, from one committee to another can be pictured as a process of achieving successive majorities.

The Trade Expansion Act of 1962 can illustrate the process. Begun as a House Resolution (HR 11970), it passed through the Rules Committee, the Ways and Means Committee, the whole House, the Finance Committee of the Senate, the Senate as a whole, a Conference Committee, and again the two chambers before arriving for signature at the White House. Many amendments were rejected and many made. Numerous controversies occurred. In the Rules Committee, one kind of microcosm of the country worked upon it, in Ways and Means another. Approvals by majorities, applied directly or implied, carried the bill in and out of committees and passed upon each change. Except where an officer presumed to be responsible to the majority of the House and possibly of the country acted in a solitary capacity, all actions were plurality or majority actions. Over ninety separate actions of a majority character were taken, in committees or on the floor.

The Civil Rights Act of 1960 affords another case. Here a House Resolution (HR 8601) was culled out of 39 bills on the agenda of the Judiciary Committee (and Sub-Committee). It went to the Rules Committee where strong opposition to the Bill set up. But threat of a Discharge Petition to force the Bill out of Committee impelled the Chairman to release it. Then followed a stream of actions, each culminating by presenting another side of Congress to consultation and voting. Seemingly everything that could happen happened to this Bill. A filibuster took place in the Senate. A vigorous struggle occurred between some House and Senate leaders. Finally after about one hundred and ten successive actions formulating majorities of one kind or another, the Act was approved for presidential signature. Most major laws have received similar, thorough processing.

Congress, that is, does not achieve its representativeness in one full swoop, one grand flash of illumination, as the executive may sometimes do, nor by an easy reconciliation of prejudices with decisions as occurs in the presidency or bureaucracy or Supreme Court. Such sublime self-delusion is not permitted Congress. In the congressional process, a will has to prove itself through a chain of subjective wills and thus become an objectified will.

It must be submitted that this procedure is not chaos. It is not irresponsibility. It is not unrepresentative. It is not against the national interest. It is none of these, save by definition. Rather it is a way of doing business that is elegantly and elaborately suited to the kind of business that is to be done. It is a great demonstration of the pragmatic and operational philosophical thesis that the means and the end ought to be reconciled and alike. Here it is republican principles being enacted by republican means.

Very few men in the world are conversant with the rules of the House and the Senate. Few congressmen are. Yet it would be fallacious to think that these rules are too complex to have reason in them. They are complicated precisely because they have to reconcile irreconcilables. They have to do something that the President does not have to do, nor the executive agency; they have to promote equality, pluralism, consensus, and at the same time produce decisions, acts of will of moment to the whole society. The constant accretion of rule, the innumerable small exceptions and change, the whole procedure of the House Rules Committee which significantly has to pass a *special* rule to get an ordinary important bill of the type Congress was created to enact onto the floor—all of this signals the throes of creativity of a kind peculiar to Congress.

Given the philosophy of republicanism, the oligarchy is an efficient idea; so are the limitations upon oligarchy; so are the complicated rules that seek to apply multiple and conflicting values at the same time, tearing apart and reconstructing the same principles of one . . many . . all . . one . . many . . all, in endless succession. The system of successive majorities, to conclude, is unique and potentially of wide applicability in many reaches of society and in many lands. It is stabilizing. It is pluralistic. It is powerful when it reaches completion. And it is, in the senses described, representative.

The weaknesses of the system of successive majorities are not wanting. Its complexity and vulnerability to the simplistic popular mind have already been alluded to. The presidency can also interfere with the process at many points, choosing precisely those points where he knows he can engage popular opinion. The obdurate refusal of many past and present leaders of Congress to countenance any form of cooperation with the President and his advisers stems largely from their experience that such "cooperation" can easily result in a breach of their defenses.

In recent years the presidency has expressed itself also through the Bureau of the Budget. There both political and technical judgments are passed upon a great many bills in the early stages of consideration and usually, when the Bureau expresses itself negatively, a bill will die. The intrusion into the system of successive majorities of this executive device which has little basis in the Constitution or laws but has acquired great informal weight has excited Senator Ribicoff, certainly no foe of the presidency, into radical protest in the pages of the *Saturday Evening Post* (March 21, 1964, p. 10). That Congress has submitted peacefully to such executive presumption demonstrates how the Executive Force benefits from drift even more than from diabolism.

Conference committees are one of the set of majorities that has typically power beyond what is acceptable to majorities of both chambers. It is possible that this situation is inevitable. The main remedy lies in reducing the scope of decision of the conference committees by maintaining and passing closely similar bills in both Senate and House. This is not always possible, not only because the two chambers may have sharply contrasting views, but also because one chamber's version may be exaggerated in order to provide more apparent "surrenders" in the bargaining and compromising of the conference.

There is the further question of the extravagant importance of certain influences in other majority-constructing settings. The domination of a powerful committee by a single man over a long period of time is often regretted. It may not be consoling to point out that the incumbency of a given President may be regretted for eight years by nearly half the people. Perhaps it is not consoling either to read the words of an historian of the House of Representatives concerning the Committee on Rules of the House:

> While the Committee on Rules failed to function during the decade under review (1937-1946) as the responsible instrument of majority party government in the House of Representatives, nevertheless it apparently did faithfully reflect majority sentiment in the House. The rules it granted or denied were calculated to facilitate the expression of the will of a bipartisan majority in the House, which may or may not have reflected majority sentiment in the country, while obstructing adoption of the program of the majority party.*

The question then resolves into whether the republican force or the executive force represents the country.

Consolation may come hard. In the end, to be consoled, a person may want only *his* special majority to win in the legislative struggle. To that end, he may be willing to sacrifice all institutions and principles of government other than his favored ones. There can be no logical refutation

---

* George B. Galloway, *History of the United States House of Representatives, op. cit.,* pp. 136-137.

of such a position, which is essentially philosophical or dogmatic. He (and others) may be asked, however, whether they are so certain either of the effects of the laws they wish or of the consistently favorable behavior of the institution they would empower.

A related question may be asked of the representation of views in committees, which do 90% of the business of Congress. A committee's roster is prepared usually, as Charles Jones and others have shown by careful analysis, to include members whose constituencies have unusually strong interests in the committee's area of interest. Thus the Committees on Agriculture are ruled by members from heavily agricultural areas. Cotton-area representatives are on the sub-committee that deals with cotton. Is this representation by skilled men; is it interest representation; is it conflict of interests? It is all three.

Pursuing the theory of successive majorities, however, it is immediately apparent that these conditions are all checked before and after matters pass through the sub-committees on Agriculture. Even in the Committee as a whole, diverse agricultural interests will watch and check one another. We note also that "on House Appropriations (in contrast to the practice followed by its Senate counterpart), a congressman generally is not assigned to a sub-committee of special concern to his district, on the grounds that his judgment would be less objective than that of a member whose constituency is less directly involved." * But this may also be the way in which the fiscal conservatives in Congress can hold down appropriations.

The staffing of committees cannot be said to be well-handled, though experts now say it has greatly improved

---

* Clapp, *op. cit.*, p. 242.

in recent years. There are only 500 people working for all the House Committees, most of them on select committees and special investigations. The number is far too few for the intelligence function of Congress, just as the number of personal assistants is too few for the administrative and constituency obligations of congressmen. Furthermore, the provision for dissenting views on committees is often defective, if full intelligence and representation should be brought to bear upon congressional operations: "The House Science and Astronautics Committee is responsible for the oversight of NASA, the civilian space agency, whose budget this year is $5.2 billion, the fourth largest budget of any Government agency. Yet the Committee has 10 professional staff members, the smallest committee in Congress, and none of these is responsible to the Minority." [*] Of course, committees will have dissension among the majority members too, which will promote thought and care. Still the greatest value of the congressional system of successive majorities is its merging of different views in a single decision, the law. The presidency and executive establishment cannot produce the likes. It must therefore be cared for.

Generalizing is risky. The pattern of representation changes, often subtly, with none of the figures so dearly beloved by scientists, to mark the passage from one condition to another. The cause of change is often so "simple" as that congressmen learn; they adapt; they fashion themselves in a new role. "Members of the Senate Foreign Relations Committee and the House Foreign Affairs Committee . . . tend to be less bound by segmental approaches to foreign policy issues than are other Congressmen. Their special responsibilities in the international field foster a

---

[*] Fred Schwengel, "An Open Letter to Members and Friends of the American Political Science Association," September, 1963.

broad-gauged attitudinal framework. . . ." So writes Professor James Rosenau, in his book on *National Leadership and Foreign Policy.*

A rich variety of representative forces filters through the system of successive majorities. Neither the presidency, nor the civil service, nor the pressure groups, nor the courts, nor the political party, nor the press could individually or all together duplicate the process and provide the same "product mix."

The process may suffer from not being brought to a focus, so as to achieve technical coordination and to get an improved sensing of the congressional "majority." There is, for example, no formal assembly of congressional leaders. On the other hand, the Speaker and Majority Leader of the House deal with committee chairmen as informal group members, often quite effectively. Whether the group comes together informally or by rule, it should convene in some manner to discuss the prospects of a session, any highly controversial bills, and to formulate proclamations on behalf of the whole Congress, which are to be set forth in a later chapter.

The process of communication between leadership and newcomers has been described as weak. The oligarchy, in the House especially, would appear well-advised to give more attention to assimilating the first and second term members. Since rarely does a leadership which is under pressure act save under greater pressure, and since the normal pressure mounting up presently is directed at the destruction of the independence of the leadership, a device to create the appropriate pressure is needed.

Pressure is usually more effective when it provides a benefit while asking one. Therefore, one asks: "What do the oligarchs need that freshmen can provide?" Strangely,

it is public prestige. For, while the oligarchs have great
prestige in the Congress, they are not respected in the
country at large. It is for this reason that, also in a later
chapter, a set of Halls of Congress are recommended; in
their establishment and management, the freshmen must be
agents, while in filling them the leaders are principals. Both
groups would gain new public stature.

THE INTELLIGENCE FUNCTION

> *The world is not led by long or learned demonstration; a rapid glance
> at particular incidents, the daily study of the fleeting passions of the
> multitude, the accidents of the moment, and the art of turning them
> to account decide all its affairs.*
>
> de Tocqueville

Neither the public nor congressmen are apt to take seriously enough the delinquencies of Congress in the matter
of planning, programming, and researching legislation. Consequently, a common source of disappointment with legislative institutions and with legislation is not explored and
corrected while above there rages controversy of a specious
political nature. Congress lacks the comprehension of research and development in its own work even while it spends
15 billion dollars a year for research and development in
the agencies of the executive branch.

Let us scan the ways of knowing that a new congressman
possesses. There are twenty of them at least. He learns,
of course, from his colleagues, just as a student learns from
his classmates. His family and "nuclear constituency" ply
him with information and advice. He forms groups and in
the group is educated. He learns through committee staffs,
and from the hearings and reports of committees. The pressure groups provide him with services and information. The
executive agencies are usually ready to answer inquiries and

often provide staff assistance on a temporary basis. Their
liaison personnel stand ready to assist when required. Their
dissident members brave retaliation to "leak" information
or, as in the Jerry Jackis case (1963), to testify about internal problems before congressional committees.

The mail is a continuous source of ideas and information. The debates are not as uninstructive as many believe.
Newspapers, magazines, and books are everyday intellectual
fare. Radio, television and films form some small part, but
are followed more as plays in the game of politics or for
sheer entertainment than for acquiring knowledge.

University professors are used frequently as consultants.
Private research organizations may do special studies, especially of the type of a personal public opinion poll. Lec-
tures, meetings, and travel, where the congressman is both
teacher and learner, provide many stimuli and much social
information. The research divisions of the national, state,
and local parties furnish more carefully prepared information on trends of opinion, voting behavior, and political
argumentation. The office of legislative counsel provides
legal advice and help in the drafting of bills.

The Legislative Reference Service of the Library of Congress, which has doubled its work in the past decade,
answered about one hundred thousand inquiries from congressmen in 1963. Other units of the Library of Congress
responded to another fifty thousand requests for information. The vast bulk of these are trivial. They may be merely
lists of books prepared on a constituent's request for information. On the other hand, many of the reliable and
systematic studies that a congressman receives are prepared
by the Legislative Reference Service.

The best is none too good. Without exception, the ways
of knowing are inadequate and shallow. Only a small frac-

tion of what the scientific method can contribute to informed legislative action is known and used. In this sense Congress is more backward than practically all large American corporations. Business concerns typically calculate carefully and plan systematically before deciding on a course of action.

An example of what regularly occurs is afforded by the Economic Opportunity Act of 1964. Originating with President Johnson as a slogan, "War Against Poverty," the legislation was probably intended to bring high political status to the new President, who had to win popular election within a year, as well as to help the poor. The canny President combined old "New Deal" ideas to appeal to centers of organized voting but disorganized economies in the old industrial areas of Pennsylvania, West Virginia, and elsewhere; he repackaged a number of existing programs in welfare, education, business, and labor; he promised to appoint the governmental "Hollywood Star" of the time, Sargent Shriver, as the program's Director; he and his staff "updated" the phraseology of reform to include many research, experimental, and training programs; and to reduce opposition from local quarters as well as to try not to harm voluntary and local activities, he and his staff provided that the federal government cooperate with local and voluntary groups in many instances. Almost a billion dollars was to be authorized, with promises of a great deal more later on.

The House Committee on Education and Labor was assigned the bill and called in a set of favorable witnesses. Department heads, governors, and mayors attested to its value. Vigorous efforts on the part of Republican members of the committee were required to bring objective and unfriendly experts into the hearings. Only several could come, unpaid, in a hurry, without preparation. The hearings were

promptly closed and the bill went to the Rules Committee
where questions of a rhetorical, legal, and political nature
were asked. In the Senate, a similar procedure occurred.
Favorable witnesses urged adopting the bill. Others were
crammed in on a moment's notice.

There was no systematic study prepared for one or another of the several viewpoints that might be held in respect
to the legislation. The most elementary precaution of
straight thinking, namely the definition of basic words such
as "poverty," was not taken and the issue of defining them
fought off until the end for political reasons, and out of
sheer ignorance of the benefits to be derived from logical
clarity. A mess of vague statistics was dished out; references to the specific features of the proposed legislation
were in lofty abstracted language as if poverty were such
a holy subject that it should not be pried into. Large grants
of undefined powers were to be assigned the Director, but
effects of such delegations upon the other agencies in education and welfare, upon voluntary welfare groups, upon
the powers and functions of Congress and upon federalism
were not contemplated.

Nor was serious attention given to the primary question:
"What effects would all the money, personnel, activity, and
power really have upon poverty in America?"

To take one instance of the failure of intelligence. A
single national sample survey, requiring three months and
one quarter of a million dollars, would have told Congress
(and the whole country) for the first time who was poor,
where the poor were located, what combination of problems
made some of the poor handicapped, and how could the
poor be approached so as to help them with the least bad
side-effects upon other people, institutions, and ideals.
Sargent Shriver declared before the House Committee on

Education and Labor, "We wanted this program with the maximum amount of objectivity that we could bring to it; namely, we tried to find out very accurately who the poor people are, where they were, and what could be done by government in cooperation with the private sector that was workable, that could affect them and help them." If this were so and the voluminous material introduced at the hearings reflected it, as was certainly intended, then the conclusion must be that the standards of scientific inquiry on matters of legislative policy are as low in the executive branch as in the legislative.

The courts of the federal government have gross appetites for law-making that extend far beyond their ability to gather and prepare social intelligence. The President, who has been granted truly wonderful resources to obtain social and economic information, often fails, as in the present case, to avail himself of his chances. (Indeed, nearly every statement in this book concerning the presidency and Congress can be illustrated from the history of the Economic Opportunity Act of 1964.) Congress, in turn, has never consciously, in full self-awareness, asked itself how it should go about incorporating into its operations the arsenal of techniques of intelligence recently developed by the behavioral and natural sciences. Were it to do so, legislative histories as damaging to the republic as that described here would become more rare. If a technically equipped Congress, as Professor Griffith has suggested, can handle any complex problems before it, the total problem of Congress in the framework of American society would be clarified. The total problem will become then basically a political one. On what issues and with what ideology *should* Congress be made to work? And, how much power, given the

"correct" issues and ideology, *should* Congress have in proportion to other powerful agencies of government?

However, the problem of adopting the most modern instruments of intelligence will not result simply from edu-
cating congressmen concerning their possibilities. Planned
ignorance can be a tool of shrewd policy. Cutting off Congressmen's independent sources of knowledge or maintaining them at a low level of efficiency is an excellent method
of making Congress dependent upon the executive branch.
It is a sociological paradox, one of the many that block
reconstruction of the republic, that the supports of the
Republican Force are anti-intellectual, even while the survival of the republic depends upon maximizing control over
the intelligence machinery of society.

Congress needs more than one official intelligence and
research group. A congressman should be able to call upon
any one of a large number of certified research agencies to
prepare a study for him. The Legislative Reference Service
must of necessity be superficial, non-philosophical, and narrow in its range of research instruments. A congressman
should be able to call for whatever instrument he wishes
from those who know how to employ them. The money
presently available for ordering studies is inadequate. Within a decade or so it should be multiplied ten-fold. One
hundred million dollars for congressional research would
provide congressmen with the "Great Equalizer" to the
bureaucracy, executive, and major interest groups. One-
tenth of one per cent of expenditures for research is scarcely
excessive. It is one dollar out of every thousand spent. With
that sum, two parallel organizations might be set up in the
Library of Congress from which a congressman might choose
his research (never mind the shibboleth of "avoid duplicating a service"). The leadership could prepare policy

programs. The individual congressman could go far to develop social and economic intelligence. The whole output of Congress would rise to a superior level.

CONTROL SYSTEMS

> *The medieval parliaments might appear, and perhaps appeared, to an uninformed or prejudiced observer as champions and instruments of conservatism. Actually they were; however, opposition to the new meant not only the defence of special interests but also resistance to novel directions—especially the attempts of power to unbind itself— granted in the name of this or that promising ideal—from every brake and control of its subjects.*
>
> A. Marongiu, *Il Parlamento in Italia* (1962)

Corresponding to Congress' peculiar mode of achieving consensus by the system of successive majorities, is its special way of governing the executive branch. ("Governing" is too strong a word since the power of governance is in process of shifting around and the executive is coming in from another side, so to speak.) The unorthodoxy of Congress' method of dealing with the executive is more theoretical than real. That is, it is unorthodox when compared with textbooks on administration; it is not so unusual when compared with what actually occurs in the struggle to control large-scale organizations.

Of what does this unorthodoxy consist? Essentially it consists of a willingness of Congress as a body and as individuals to come to grips with problems of controlling the executive wherever it can grab hold. It consists on the other side, of releasing its grasp of anything that gets too "hot" or too "cold."

The principal systems of control over the executive are six: Briefly, they are:

Empowering: The granting (and shaping) of powers

Designing: The design of organizational structures

Governing: The governance of personnel

Funding: The provision of funds

Auditing: Watching the record of spending

Investigating: Investigation and research, constituent
nursing

None is unique to Congress. All are performed by cabinets, boards of directors, politburos, and boards of education.
To specify them as they occur in the legislative process, we
should need to emphasize certain variations only. For example, when Congress grants powers to the executive, it
legislates, but these orders to the executive and to the larger
population beyond differ from other decisions of other
bodies mostly in being more formally stated and covering
a great variety of subjects. The pomp and ritual of the event
combine with the fact of ultimate possible sanctions by
force to make the law of Congress appear of another kind
than the "laws" of other groups. Give a private company
a monopoly of a mysterious and dangerous product such as
dynamite, and before long its board of directors would begin
to act like a legislature.

"Excessive" delegation of powers is a second deviant
trait of Congress as a rule-making group. Nothing is excessively delegated that can be readily recalled, but Congress' assignments of authority to the President and agencies
tend to glue themselves to their assignees. When congressmen later speak of recalling or even altering such powers,
the protest that greets them appears to come from persons
whose private property from time immemorial is being taken
without compensation. Owing to the constitutional independence of the presidency and the legal and traditional
independence of administrative personnel, Congress has to
fight to regain powers it may once have blithely delegated.

Are there any clear boundary lines between admissible and inadmissible interventions by Congressmen, collectively or individually, by inquiry or by law, in the executive branch. There are such to some monomaniacs of the Executive Force: Congressmen have no right to intervene personally in any individual case before any agency; they have moreover no right to deal legislatively with any sub-agency or any internal agency affair—structurally, financially, on personnel or on substance; in short, Congress should act only as a whole, only by law, and only through the broadest policy statements possible, leaving to the President the absolute power to rule the government beginning three paces from the steps of the Capitol.

Of little use it would be to modify or subdue this extreme statement. The exceptions advanced to disprove it would be so weak as to lend it support. One could cite and quote many a document, speech, and action showing what a powerful grip this conception of the Presidency has on "the best minds" of the country.

Thus a committee of twenty-five distinguished business executives, all with governmental experience, approved in 1965 a report called "Improving Executive Management in the Federal Government." Their conclusion: "The president of any large corporation with so little effective control over his key executives would be severely restricted in his ability to accomplish corporate objectives." The remedy: transfer almost total control over all top executives to an office inside the Executive Office of the President. It scarcely occurs to these gentlemen that a) The Federal Government is much vaster and different in spirit and purpose from a corporation, b) the words "his key executives" imply a spirit of property that is certainly not derived from the Constitution, nor from the laws of Congress, nor

even from the utterances of several Presidents, but is a con-
coction of the old-fashioned textbook school of military-
civil administration, c) many corporations do not have the
absolute freedom that is premised here for them, and d) so
long as the President calls himself a legislator—as they all
do now—he must be ready to struggle for the power to
legislate with the original supreme legislator, Congress. If
a cartographer and a gold-miner meet in a valley, they might
get along splendidly until the cartographer says that he is
also a gold-miner; the first miner would scarcely be blamed
for taking an interest in cartography. The top executive
establishment is both the object and the source of power.
To surrender jurisdiction over it would greatly diminish the
general power of Congress.

Is the other extreme as ridiculous? Can the advocate of
the Republican Force reasonably say: There are no limits
to the right of Congressmen to intervene in the executive
branch, collectively or as individuals, in personal cases and
by laws? He cannot, for there are several important rules
of intervention that must be followed if other aspects of the
republican program are to be pursued consistently:

1. A congressman can justifiably intervene as advocate
   of a person being seriously harmed by the executive
   branch, or as advocate of a person receiving treat-
   ment that reveals corruption or abuse of administration.

2. A congressional committee can do the same and can
   also use its substantive and fiscal competence to
   cause agency officials to treat its views with as much
   respect as those of the President or agency head.
   The administrator has no right to "freedom from
   fear of Congress." The executive hierarchy retains,

of course, the final say on the policy or action at issue.

3. Congress as a whole can structure and restructure all agencies down to the last unit, and can give and recapture all initiatives (powers) that it believes important to have. Congress, as Professor Crosskey has elaborately demonstrated, was originally created in the model of the omnipotent eighteenth century legislature; there is no fundamental reason why that concept has to give way to a hierarchical executive walled against intrusion.

It will be said that these rules are in fact followed (and those who say so will often add "regrettably" and "unfortunately"). They are to a degree. But let us consider two examples of the moment. They are transient, yet eternal. In June of 1965, the House, aroused at the Secretary of Defense's decision to close certain defense facilities, particularly the famous Brooklyn Navy Yard, attached to a $1.9 billion military construction bill a requirement that any termination of a facility might be rejected by a majority vote of either Chamber. The administration objected that its executive prerogatives were being encroached upon.

Is the closing of a military base an executive matter? Thousands of persons suffer economic deprivation. Is Congress to permit this "legislative enactment" by a cabinet official? Would not the maintenance of the facility constitute the prevention of what was probably to become otherwise a depressed area? But the Presidents have asked Congress to legislate for depressed areas, such as the famed "Appalachia" program. Why ask Congress to legislate on this but not the other matter? Is the prevention of

Appalachia's an administrative problem, but the relief of Appalachia's a legislative one?

The mysterious White House spokesmen appear and argue with the reporters the case of the Executive Force. They argue a second case in the same month, in support of a presidential veto. Congress had provided $70 million for flood disaster relief for the Pacific Northwest; but it had also required that certain authorized projects could only be initiated following upon the approval of the Public Works Committees of the House and Senate. "It has the potentiality," says the mysterious spokesman to the *New York Times* reporter, "of making government programs the political playthings of committee chairmen." To which it might be retorted, "Whose playthings should they be?" What makes a project of a size that constitutes a *legislative* as against an *executive* matter?

The answer seems clear enough. First, the contest to make policy is a pure struggle for power, and the legislature's power is generally to be preferred to the executive's power. More significantly, if unhappily less potently, Congress is entitled to choose its means, if its policies are legitimate. That is, granted it can legislate separately on the matters in question, it can legislate *en bloc* on the same matters and others together.

Generally the Executive Force, with its command of the sword and the pen, has been successful in the "moral" and "scientific" struggles against congressional controls. Yet some congressmen are constantly alert to new possibilities of probing and mastering the vast administrative apparatus that Congress itself has created and helped to expand.

Congress has similarly lost its moorings on the philosophy of personnel governance, an area in which in truth Congress has been victimized by the textbook writers. The fact that there are several millions of government workers and armed forces personnel has made it appear "obvious" to many people that one rule should govern all. Congress has been intimidated by the statistics and by the experts.

Actually, one can well conceive of as many personnel systems in the federal government as there are agencies or as many as there would be if the agencies performed non-governmental functions. The State Department in fact has a separate civil service, the Foreign Service. Florida and other states, and other nations, have independent personnel services in the same overall executive branch of government. Creating a great monolith of the civil service works only to solidify the bureaucratic and separatistic spirit, and to make the whole body more solidly resistant against congressional governance. It is difficult, now, nearly a century from the foundation of the civil service and a generation from the major consolidating decisions to see what important economies, efficiencies, and recruitment advantages were obtained. The provisions of security, interchangeability, likenesses, uniformities, freedom from firing, and freedom from politics have worked largely to make the civil service ungovernable, indeed almost as unmanageable to the President as to the Congress. They operate like dredges to keep the currents of powers moving swiftly down from the elective institutions to the civil service, and to impede the process of bringing the same powers back up river. If once the centralization and integration of all federal personnel were needed to educate them to certain practices, that time may have gone now and a series of independent structures may be more in keeping with a spirit of republicanism. At the least, the personnel of the General Accounting Office, which is a particular instrumentality of Congress, might be organized in an independent civil service, to accentuate their special congressional mission in regard to supervising expenditures of the executive agencies.

In providing funds for the agencies, Congress faces the dilemma of all who run non-profit organizations. Wants are infinite, the treasury limited, and the philosophy prevailing is that all desires are equal. It is an annual miracle that a democracy can survive its fiscal trauma. That it does so reveals how superficially the common democratic doctrine of "give everybody what he wants" penetrates the government. Other principles interfere. Some people want more than others; some people turn to government more for their wants. Various interest groups outside and inside government organize the political process. The picture is too complicated for most people to be sure of what is happening. And legislators have their own ideas of who should get what. If it were not for all of these facts, the government would reduce to chaos.

Budgeting is therefore largely a political process, as Professor Aaron Wildavsky has lately described it, and so are taxation and financing, where the bulk of all that is done has been determined by past politics and where present politics can usually make only a small impression. Nevertheless the hope must always remain that enough forces of the same persuasion may be banded together to guide taxing and spending along certain philosophical lines.

Then it would seem that the strategies of the budgetary and revenue struggles should be dictated not by the textbooks on public finance so much as by the needs to control and turn a vast machinery toward certain social ends. Thus if the textbooks read that an across-the-board cut of the Budget, affecting all agencies, is the worst form of budget management, but the alternative is to run large deficits and increase taxes (there being no chance for various reasons to cut the budget selectively), there should be no moral shock over the technique. Whatever principle is used that is better than the next best, is best. The intervention of Congress, then, which of course must mean the action of some segment of the chain of successive majorities, can justifiably occur, if the end is justified, at almost every stage of financing and spending, and in whatever depth of the executive hierarchy is necessary to attain the goal.

The same principles hold for the auditing and investigating functions. For a generation, pundits have argued that Congress should cease trying to control spending before it occurs, whether by its own actions or by those of its agents such as the Comptroller General. Congress almost as stubbornly retains the power to look into the spending process at every bend of the road. In a non-governmental organization where the formality of rule does not crystallize so rapidly into walls of dogma and law, the legislative and top executive power does not delve often into the accounting process, but it may readily do so and does so whenever it pleases. If once Congress were to agree to let the executive take over all save the ultimate post-audit of accounts it would have little more power over the conduct of government than an accounting firm such as Price Waterhouse has over the du Pont Company.

Similarly the investigating power is hugged closely and blindly, like a spoiled child. Those who have been led by the tantrums and scoundrelly tactics of various investigations to study them closely usually finish nevertheless by advocating the education of congressmen, not the abolition of investigations. It is obvious that a legislature whose probes into any part of the government or society are restricted, is limited by that degree of restriction in its ability to know, rule, and control. The education recommended follows a simple logical line: standing and select committees are in the business of learning prior to legislating. Learning may be by general study or case study. The case study is the dramatic, news-provoking search into a troublesome or criminal condition. It has reason to exist despite its teetering frequently on the edge of sheer publicity or sheer persecution. Some part of human science is founded upon case studies in which individuals and groups concerned have suffered ridicule and unfavorable discrimination.

But Congress has far to go to straighten out its character in this regard. Legislators must train themselves not to think of legislating as a game of cops and robbers and of committee work as public relations or adversary proceedings. Good government asks for scientific research, not a show. The total committee process should be reviewed in this light. Every procedure should be scrutinized by congressmen and specially equipped researchers to determine the time, motions, attitudes, and effects of the process. In the end, ways of converting the details of the process into modern means of advancing knowledge and converting knowledge into intelligent power should be achieved. Still it is difficult to recommend specific reforms that could guarantee improved attitudes and practices.

In an external context too, Congress should give greater attention to structural design. Each year brings the creation of new agencies and the proliferation of old. The determination of "who shall do what, when" is critical to everything that occurs afterwards in connection with an activity in the area covered by legislation. When Congress makes such determinations it is saying in effect, "This is the house you will live in for many years to come, and it is suited to certain ways of behaving."

Yet Congress performs this vital control operation often without full awareness. Legislators pluck conventional forms of organization out of the military and paste them on the civilian. They use financial organizational structures for community action programs and so forth. Again a complete inventory of forms of agencies is called for, and a continuing study of how to adapt all structures to republican ideals and substantive aims should be carried on. Here too, the subject is too important to be delegated to the executive branch. Intervention in the design of agencies, far from being a technical matter to be left to experts, is the key to a republican bureaucracy.

If structural design is at one end of the continuum of regulation, intervention in administrative detail goes to the other end. "There are many members who have been here a long time who still devote 90% of their time to case work," asserts one congressman, according to Dr. Charles Clapp. It is remarkable indeed that anybody can spend time on legislative business considering the much greater rewards that go to fence-mending. "You can be a great fellow with the voters," says another M. C., "and a mediocre legislator." And still another, "This life consists of preoccupation with the unimportant at the expense of the important." If "errand-boy" or "nursing" functions had no meaning besides themselves, one might find in them the ultimate destruction of legislative government. On the one hand, no one could be elected without being wholly devoted to them. On the other hand, no one could help legislate and govern wisely with them.

However, they are of larger meaning. We have already said that a million contacts with citizens on personal matters touch a sizable fraction of the country. Congressmen are busy and highly efficient social workers, earning twenty times their cost easily in the counsel and therapy they minister.

In the second place, the service function provides occupational therapy to the congressmen and their staffs, who otherwise would suffer gravely from the frustrations of trying to move business on the floor. There is only room for a select few at any given moment on the business of the chamber. The rest must occupy themselves usefully and, given the excitement of politics and its irregularity, learning in the process of human contact is much more possible and easy than through books and reports and solitary thought.

Perhaps the principal merit of the service function is to keep the congressman at grips with the giant administrative establishment. Unless they were to approach executives with a particular cause in mind, they would scarcely do so at all. Communications would languish and the only contact which civil servants might have with the political world and all the problems that well up through it would be occasional formal appearances and conferences.

If this analysis is true, there is ample reason to retain a strong service function in representative government. How much of a congressman's time should be properly allocated to services? What are dishonest services? How can the congressman's staff perform such services? How can the services be performed without disrupting relations within the agency and between the lower agency officers and its top officials? These are all questions whose answers are dictated by circumstances.

The number of personal services performed by Congress is a measure of the power of Congress. When Congress is strong, its members interrupt the bureaucratic process often. Its constituents interrupt the legislative process just as often. In times gone by, the number of requests and interruptions varied with economic conditions. As Congress set up an ever more separate and impermeable executive establishment, and provided for executive performance of some of the tasks it performed formerly itself, it could be expected to have less of such work.

On the contrary, it has had more. For the number of personal problems brought to members' attention is also related to the extent of bureaucratic intervention in society. When that is large, congressmen have more services to perform. Every increase in government's role in society—whether expressed in payrolls, activities or rules—adds new sources of complaints and inquiries. In this way, the flood of personal business reaching a congressman can be a danger signal that Congress is becoming weaker relative to the growing collectivization and bureaucratization of society.

In that case, to jettison some of the service tasks would only make the surrender of the citizenry to the bureaucracy more complete. They would have no third party to whom to bring their concerns unless a new agency or set of officers were created for the purpose. That would probably be inadequate if only because an agency is a bureaucracy and a bureaucracy sets up rules and the rules eliminate "irrelevant," "illegal," "shady," "emergency," personally-involved, and other kinds of situations. So the congressman's office, or something like it, would appear to be most efficiently designed to take human beings and their problems for what they are and to resolve them.

To conclude the discussion of congressional self-government, several assertions are made once more: Congress has great powers but exercises few. An oligarchy runs Congress but is responsive within reason to the rank and file, demands little of it, and subsists independently of the

President. The system of seniority that underlies the oligarchy is a complicated result of many motives and practices. The system of successive majorities gives solidity
and representativeness to congressional action. It is in every
sense an intelligible and defensible alternative to the means
of deciding policy in the presidency and bureaucracy. The
intelligence system is defective and Congress thereby is
deprived of the fruits of knowledge—power and prestige.

The controls systems are unlike those of the textbooks
on administration except in essence, for they permit Congress to enter into the executive process wherever it pleases
and relinquish to the executive and courts whatever it does
not wish to decide. Thus the situation of congressional government is less definable and more flexible than many another large-scale organizational system. Yet it is inferior
to them only if its objectives are made un-republican in
character. The judgment of any single device used by Congress to intervene in the work of the executive branch can
only be made on the basis of a philosophy of ends, not on
an alleged "objective" applied science of administration, a
thing that does not exist.

That many a congressman does not understand this
viewpoint is not surprising. He sees himself today in the
mirror of the executive suite. The "old type" of politician
is beyond the pale; he is supposed to be ignorant of the
science of administration. The contemporary member has
been put through a cultural training and schooling that
makes him ashamed of ways of doing things that are out of
vogue. What he does not appreciate very often is that the
way to "efficient" government is not through conventional
administrative management theory but through the human
relations techniques of mutual aid and consensual decisions
exemplified in embryo by the original legislative way of life.

Chapter Eight

A PROGRAM OF EXECUTIVE CONTROL

Repent what's past; avoid what is to come;
And do not spread the compost on the weeds
To make them ranker.

Shakespeare, *Hamlet*

There are a whole series of valid objections to the traditional methods of conducting Parliaments, but if they are taken one by one, it is seen that none of them justifies the conclusion that Parliaments ought to be suppressed, but all, on the contrary, indicate directly and plainly that they should be reformed. Now the best that humanly speaking can be said of anything is that it requires to be reformed, for that fact implies that it is indispensable, and that it is capable of new life. The automobile of today is the result of all the objections that were made against the automobile of 1910.

José Ortega y Gasset, *La Rebelión de las Masas* (1930)

PROPOSALS FOR THE REFORM of Congress are as the sands of the beach—innumerable and small. They vary by a little, but usually have to do with rather minor corrections, at least when viewed from the broad rises of this book. They are furthermore colored generally according to the myth of an ideal Congress; they reflect an absolute notion that a legislature has some kind of fixed constitution.

To the contrary, a legislature is what it is made to be. The proposal for an "effective Congress" may be a republican proposal or it may be an executive appeal. When its details are spelled out, it is never neutral; it usually favors one or another force in the nation to some degree. It so happens, under the conditions of recent political life, that the slogan of an effective Congress has been the property of those who would in effect displace Congress as the supreme legislative body.

193

It is not always easy to distinguish the ultimate consequences of the many proposals of reform that are offered. Each is usually examined as if its only meanings were on its face. Not long ago, Dr. George Galloway, a senior research officer of the Library of Congress and expert upon Congress, collected about 180 recommendations received during one month of hearings on the organization and operation of Congress. Classified according to the topics with which they treat, they are carried as an appendix to this book (pages 265-74). They display fully the universe of congressional reform proposals.

It develops that many of these recommendations for reform are innocuous with respect to the major thesis of this book. They have to do with minor modifications of pay, tenure, the number of committees, committee allowances, increased publicity about lobbies, expense money, and the like. Some are ambivalent: depending upon their specific provisions, they may be biased towards the Executive or the Republican Force. Of the remainder that have relevance to the struggle between the two forces, most would benefit the Republican Force, but in numerous cases, the beneficiary would be the executive branch of government. The great majority of proposals, especially those bolstering up republican principles, are low-powered. They would not have much impact on the great issues of republican government.

Another way of studying the scope of reform of the Congress is to see what congressmen view as the *problem areas* to be explored by proposed commissions on congressional reorganization. Perhaps these too will indicate the priorities of congressional reforms. Thus, Senator Clifford P. Case, in his bill for congressional reform (S177-1963) lists twelve specific problem areas. They are:

1) The scheduling of measures for consideration and action;

2) The structure, staffing, and operation of congressional committees;

3) The workload of the Congress and the committees thereof;

4) Congressional rules and floor procedures;

5) Conflicts of interest of Members of the Congress;

6) The term of office of Members of the House of Representatives;

7) Communications, travel, and other allowances of Members of the Congress.

8) The financing of congressional election campaigns;

9) The duties of Members of Congress incident to the appointment of postmasters and the making of appointments to military service academies and other government academies;

10) The legislative oversight of the administration of laws;

11) The strengthening of the congressional power of the purse; and

12) The operation and effectiveness of existing laws with respect to lobbying.

The list in itself reveals a preoccupation with areas of reform that are pitched towards the strengthening of executive forces. They are offered apparently in a neutral and objective spirit but this is all the more demonstrative of the way in which the reform of Congress has been embraced

by the ideology of the executive branch. Behind each "area
of proposed investigation" we may suspect that there is
standing prominently as candidate for favorable consideration some executive-biased scheme.

Behind (1) the scheduling of measures, stands the idea
of forcing Congress to act on the President's program.
Behind (2) and (3) stands the resolve to "streamline" Congress by taking away the independence and nuclear constituencies of its members. Behind (4), the interest in
rules, lies the hostility towards the congressional oligarchy.
Behind (5) lurks the desire to sever connections between
congressmen and the world they represent. In (6) is the
desire to tie a congressman's election to the President's.
In (7) is the possibility of diminishing a congressman's
means of operating freely. Behind (8) may be the restriction of independent campaign funds and a desire to unite
congressional and presidential fortunes. In (9) are implied
cuts in control and patronage of congressmen. In (10)
and (11) might be limitations on the right of Congress to
specific oversight over administration. And (12) suggests
that Congress is a victim of nefarious lobbies.

Perhaps these suspicions may still appear unwarranted
to some. They should no longer seem so, given the analysis
in earlier chapters of the ideology of the executive force.
Moreover, speaking in support of his bill, Senator Case reveals a view of the congressional process that is strongly
biased toward the executive branch of government. (See
pages 15-16.) He may not himself perceive the extent to
which several of his major wishes, if realized, would project
the nation toward centralization, although the Senator's
critics may be well persuaded that he must know so. Still,
there is no reason why the list of reform areas put forward
by him should constitute the basis of discussion here.

For present purposes, the great dividing line is apparent: *there are two major categories of proposals, those that tend to carry out the program of executive control, and those that tend toward republicanism.* In this chapter, executive control shall be the aim of a set of proposals for the reform of Congress. If these reforms, and it must be admitted that they are the most popular of those being proposed, are carried into effect, Congress would shortly lose its character as an independent and powerful legislature.

In the next chapter, different proposals for the reform of Congress are set forth; they consist of a set of ideas, which, if adopted, would establish Congress as the supreme governing force. Which of the two is to be preferred is a matter for individual choice. But friends of Congress are fools to let congressional government be destroyed on the pretext of making it efficient.

The set of reform proposals that would bring about the victory of the executive force may be grouped into several categories and discussed in that order. There are reforms of the constituency; there are reforms of the parties. There are reforms of the presidency, and reforms of the executive establishment. Finally, there is a group of reforms proposed for the Congress, which, like all of the others treated here together, would tend to change congressional government in the direction of presidential and executive control.

EXECUTIVE'S MODEL OF THE CONSTITUENCY AND PARTY

> *When a majority is included in a faction, the form of popular government . . . enables it to sacrifice to its ruling passion or interest both the public good and the rights of other citizens.*
>
> Madison, *The Federalist* (1787)

The ideal constituency of the executive force is one well-organized by the political party, led and instructed by the

President via the mass media, and directed at and responsive to national issues. Adherents to this conception of the
electorate look back upon the somewhat mythical Jack-
sonian and Rooseveltian constituencies as the model. Actually, in some critical cases such as going to war, and
curbing the legislative power of the Supreme Court, the
commitment of the constituency to the presidency was most
doubtful. The considerable evidence available about the
nature of constituencies and the active or even attentive
public would lead us to doubt that the majority here thought
to exist ever corresponds to a true majority in being. In
other words, involved is again a myth, the components of
which hold that government by majority is a possibility,
that the aim of government is egalitarianism, and the road
to this condition lies via the politically organized electorate
under the leadership of a national executive.

The greatest structural reforms of recent years contributing to this desired condition came with the decisions of
the Supreme Court in the cases of *Baker* vs. *Carr* (and its
successors, *Reynolds* vs. *Sims*, etc.) and *Wesberry* vs.
Sanders. The doctrines of these cases encourage a complete
reorganization of the apportionment systems of the state
governments to provide for equal-population districts in the
state senates and assemblies and equal-population districts
in the House of Representatives. Should an amendment to
the Constitution later permit a Senate shifted to a proportionate population basis, in weighting of the votes if not
in actual membership, so much the better for the Executive
Force.

Meanwhile it may be expected that the reapportionment
of the state legislatures will increase the power of party-
organized constituencies, since many new seats are going
to urban areas of strong party affiliation. Since these in

turn are correlated with party-controlled congressional constituencies, and since they both in turn are correlated with
the more highly presidential and nation-directed constituents, then the whole effect will tend to tie the state governments more closely into the national parties and the national
parties on the state level with the presidential parties. This
effect will be bolstered by changes occurring at the same
time in the House, whereby congressional districts will become more equal in population, and urban areas in some
states, suburban in most—both of them presidentially and
executive-minded—will be given as many as fifty seats, tip-
ping the balance on many issues to the Executive Force.
The Executive Force should pursue these developments
enthusiastically.

The suffrage is still in process of enlarging in the United
States. The most important and largest new element
consists of Negro voters, hitherto denied the right un-
constitutionally or kept from it by social, economic and
psychological causes. That this electorate, prevented from
self-realization by a system of local autonomy and battered
economically by a "free" system mirroring faithfully social
prejudices, will be pro-centralization and pro-presidential is
fairly plain.

The new electorate generally, whether it is of youth or
women, or the economically depressed or Negroes, tends
to be very largely pro-executive. Elimination of the poll tax
payment, as a prerequisite to voting, and diminishing the
length of residence required for voting have similar effects.
Completing the task of universalizing the vote can help the
Executive Force, and, should the Republican Force be
goaded into resisting these changes, so much the worse for
its reactionary image.

It is also proposed from time to time that Congress be reformed by the removal from its competence of the government of the District of Columbia, a proposal often sincerely meant to relieve Congress of the burden of governing a single city as if it were a city council. Of course, Washington is no ordinary city, as those who planned its birth knew beforehand. The government of the District of Columbia presents opportunities to control the total government that cannot be overlooked in the long stretches of history to be written.

That Washington is worse governed than other cities would be difficult to prove, although it is often asserted; that it is not self-governed is somewhat easier to prove, beginning with the fact that its residents do not cast ballots that control its government. An extension of self-government to the city, which would remain still under congressional rule, would appear possible, and would encourage the development of those local qualities of initiative and self-government that republicans should espouse. At the same time, the voters of the district would be largely pro-executive by profession and attitude. That has to be granted.

But the executive should never have in its hands the power to turn a local or national police force against a legislature. For this last reason, any reform of the District that would remove completely its government from congressional hands may be considered anti-republican, and most reforms towards self-government short of that would probably be considered pro-republican.

The proposal to organize constituents more tightly along party lines by requiring payment of membership dues and issuing membership cards pledging certain attitudes and activities on behalf of the party would also promote executive centralism; part of the constituencies would be mobilized, and this always helps mobilize the rest, because they are deprived of choice and influence. The parties should seek financing, too, on a mass basis; small contributions from a multitude mean that the party leaders will be accountable to no "wicked special interests." They will in fact be accountable to no one and in a happy condition of fiscal solvency.

Appeals for centralized and integrated parties should be widely disseminated by advocates of the Executive Force. Professor Burns's proposal that the presidential and congressional factions of each party in Congress should be merged is characteristic of the reforms needed. His plea for cooperation meanwhile between the presidentially favorable branches of both parties in Congress is significant and understandable too. Actually, what appears to be a contradictory demand on the one hand for the merger of the two parties in support of the presidency, and on the other for greater party responsibility is resolved when it is realized that the ultimate goal is rational one-party, one-force government, the efficient, effective, responsible executive leading the whole country.

One of the weakest points in the establishment of executive dominance has been the collapse of the presidential leadership of the party once the party does not hold the presidency. Thus all the strength, integration, issues, and organization built up in the halcyon days of office are washed away in the defeat. The obvious solution would be modes of creating a strong party directorate carrying on as if nothing much had happened. To this end, Professor Burns, for example, calls for a permanent national conference of the opposition party. Something like this occurs now; the defeated are forever organizing groups, conferences, assemblies to perpetuate their memory, hold onto internal party power, and plot for the day of return. But the ultimate aim of a true executive system would be permanent, unified, disciplined party leadership, in office and out.

Within Congress itself, the path to executive dominance is clear. Professor Daniel Berman ends a recent textbook typically with the word that congressional "localism and party irresponsibility fairly cry out for solution." There is fairly general agreement among the Executive Force on the solution. The minorities within a party should not be permitted to join the opposition party, organize themselves, hold any of the several dozen posts of leadership in Congress whether in opposition or in office. They should be confined to necessarily curtailed rights of debate, and their opposition to party positions should be reserved for caucuses. The majority of each party will be thoroughly coordinated with its national leadership. Several devices will promote this condition. Compulsory party councils under presidential chairmanship, extension of presidential patronage, control of party funds by the President, amalgamation of presidential and congressional campaigns, extension of party organization into the areas where maverick party candidates reside—all of these and more will help to strengthen the presidential party in Congress and to tie it into the presidency and executive branch of government. As Robert Bendiner, who wrote of the difficulties of federal aid to education legislation, sighed and said, "In our dream arrangement the President's party naturally is in control of Congress."

The presidency itself requires some considerable reforms if it is to lead Congress. The State of the Nation address has become an excursion into dreamland; it contains all the wishes that the President may have or indulge his followers and would-be supporters with. It has nevertheless tended to increase presidential prestige; it has meant to millions that the President can be counted upon to be active and constructive. However, he should also have more exclusive rights to initiate legislative proposals. In recent years it has come about that legislative proposals, even those generated in Congress, have been forwarded as a matter of course to the Bureau of the Budget in the Executive Office of the President. This practice, originating out of a desire to inform and coordinate, has gradually assumed an influential role in eliminating bills unsatisfactory to the executive branch. Formal adoption of this procedure would further strengthen its role.

The right to veto individual items in appropriation bills passed by Congress would facilitate executive control over the finances of the government. Not only could policies be selectively promoted and enforced, but friends could be helped and enemies punished. What the bill of attainder could be for Congress, the item veto could be for the President.

Moreover, tendencies to vote money to agencies for periods in excess of one year, or at least to authorize programs that must then be funded, aids the executive. Some three-quarters of civilian programs and a third of the defense programs are already of this kind. If to this practice could be added the procedure whereby funds are generally voted for a long period, with liberal powers to the President and agency officials to rule on the manner and amount of their expenditure, then would the scope of executive power broaden indeed. It was probably owing to such a power as this that Governor Talmadge and his successors could erect a kind of dictatorship in Georgia between 1932 and 1961; the Governor controlled the second year of appropriations voted for a two-year period of time.

The Twenty-second Amendment to the Constitution should be repealed, if the position of the executive branch is to be enhanced. Limiting the terms of the President to two may preclude a popular dynamic figure from retaining office. Professor Burns, who is the most consistent reformer among the executive force, urges this action. Similarly the Electoral College is to be made "more responsible to the people." Several devices can be employed for this purpose. The ideal would be to abolish the college entirely in favor of a single national majority vote. Another method would keep the College, but split each state's vote among the candidates in proportion to the votes they win. Either way would allow the presidential candidates to drive at a central majority in the American electorate, and to exploit the mass media to the fullest extent.

THE PRESIDENT'S IDEAL ADMINISTRATION

Several reforms within the executive establishment would strengthen its position. The affirmation and continuation of the absolute power to determine that certain secrets and documents belong to the executive branch and are not to be released to Congress is a logical step. Extension of the single civil service merit system to the furthest reaches of government employment is also desirable. The President may be assumed to use his patronage to affirm his position as head of the executive and political branches of government, but actually, so long as the political system is decentralized, and attention has to be paid to local autonomous groups in making appointments, the President is better off without the appointive power. He can get stricter obedience and readier response from a civil servant than from one of his own appointees, on the average, under a decentralized party system.

Furthermore, though it may be difficult for people to imagine how it works, the administrative service is the savings bank of presidential power. What he earns, it keeps. Even more, it acts as trustee. His successors cannot spend this capital. And therefore it accumulates more and more.

The unfettered power to reorganize agencies of government has long been the aim of administrative reformers such as the Brownlow Committee and the Hoover Commission. They appreciate that with a wholesale delegation of power to create, change, and abolish agencies of government less than giant size, the presidency can effectively uproot the sources of congressional power in the agencies.

A companion reform, as urged by Louis Brownlow, among many others, would prevent congressional interference in the "details" of administrative management. Though difficult to carry into effect by formal enactment, this reform, formal or informal, would also cut out the numerous relations between congressmen and officials that presently lend a special character to American federal government.

The fiscal accounting system is also unsatisfactory at present from the standpoint of the executive force. The General Accounting Office is concerned with the auditing of expenditures to the point where often administrators are intimidated in making them. Louis Brownlow and others would have a strict accountability assured through the executive branch with selective post-auditing. Thus the departments and agencies would be able to manage all except post-auditing without concern for how a congressionally-minded official might interpret congressional policy, and in the final analysis some would have even post-auditing done by a top executive agency, as occurs in Britain. This is said to provide perfect honesty and efficiency—two terms however that do not include the appropriate representation of the appropriate policy-making groups and therefore are incomplete with reference to the total range of functions within the scope of auditing and financial accounting.

Generally speaking, the aim of Executive Force reform is to elevate the bureaucracy fully to legislative status. There is no structural reason why the administrative branch of government cannot operate as a congress of the United States. It can employ the full collection of devices of representative government. It can take public opinion polls, set up representative councils of industry, commerce, agriculture, the arts, and foreign affairs. It can create dozens of representative bodies and employ thousand of consultants and service agencies to keep close watch on whatever may be the aspirations and wants of the American people. Its rules and regulations already have a scope, domain, and intensity that would make the average pronouncement appear to the casual eye to be more important than the average enactment of Congress. Most citizens and businessmen, when told something "is the law" already obey without knowing that most of the time it is an administrator's rule that they obey, not a law of Congress. The bureaucracy-as-Congress is well over half-way established, more by the method of the *tour de force* than by taking from Congress any powers.

The enactment of more programs and engagement in more activities will of course increase the trend; the intent may not be present but the effect will be there, for it is impossible to add to the functions of government without diminishing the possibilities for organizing enclaves of libertarian and voluntary action in the population at large. In the process of executive reformation of American government, therefore, the venturing upon new forms of regulation and government enterprise is the massive core.

EXECUTIVE'S MODEL OF CONGRESS

> . . . *He begins an oration with so quick and loud a voice, that, at a distance, it might be imagined they are all making a noise together. During the whole discourse the rest keep a profound silence, and when it is ended, he makes signal to the rest to answer him, and immediately they all set up a cry together, till such time as by another sign with his hand, he orders them to be silent: when they are immediately obedient and quiet. Then the first renews his discourse, or his song, which, when finished, and the others have paid the utmost attention to, the whole assembly breaks up and separates.*

> Buffon, on the Howler Monkeys

The reforms of Congress itself are less important to the success of the executive force than the development of a large administrative establishment. No matter how keenly adjusted a mechanism to the tasks desired of it, it will not have an effect on a larger setting in which its tasks are limited. Still consideration of reforms of Congress is of large interest to this study.

A favorite reform among executive advocates is the four-year synchronized term for congressmen and President, preferably with a four-year Senate as well. Then the whole political machine will turn over at the same time; all will depend upon coordinated integrated campaigning behind the banner of the presidential candidate. (Is it too much to hope that the Supreme Court or a constitutional amendment will reapportion the Senate by equal-population districts?)

Restricting freedom of debate is also recommended, from the executive's standpoint. Since the House has already rather severe restrictions upon debate, save in respect to the final decisive element of placing a partisan presidential limit on who may speak, the proposed reform concerns only the Senate. There the notorious filibuster stands as an insufferable bar to presidential ambitions.

The filibuster, it perhaps needs asserting, is not absolute. Two-thirds of the total membership of the Senate, after a short delay, can impose closure upon debate. Closure was imposed during the debate of the civil rights bill of 1964. Obviously the Senators, who are 100 well-educated, well-informed, and rather "liberal" men prone to spend money more freely than the House and support the President on welfare legislation more than the House, see something exceedingly valuable to their corporate and individual status in the privilege of unrestrained debate. That value is the right to resist in a most public manner policies that a President desires. Considering the losses of policies and time occasioned by filibustering and the fact that the target is almost invariably the executive, it would appear necessary, to those who feel that the executive in America has little enough power to consummate its will, to limit further the personal liberty of Senators in this regard. Making closure of debate easier, by a majority of the membership, say, would be the solution.

Next in importance to abolishing the filibuster would be circumventing the powers of committees to bottle up legislation. As Senator Case put it in one place: "A President who has been elected by the people of the United States and who has a majority in both houses has a right to believe that his major legislative proposals will be brought to a vote." And elsewhere he says, "This is the forthright way to deal with legislation and is highly preferable to a procedure under which bills are buried without a hearing, without a vote, often by the action of one man, a committee or subcommittee chairman." Though not accurate as fact, the statements have a logic that is admissible: the Rules Committee, the leadership, the committee system, whatever may be the dilatory element in the legislative process must be forced to stand aside and permit a vote on a proposal of the President, substantially in the form in which he requests it and with only so much legislative consideration of it as he feels necessary under the circumstance.

It would be better in fact, by this view, to reorganize the method of selecting committee chairmen and appointing members to committees. One of the primary sources of trouble is the modified seniority system that prevails. This should be replaced by a partisan system, which would essentially place power in the hands of the party leaders, acting under the national authority of their party, to designate their committee chairmen and members. A change in the rules of the House and Senate would be adequate for these purposes and would require "only" a majority vote in each case.

That this is not done forthwith or even seriously considered must come as another of those surprises that baffle the superficial observer of the American political scene. Without discussing it further, it must be stated flatly that a simple resolution by each House to the effect that the President or the national party leadership will designate representatives in each House who will in turn organize the appointments to committee is inconceivable.

That such a popular idea could be carried out by such a simple mechanism, and yet is not, should be a flashing signal to everyone that something more than a love of old men is involved. Therefore, to reform Congress in accord with the desire to make it more responsive to the presidency requires more devious and half-way measures. Such would be the organization of policy committees in each chamber that would voluntarily settle upon modes of cooperating within their parties and with the national party leadership.

The same might be said for the proposal of joint policy committees of congressmen and the President, whereby the leadership of each party could meet in both its executive and congressional manifestations, for the purpose of determining a united course of action. Many proposals that would fall into this category could be specified.

In fact, each President is entitled, if he pleases, to call upon congressional leaders of his own party, or of both parties, and may together with them plan a strategy about one or more problems before the nation. Congressional leaders might also request such encounters.

Since meetings conducted in an atmosphere of hostility or reluctance would not at all be conducive to the settlement of any issue before them, it would appear that legislation in this area would avail the Executive Force little. A forced meeting might be the occasion for an unconstitutional showdown. In sum, peaceful and voluntary meetings, and policy committees can be set up whenever they may be desired. Where they are not desired, the power to compel them would only goad the White House group into extreme measures to obtain consensus from them.

As the number of presidential faction adherents grows in the next few years owing to changes in apportionment and other factors, it may also be possible to guarantee a Speaker who will be favorable to the President or to the presidential candidate's ideas. In that case, the cry that the House is oligarchically run will have to give way to the "need" to give the Speaker more power so that he can appoint more committee heads and members favorably disposed to the presidential party. If the Speaker does what the President tells him to, he is no longer, miraculously, a boss.

The reduction of the number of committees is often recommended as a means of obtaining stern public scrutiny and improving the "efficiency" of Congress. This does not usually work, because it is accompanied by an increase in the number of subcommittees, who have almost as much authority as the original committee would have had. Furthermore, the persons whose ambitions are most likely to be suppressed by the reform would be presidential adherents. And the public cannot visibly impress itself upon fifteen committees any more than on thirty.

It would be better to force matters out of the committees earlier, if only the floors could be cleared for them. But the floors are always crowded or somehow unavailable. Whence the correct tactic is to reduce the ability of a member to command the consideration of his fellow members for private bills. Further to save time by electric voting. Further to insist upon bills of a more general rather than specific nature, to "get Congress out of the business of administrative management."

There is a great deal of circumlocution in all of these proposals. Proposals to clear the floor as a means of making Congress effective are countered by proposals to bring new matters upon the floor; take away merely personal legislation but bring in a question period. Let matters be decided on the floor; but keep raw material off the floor. All of which inclines one to believe that on some matters there is either no important reform to be desired from the standpoint of the executive branch or that the simple reforms, the direct ones, that place congressional officers at the command of the presidential ones, are ultimately the ones to concentrate upon.

Other reforms come to mind. It is a pretty thought to permit former presidents to address Congress and take the floor; and it has recently been effected. It enhances the dignity of the office of President and queues them up ahead of hundreds of equally good orators. But it will not advance the cause of executive government by more than that.

A more promising avenue of executive leadership is by way of reforming the ethics of Congress. For instance, the public and the bureaucracy can be easily aroused to moral indignation by accounts of congressional travel abroad and within the country. Congressional "interference" with the administration can be curtailed if congressmen spend less on travel. It will be also clear that they will be less prone to travel needlessly. Hence a stingy attitude toward congressional movements and travel expenditures is desirable from a strictly executive point of view.

On a broader scale but resting upon the same principle is the question of congressional conflict of interests. If congressmen are restrained by ever tighter definitions of conflicts of interests, two results will occur. Fewer candidates will offer themselves from among elements in the population who have free-wheeling, libertarian, independent professional backgrounds and humble origins. The reputation of Congress will decline as impossible standards of conduct are imposed. Meanwhile, the moral stature of the civil servant and presidency will be in the ascendant.

In addition, if conflict of interests statutes can be tightened up throughout the government, fewer elements of a republican nature will be invited into the government; their quality will go down, and therefore, their reason for being invited in the first place will no longer exist; and thus those who know about government are least likely to have a hand in determining the course of government, unless they join the civil service—the professional soldiery of government— and thus disown their membership in the general public.

For these several reasons, campaigns aimed at tightening rules against situations where conflicts of interests might exist are of benefit in establishing the greater neutrality, objectivity, and publc interest of the executive establishment and the presidency.

If all or most of the proposals recited above are carried into being, whether by law or by informal practice, the chances for the early success of the executive force in government will be measurably increased. Taken together they add up to the accepted definition of "effective, modern government." They are "constructive, moral" reforms. They will give a "badly needed integration and coordination to national government in America." They will "promote a stronger, more favorable image of America abroad." Congress will be adequate—adequate, that is, to the role provided for it in the executive government of the future.

Chapter Nine

A CONGRESS OF REPUBLICAN PRINCIPLES

Concilium totam civitatem repraesentat. *

Bartolus de Saxoferrato (1314-1357)

To THE ADVOCATE of republican government, with its principle of congressional supremacy, reforms of the system come less easily to mind than they do to the executive reformer. The typical congressional leader still believes, though anxiously, that the Constitution carries Congress at anchorage. But the Constitution has lost its moorings in the Courts, and the institutions of government are now determined largely by reason and power. Professor Aikin states the situation thus: "The modern basis of a genuine separation lies in political facts, not in juristic theory." **

Political scientists have also been less commonly at work upon pro-congressional reforms. The morale of the republicans is weaker. More has to be invented. The force of the century has been moving in the opposite direction;

---

* (The Council represents the Whole Civic Body).

** Charles Aikin, "The Regime of Assembly and Responsible Government" (Berkeley, Calif.: Dept. of Political Science, U. of California), p. 358.

therefore the congressional force, far from being conservative, must be more disposed to change than the Executive
Force.

Again, however, the reforms fall into natural categories
insofar as they concern first the constituency and party, then
the presidency, then Congress itself, and finally the executive establishment. It should be remembered too that some
reforms have an ambiguous effect. For example, electronic
roll-call voting and the question period, by slight twists of
detail, can be converted from pro-Congress to pro-executive.
Also, the tying of congressional elections to presidential ones
will favor the strong executive, whereas varying the time-
table so that the two do not coincide will favor the independent Congress. Finally certain recommendations presented as reforms for the executive can be reversed and
become advantageous to Congress. An example would be
the opening up of *greater*, not lesser, travel privileges for
congressmen.

REFORMS OF THE CONSTITUENCY

> *The Venetian Senate is so courteous in modern times that in the dis-
> tribution of offices, when there is one who asks for an office and many
> who refuse it, it finds it easier to satisfy both the former and the
> latter, without considering whether it might be better to send the man
> who refuses and hold back the one who requests it, so that the former
> may use the ability he has acquired and the other, who does not have
> it, may acquire it.*
>
> *Esame Istorico Politico*, Anon. Venetian, 1675

Congress lacks what is called these days a "good public
image." This is partly because the corporate workings of
Congress are unknown to persons even of educated status.
The content of the laws reaches lawyers in correct form;
it reaches the public through the press in a garbled form,
if at all. A reporting service that would translate legisla-

tion into language understood by the average educated person would clarify and support the functions of Congress.

One member of the House has declared: "The media today are so poor in reporting what is going on, that a Member has a double responsibility to report to his constituents about legislation." As a result, ninety per cent of the congressmen employ newsletters to their constituents. Newsletters usually play up the work of an individual congressman and they also support Congress as a whole. Not infrequently, however, a congressman will use his newsletter to denounce Congress and its procedures for opposing his good works. There is no continuous output of information in support of Congress.

It would be well, if possible, to establish Halls of Congress in a central city of each state, where a kind of dynamic museum of the history and present operations of Congress would enlighten the public. The same Halls would contain "exhibits" leading into the future, showing that Congress, while retaining its historic character, will be changing, like every other progressive institution. Certain kinds of projections can be made of congressional business; for example, it can be graphically displayed as it may be experienced ten years, a generation, or a century from now.

Broadcasting and telecasting of Congress have also been suggested. This proposal seems on the surface to be pro-republican, but might have anti-congressional results unless the Congress invested much energy and time into the work happening on the floor. Actually, unless some exceedingly clever means were devised for conducting work while under the eyes of the television cameras, the telecasting would prove to be a great waster of congressional time. Congressmen would come on the floor solely to be "mugged" by the cameras, when they would have more serious work to do elsewhere.

Certainly, however, more frequent expositions of congressional work via the mass media would be valuable. It can be said that at any given time, there will be something important occurring. If it is not on the floor, it may be in a committee meeting, a congressional caucus, or in some encounter of Congress and the outside world of the executive branch or the public. The proper use of television or related media could bring about a deeper public appreciation of the intricacies of the congressional processes.

A National Civic Service should benefit directly and indirectly the congressional system. By a National Civic Service is meant the requirement that all persons of a certain degree of education in America devote some part of their time to meritorious associational activity or political activity. This project would only extend the precedents and experiences incorporated in military service, Red Cross service, jury duty, charitable activity, educational work, and other manifestations of civic energy.

The present active constituency of Congress is too small and there is a danger that Congress may be fatally weakened by lack of support from the grass roots. Encouraging much variety in types of civic service would eliminate the danger of a single group monopolizing civic skills. Any kind of legitimate service would become an acceptable fulfillment of the duty. Setting a limit on who is compelled to enter the service by setting a minimum level of education or a test of achievement would assure that an increasing proportion of relatively well-informed and interested persons would be found in the active constituencies. In effect, the National Civic Service could provide Congress with a more broadly-

based and a more competent public than presently engages it.

Congress needs more help. This point is clear in several regards and will be mentioned again. But here the
emphasis is upon providing congressmen with *personal* followers. A larger nuclear constituency is needed. It is most
unreasonable and anti-congressional to strip the support of
congressmen away, leaving them to perform heavy tasks
with help that is numerically and quantitatively inferior to
that provided for a middle-level bureaucrat. The Congressional Internship program of the American Political Science
Association, supported by foundation funds and providing
young professional assistants, has in recent years been a
boon to many congressmen. The auxiliary services provided
congressmen could be improved too. Within limits, whatever adds to the personal efficiency and comfort of the congressman will aid republican government.

The power of Congress to control the apportionment of
its seats within the states may have slipped out of its hands.
The Courts have usurped it. Constitutional amendments
may possibly reestablish congressional control. Actually
such congressional control has meant in the past largely an
abstinence from exercise of control. If Congress, following
the Courts, determines that all districts must be so far as
possible of equal population, contiguous, and compact, then
little variety may be expected in future apportionment systems. Otherwise, it is conceivable that some states would
experiment with modes of apportionment more in accord
with future stages of society.

Particularly important in this regard would be some
means of conceding to major interests in a state recognition
that congressional districts may be based only partly upon
population, and otherwise upon vocational or ideal concerns.

At present this would be discouraged by the Courts. Furthermore, the court rulings would appear to prevent experiment with systems of proportional representation, community representation, representation that follows socio-economic and geographic boundaries in the state, and other types of groupings, besides those based strictly upon equal-population districts.

A republican position would call for strong opposition to the Courts or executive branch taking over any part of the legislative function, including apportionment. It would entail apportionment wherever possible according to rules that would favor strong local and state bases for the support of individual congressmen, and a moderate weighting of electoral systems in favor of republican ideological and social groupings of the population. In the metropolitan regions of the country, a plan that would typically elect about half of each metropolitan congressional delegation at-large would speed up the self-government of the region.

Many government agencies use non-governmental personnel in a representative capacity. There are probably hundreds of instances of private persons participating in governmental decisions in an official capacity, alongside or within agencies of the government. This is as true of the Department of Defense as it is of the Department of Labor. Since the effect of these panels that give functional representation is to incorporate into government policies the ideas of groups affected by the policies, the selection of such persons should not be left entirely to officials of the permanent services. They should satisfy a formal, cultural test, laid down by the Congress. It would require an understanding of the nature of federal government, of the doctrines of congressional control over administration, and of other principles so often overlooked in day-to-day activity.

The roster of the qualified could be drawn upon in filling hundreds of positions in a way that would be conducive to republican government.

REFORMS OF THE PARTY

> *Democratic Government is sure to degenerate if we drift into a position in which the only, or the most effective means by which the servants of the State can get their special ideas, or their special prospects, attended to is by canvassing indifferent electors; or if the privileges of large property-organisations are permitted to exist, but are exposed in every session of the legislature to ignorant or interested attacks, and are allowed to defend themselves by huge subscriptions to party funds.*
>
> Graham Wallas, *The Great Society* (1914)

The political party system, except as it responds to the mass media and is taken over from time to time by gusts of popular emotion, has been tamed over the years. When it first appeared, party was the chief instrument for the democratization of the federal government. Fortunately at the same time, it reflected a sentiment against the federal government and therefore could not achieve its ultimate natural target, that of raising up the President to great heights of power and influence. The present party is weaker than its ancestor but the opportunities afforded it, if ever it were to control the government, are much greater than they originally were. Hence the true republican seeks no increase in the centralization or integration of the party.

For the Republican Force, the party appears to have two functions: they are highly important functions, even indispensable. They are not of the type that rationalists or party reformists would regard as advantageous. The history of political parties largely ignores them. They are not even admissible in polite political discourse. Still, through them the party operates from beginning to end, and in the Congress especially, usefully to organize non-justifiable, non-rationalized behavior.

The party does so by organizing frequently occurring situations, where which way one should go as a member of the House or Senate is a "toss up," that is, where two sides are needed and there is no other way of organizing the sides that is as easy and seemingly rational to do as by party. Thus, the party forms committees for the House and Senate; it sets up the choice of leadership; it organizes necessary propaganda; it urges and opposes, often taking both sides of an issue within a relatively short time.

In addition, the party rationalizes ignorant behavior. This occurs all the way from the constituent to the President and the leadership of Congress. The people are diverted by the party into accepting the disappearance of direct democracy, with its attractive but impossible promises, while keeping the myth. In place of wholesale ignorance, which would damage the myth of popular omniscience, the party label can be pleaded.

When there is a doubt as to what to do, a representative can cast a blind vote or a recommended vote and say that it was a party vote, justifying his action as being that of a loyal party supporter, a vote of principle against local, personal, national, or international interests of all kinds. This happens "frequently," regularly, reports Charles Clapp on the basis of prolonged discussions among congressmen. When the representative does not know what an issue is about, his party vote becomes a safe vote. It requires little defense other than that afforded by party label.

It is amusing that so much intellectual effort has gone into discovering the rational meaning of party voting or lack of party voting in the Senate and House of Representatives, when what would apparently be required to solve the problem would be an ability to face the somewhat outrageous non-rationality of the political system. The political party incorporates ignorance into the government as a working force. The political party in the United States is a catch-all, a carry-all, and a cover-all. This situation, to a republican, is good.

REFORMS OF THE PRESIDENCY

It will be . . . far more congenial with the feelings that actuate me, to substitute, in place of a recommendation of particular measures, the tribute that is due to the talents, the rectitude, and the patriotism which adorn the characters selected to devise and adopt them.

Washington, "First Inaugural Address to the Congress" (1789)

Precise reforms of the presidency are more desirable from a republican point of view. Probably the most important of all is to reduce the terms permitted to any single man as President from two to one, and to lengthen his single term to that of a United States Senator, namely six years. Four years is insufficient to permit the President to develop a program and make lasting contributions to the reform of the civil service. The four-year term is short enough to entice opponents of the President to delay his every wish and to tie up government while waiting for a change of office. Six years (five is not impossible) is adequate for these tasks of the President and would let him develop a wealth of experience.

At the same time he would stop running for re-election. Presently much of the first term of the President is devoted to assuring re-election. Only rarely does the President during the first term of office stand for principles that can be construed as hurting his chances of re-election. There has been no systematic study of the first term-second term difference, but it is widely believed to exist by friends as well as foes of the presidency. It may therefore be given some credence.

The advantage of the incumbent President in seeking re-election is formidable. The late Professor V. O. Key and many another political scientist have said upon occasion, though rarely do they put words into print, that the incumbent is as good as re-elected, barring some extreme personal or national ignominy. Estimates of his electoral advantage in pecuniary terms can reasonably reach the sum of $60,000,000. quite outside of the sums expended *officially* for the incumbent's re-election. Included in such an estimate would be the political services of government officials, the news media coverage of the incumbent, the patronage that can be tied to work and contributions in the election campaign, planes, ships, cars, staff services, and numerous other perquisites directly promoting re-election.

This advantage refutes the defenders of two and more terms who assert that the President behaves better in his first term if he knows he can win another. It also suggests that another reform may be in order. In a welfare state, the months before election can be used to release a number of benefits to the population. Increases in pensions, tax rebates, concessions, relaxation of administrative rules and other actions, shrewdly timed, may influence large numbers of voters. Admittedly, the wheels of government cannot be braked before every election; still, in the interest of fair and equal elections, a law halting the conveyance of direct material benefits to any group of the population by presidential or executive agency order in the six months prior to a presidential election may deserve consideration.

The presidency holds a number of powers granted it in emergencies of the past. These powers can be recuperated through an omnibus bill for the restoration of normalcy.

The President's State of the Union message and other special messages have come to be regarded as official and authoritative statements of the policy of the United States. This is wholly erroneous. It is constitutionally a report that could presumably be given over to past affairs. But as the ambitions of the President have expanded, so have the contents and scope of the presidential messages.

Inasmuch as there is little likelihood that the President will become more modest in his messages, Congress may wish to develop a collegiate response. Whenever the President delivers a message to Congress, the Congress would be entitled to deliver a message to the President. Something like this practice was initiated by the very first Congress. This need not be a perfect representation of consensus in Congress, but for that matter, the President's State of the Union and other messages do not represent unanimity in the executive branch. The public might compare each set of messages and decide which had a more attractive sound.

The ideal President, in the eyes of the Republican Force, would not at all be a weak-minded person, or merely a figurehead, nor a person at the beck and call of Congress. What would be essential in his character and office, and it must be said that American Presidents on the whole have had generous doses of such qualities, would be a serious understanding of the congressional system, a free and undogmatic approach to problems of administrative management, and a patient willingness to carry on an endless discourse with Congress, while maintaining an appropriate social and political distance. He must be a pluralist at heart and in mind.

REFORM OF THE COURTS

> *Shout it! Shout it! Cry out!*
> *Run and cry! ... Only—it*
> *Won't do any good—now.*

Maxwell Anderson
Gods of the Lightning (1928)

It is tempting to offer a set of reforms of the Courts on the ground that all of the work of the Courts is pertinent to the position of Congress. But the same could be said of the whole of American society. It is particularly important to raise up as possible reforms, according to the republican viewpoint, first, some kind of legislative approval to decisions of the Supreme Court when the Court has apparently damaged the position of Congress in the governmental and social structure.

A Constitutional Amendment has been introduced in the state legislatures providing that in matters affecting the federal union a Supreme Court of the Union be specially constituted to include elements from all the state courts, as well as from the Supreme Court. There is no question that such a proposal would result in the strengthening of the republican element in American society and government, without damaging the essential position of the Supreme Court in all other matters. This would be preferable to attempting to give Congress that power of declaring the meaning of the Constitution which has, in the course of history, been assumed by the Courts. It would be less dangerous to political stability and private rights than the latter power and it would not interfere in those areas of traditional review where the Supreme Court has admittedly done well.

Secondly, the size of the Supreme Court might well be increased to permit its dealing with cases in panel form, to speed up the dreadfully slow wheels of justice in America, without loss of careful consideration of the merits of cases. The same reform would, by promoting an internal division of labor, diminish the unprofessional and political character of judicial behavior. More and more, Supreme Court justices appear to be chasing after exotic cases, letting the essential body of judicial work be handled by lower courts and law clerks.

Moreover, it would seem advisable to provide the Court, and indeed all federal courts, with better research facilities on social affairs. Insofar as there must be ascertainment of sociological and economic fact, going in many instances beyond the ability of law clerks and opposing attorneys to provide, the courts should have personnel, funds, and techniques—perhaps research institutes—to make such studies. As Professor John Roche and the late Professor Edmond Cahn showed, the touted assertion that the Supreme Court has come around to being sociological and psychological is not only not true—for it has always been so—but it has not shown any signs of doing a better job of social science than it did in the past. It is at least possible that the Supreme Court, properly equipped to get scientific assessments (including appraisals of what science cannot say) on matters of fact, will regain some measure of judicial objectivity. This in turn would enhance the great ideal of *objectivity of the law* which is that idealized conditions when all informed and reasonable persons agree that the application of a law to a case does not deviate from previous applications to similar cases except by the rules of empirical and deductive logic. There exists a continuous abuse of republican government in America so long as the Supreme Court engages unrestrainedly in legislation. The careful plans of a generation of statesmen, backed by substantial and leading segments of the public, can be destroyed after a single day of argument by a one-man majority of the Court.

REFORMS INSIDE CONGRESS

> *At first it was, 'Your humble poor Commons beg and pray, for God's sake, as an act of charity.' By the time of Richard II, the 'humbles pauvres communes' had become, in the royal eyes, 'the right wise, right honourable, worthy and discreet Commons.'*
>
> R. Luce, *Legislative Principles*

The reform of Congress can be divided into changes intended to bolster its authority and morale, changes meant to increase its efficient intelligence, changes of its ways of making decisions, and changes in its powers.

The authority and morale of Congress have suffered losses in recent years. This has been elaborately demonstrated in these pages and elsewhere. The remedies are several. Congress should prepare a Charter of Legislative Authority. In this charter, it would declare the principle of legislative supremacy of the Congress, the position of the Congress with relation to the executive branch, the aims of congressional legislation, and the farther limits of congressional authority, which are less and less known to officials and public. It should, as mentioned, produce more collective messages, resolutions declaring the congressional view of life, so to speak.

An omnibus bill repealing all emergency laws, already mentioned in its precise reference to reducing presidential powers, is needed. Emergency laws have tended to become permanent. Their repeal would enhance the prestige and reestablish the authority of Congress in areas presently lost to it.

Congressional academies might be formed in a number of states or groups of states and attached to universities.

These academies, which might serve the state legislatures as well, would prepare students for the legislative way of life. They would not teach executive management of the conventional type, which stresses one man's power and capacity to discipline others. They would emphasize the skills of understanding people and bringing them together. It would even be desirable to give such academies the right to assemble courses of study and do research in conciliar bodies of all types—in business, in voluntary associations, in churches and in historical and primitive societies.

There clearly emerges from various studies of congressional operations a picture of low morale among freshmen and even second-term congressmen. The lot of the freshman congressman who takes his work seriously can be sad. There is always a pathos to the freshman, but the lot of the congressional freshman is excessively hard. He is given very little influence, he has little explained to him, he is an outside individual groping for ways of entering a mysterious, over-occupied, rather indifferent collectivity.

To increase the efficiency of Congress for republican work and to slow down rebellious movements among freshmen leading to presidential supremacy, the congressional leadership could well take a greater hand in orienting, organizing, and apprenticing newcomers. The leadership should seek to employ the talents of every freshman as an individual in the admittedly overwhelming mass of work devolving upon Congress as a whole. The Halls of Congress (see above, page 217) could be directed by first-term Representatives and Senators.

In the sphere of intelligence operations, much reform is needed. Committee staffs of Congress, though they are the peak intelligence center of the legislature, are already far behind times. Several changes are necessary. We have already referred to the need of increased personal staffs for congressmen. These would be separated from committee staffs, which should be increased moderately all along the line.

The committee or subcommittee, acting in its corporate capacity, should plan the work of the staff. At the beginning of each session and at intervals thereafter, the chairman, ranking minority member, and any or all other members of the committee should submit for discussion proposals for study and work, accompanied by a work budget and a research budget, both of which should be adopted or rejected by the committee.

A battery of qualifying tests should be imposed upon congressional staff members, but it is important that the congressional staff members remain responsible personally and loyal to their appointing committee and/or committee chairman. There seems to be little to be done and less reason to be doing it, in respect to the controversy as to whether chairmen or the whole committee should choose staff members. The provision for a kind of "bar examination" for congressional staff members is intended solely to require a basic level of high performance and philosophic principle in the office of Congress.

The committee should be able to call upon the Legislative Reference Service for the assignment of experts from various fields to the work of the committee. The experts should come from a roster composed of members of the LRS staff, persons outside of the federal government, and federal experts.

Factual inquiries and "crash" reports should be referred to the Legislative Reference Service. These are conventional on the whole and lend themselves to the broader capabilities of the Legislative Reference Service—at least as the LRS should be organized.

A Social and Behavioral Science Institute should be founded in the Library of Congress. Studies of controversial problems are denied support at present by the National Science Foundation. That is as it should be. The agencies undertake controversial research in abundance, but usually, if there is a presidential policy on the matter, the results are a foregone conclusion. Congress is naturally suspicious of work conducted in the executive or in the National Science Foundation, even though the work is allegedly "non-political."

Actually Congress would probably be more lenient and liberal in its aid to the development of the social sciences if those fields, in their controversial aspects, were supported by research even in part controlled directly under Congress. The place for this would seem to be naturally the Library of Congress, but the Institute would be separate from the Legislative Reference Service and would probably do most of its work by means of grants, where the research is of a basic and pure nature, unconnected with legislation, and by contract with outside agencies in the numerous instances where the job is being done in connection with impending or past legislation.

The central staff of Congress needs strengthening. An office for public relations has already been suggested. The congressmen themselves need information and popularization about what is going on in Congress. A daily, trustworthy popularization of the contents of pending laws and issues before the Congress would improve the intelligence of voting among the members. Professors Bailey and Samuels were among the first to make this suggestion.

An Inventory of Freedom and Restrictions should be built up and permanently maintained by congressional appropriation. The inventory should be in the hands of congressional officers and should keep a national set of accounts of the numbers of ways in which, as time goes on, the liberties of individual Americans are promoted or infringed upon by non-governmental and governmental agencies alike. The stated policy of Congress should be to increase over a period of time the liberal capacity of American society and to reduce the restrictive capacity of society.

Such a policy is just as much and indeed more needed than the vaunted goal of assuring that the Gross National Product maintains a respectable rate of increase. Socrates once scorned the Athenians, who applauded the aggrandizement of the state, saying "They do not see that this enlargement is nothing but a swelling, a tumor filled with corruption. This is all that has been achieved by these former politicians by filling the city with ports, arsenals, walls, tributes, and the like follies, and by not adding temperance and justice."

Indeed it would be best if Congress not only required the Inventory to be kept of the bureaucracy but kept a similar set of books on its own conduct, so that the inevitable measure of restraint entailed by every law would be balanced against the freedoms tendered by it. And all laws would finally be tallied together at the end of a year, a session, and a decade, telling the people the fatal news whether all that was done in their name gave them less or more of liberty. The same set of books would have facilitated, as a by-product, the appropriate compensation, wherever possible, of those who by the legislation were damaged, and, in the fine language of the Common Law, needed to be "made whole."

Attached to the Social and Behavioral Science Institute of the Library of Congress, and relevant also to the Inventory of Freedom and Restrictions, would be a Sanctions Institute. Its purpose would be to perform research and make recommendations to Congress concerning all the modes of social control that are used to implement congressional policy. The techniques of obtaining conformity to law and public policy are practically unknown in their range and effects. Imprisonment, fines, adverse publicity, cease-and-desist orders and a hundred other means are used to see that public policies are universally observed. Yet no reliable body of science exists concerning them.

Although already indicated, it should be emphasized that the Legislative Reference Service is too small and too conventionally operated for the intelligence requirements of the modern Congress. To strengthen the competency and control of Congress requires a creative and well-equipped establishment, larger than the present one, authorized to undertake a variety of investigations in the country-at-large, upon the request of individual congressmen. If a representative wishes any kind of field study made, he should be privileged to have it. To avoid handicapping unduly any potential opponents, the findings should be available as a matter of public record.

Minority staff should be increased in order to provide opportunities for an opposition to generate intelligence. Disregard of the need of minority party members for research and intelligence merely promotes discord, increases the crises of party turnover, and diminishes by far the value of the legislative product. Granted that it is not the party issue that requires protecting so much as it is some principle whereby intelligent opposition and control may be aroused, there appears to be no reason to deny minority members on any committee a third of the staff personnel and facilities used by the committee. In view of the sums presently made available, enlarging the staff budget will have to follow to insure against starving the necessary majority service.

Reduction of the special interest representation now to be found in certain committees is in order. The agricultural committee, to isolate an example, is too heavily weighted in favor of the interests being helped or regulated. On the one hand this strengthens the power of individual congressmen and therefore the power of Congress as a whole; on the other hand, the interests of Congress as a whole do not find their way far enough into the vital committee stage of legislation. A more formal representation of the unspecialized collective interest on all committees where precise interests are served—and this may indeed mean all committees—is recommended.

As to the committees and their names, very little advice can be offered. A committee on federal relations, metropolitan problems, and regionalism, would seem to have meaning for now and the future. So also would a committee on social and racial relations. Yet, no matter how these problems are divided, they will in turn invite new divisions to remedy the new defects they will cause. There seems to be no interest of a major kind which is not a major concern of an important congressional committee.

Proposals for the rule of germaneness in debate must be treated with less urgency than is often demanded. The House has such a rule. The Senate struggles to achieve one. Actually, germaneness will always rest in the gavel of the presiding officer. If he has power, he will introduce germaneness, except when to his interest; therefore there will be much more germaneness to debate. If he has no power, but power resides in the individual members, they will employ irrelevant debate whenever it suits their purpose.

Of course, most of what is regarded as not germane in debate, say in the Senate, turns out upon analysis to be a crowding of the communication lines, very much as telephone messages are deliberately garbled in transit across the country, and disentangled upon reaching their destination. Two or more tasks are being moved along at the same time.

Moreover, irrelevancies and verbosity are utilized to delay proceedings and the question is not one of germaneness, therefore, but one of whether individuals should be allowed to delay a legislative process with which they are momentarily in disagreement. It is a question of values, and not of efficiency.

There is finally a rule of germaneness that is logically such. When a man wishes to be brief and to the point, but cannot, either from psychological causes or for reason of misunderstanding, he unwittingly, or at least without malice or plan, disturbs the routines of the body. This, the true logical form of non-germaneness, is difficult to analyze and control. There is reason to think that its control would help the republican force, because floor time would be saved for other purposes, and proceedings might be more impressive.

Other matters are also of uncertain character. The proposal that no committee should meet while its parent body is in session is met with in various forms. It appears to present an almost impossible contradiction because the desire to succeed in floor business and the wish to succeed in committee business must express themselves within a time span too limited for both.

Electrical voting equipment is not so important as some of its proponents would have us believe. It may appear that

Congress wastes time in elaborate roll calls, but much necessary work goes on in the course of a roll call, and many little adjustments have been conditioned by knowledge that a roll call will be occurring as it now does; such arrangements would require new forms if electrical equipment were set up.

The policies of Congress are often left to the President and to several vigorous leaders, or even to chance, as an issue of one kind or another plays across the nation. If Congress were to deliver messages to the nation, assemble its leaders from time to time, and resolve upon other reforms advocated here, it might well finish by setting up central planning machinery. Such machinery exists now, but lacks one important element, and that is the forthright enunciation of the policies it is actually grinding out.

There is planning of policy taking place in the substantive committees and in the committees on rules, appropriations, and other groups. A method of extracting from such committees a sort of statement of policy and program would lend forthrightness and disinterestedness to the image of Congress. The results need not be more precise than those of the President or other groups in the nation. They might resemble, for instance, the program statement enunciated and advocated by Senator Taft in the 80th Congress. The nation would be told that there is a meaning in the work intended and performed by Congress.

REFORMS OF THE EXECUTIVE ESTABLISHMENT

A class of experts is inevitably so removed from common interests as to become a class with private interests and private knowledge, which in social matters is not knowledge at all.

John Dewey, *The Public and Its Problems*

A set of changes is required in the relations of the executive establishment to Congress. In the first place, much stronger action on the part of Congress is needed to insure it access to the operations and materials of the executive agencies. As a corollary, strong laws against secrecy, where that secrecy cannot be clearly demonstrated to be vital to national security, are in order. The number of areas that are off-bounds to Congress and the public and press should be reduced considerably.

Question periods have been advocated for many years. Stemming from the British practice of permitting the Ministers of the government to be present on the floor to answer inquiries publicly posed by members of the House of Commons, the American proposals vary the circumstances to what they believe would be American habit and the threshold of congressional acceptability. It is only fair to say that as the recommendations have come nearer to passage into legislation in America, they have become weaker and weaker in substance. The American executive, and congressmen as well, are disinclined to subject themselves to the rigors of thorough public examination.

On the anti-republican side, it should be indicated that congressional leaders have not been inclined to favor such proposals, whereas more of the uninfluential or younger congressmen have been favorably inclined, for obvious reasons. Stephen Horn has indicated so much in his study of *Cabinet and Congress.* Moreover, the old-timers of Congress smell a rat. The asking of leading questions can be practiced not only by opponents of the executives, but by the presidential party as well. The struggle to get the floor would also, in both houses, present difficulties to the presiding officers.

On their side, the executives of the government, while welcoming the chance occasionally to present their programs in debate, are appalled by the time that would be taken, and frequently water down the proposed legislation by suggesting that they be entitled to send junior staff members in their place. They furthermore visualize hostile interrogation.

Actually, the net effects of the question period are difficult to assess and a proposal for one kind of question period would result in a reform that must be considered part of the program of executive control, while that for another type of question period would nestle well in the package to be enacted for republican control.

Congressional Tribunes should be designated from a panel of qualified persons serving under the Congress. The Tribunes would be responsible for recommending that the government be disengaged from activities that might better be performed by non-governmental agencies, or other governments, or not at all. They would be assigned as individuals to all bureaus and offices of the government. Their task would be to report to the Congress each year on reasons for closing down or diminishing the functions of their agencies and practical means of doing so.

Each year, when hearings are held and authorizations and appropriations are voted, the reports and testimony of the Tribunes should be heard. Such a built-in antibody is probably the only method that can guarantee the control and reduction of bureaucracy.

Congress requires a more sympathetic officialdom; short of placing officials under the rule of Congress in their daily operations, a method of inculcating of congressional perspectives is difficult. A Sub-Legislative Corps might be created. This group of officers would consist of all persons who are given considerable delegated legislative power. They would be certificated by Congress itself and would be directly responsible to Congress in some way, especially with regard to the quality of their legislative promulgations. There is no paramount reason why the accident of history which has allowed the executive branch to become the legislative branch should not sooner or later be corrected.

The very existence of the Sub-Legislative Corps would recognize that there are politics and public policies made in the course of the administrative process; that there is a new type of official; and that this official requires a new type of connection with the Congress. It should not be necessarily the "crony" type of connection, or the illegal informant. But neither should the fact of delegation of power be permitted to cut away more and more of the influence of Congress under guise of its being merely "administrative" in character. By being qualified according to regulations of Congress and by being required regularly to answer to Congress in certain basic ways, the higher executive officers of the government would contribute to the maintenance of the balance of power between the legislative and executive branches.

It is quite possible to adopt a policy of requiring the cancelling of an old activity in order to begin a new activity in government. Plus/one/minus/one equals zero increase in activity. This should be called the Zero Sum Activity policy of government. The responsibility for devising a precise means of carrying out this policy should be assigned jointly to congressional leadership, to the Legislative Reference Service, to the Social and Behavioral Science Institute, to the Tribunes of Congress and to the Sub-Legislative Corps.

Congress must watch its tendencies to authorize more and more scientific experts in the executive branch of government. Scientists, whether of natural science or behavioral science persuasion, tend to serve the interest of the executive branch, advocating the causes of the presidency or other executives, and doing so with great force because they speak from the pulpit of science.

As science grows in reputation and mystery, this obstacle will become ever more difficult for Congress to surmount. It is not necessary to convert congressmen into scientists or elect scientists to Congress; it is necessary to adopt some of the preceding measures advocated for enlightening the Congress, for enlightening the public and assembling the intelligence apparatus for scientific policy-making. Science needs help, but that help is best provided while moving it out of the government, even at the risk of some waste and some loss of control.

A common proposal nowadays is to establish an agent of Congress, a so-called *"ombudsman,"* modelled along the lines of a Danish and Swedish official of recent origin. The *ombudsman* responds to a private citizen's complaints against an official by an investigation and a court procedure, if called for. Rather than recommend this *ombudsman* who might undermine the activity of the legislators, there is recommended a reform of the Courts. The procedures for redress of grievances against government agencies by persons or groups should be greatly simplified and speeded up.

There appears to be little reason for denying congressmen adequate facilities for handling similar types of cases by personal intervention. They might refer legal cases to the Courts, and would themselves be the *ombudsman.* If investigation is required, and the Department of Justice appears inadequate to the task, whether because the matter concerned is not a crime, or because the Department involved is biased for the executive branch, then such a task may be assigned to a Central Office of Congress, something like that of the General Accounting Office, composed of a number of Agents. The congressional Agent could then bring the case before the Courts, or, if not sanctionable by legal means, carry it back into the political process, for sanction by publicity, by political pressure, or other means at the command of Congress.

Precedent and Possession are politically compelling. There should be current exercises of law for as many principles as there are of congressional authority. If secrecy is a threat, then a bill, not necessarily one of substantive importance, should be introduced and passed to establish and confirm the congressional principle regarding secrecy. If the structure of a minor agency is said by the executive advocates to be solely executive business, Congress should pass a bill, again without substantive importance, creating a minor office, stating its powers, and providing for its review. If the power to screen appointments is being denied and limited to Congress, as it frequently is, then a bill should be passed providing that certain minor officials are to be appointed by Congress for essentially "administrative" tasks. It is equally necessary to legislate for the control of interest representative groups, administrative lobbyists, public relations groups and other external connectors of the agencies, so that the total representative role of Congress is perceived to govern a great many persons who have come to make a way of life from getting by way of agency rules what they cannot get by legislation.

Withal, congressional rule in the government may be established best by a determination of the nature of all forms, devices, and tactics that produce such rule, and a biennial enactment in an Exemplary Legislation bill of measures incorporating each and every one of them—the congressional veto of agency rules handed down under a law, the spelling out of structural details, the requirement of approval by a committee, the requirement of advance information on a rule, the reporting of all new boards and appointments (paid or unpaid) that have representative and public relations functions and so on.

Thus each session of Congress will reaffirm and strengthen the theory of rule by representative government as opposed to rule by the executive. In consequence of these measures, special stages would be required to handle judicial litigation, since the theory of congressional authority is unlikely to be second nature to attorneys for the executive branch. For this kind of work, it would be best to have a General Counsel of Congress, working under a joint committee of Congress, to expound congressional intent and prerogatives at the bar.

In the end, an increase in the long-range policy function of Congress is required, with a corresponding diminution of that function by the agencies. Three-quarters of the congressmen, reported a Dartmouth College study group in 1964, believe in legislative activism, or congressional supremacy. Since Congress has to be elected, and the Civil Service is long-enduring, this may seem to be an impossible task, but if several of the preceding recommendations are followed, especially that of expanding the research facilities and central planning of Congress, the objective may be attained. Furthermore, all those steps which would be taken to increase the congressional perspectives of officers in the executive branch of government would indirectly result in introducing more congressional perspective into the planning of future legislation.

In the final analysis, the need for a society fit for Congress to serve and work in is evident. Yet this society depends upon the positive character of congressional legislation. The substance of the laws—economic, social, welfare, military—brings about changes in society and then again in the role of Congress. There is an ascending cycle of causation: from republican substantive principles comes a republican society, and from a republican society a republican Congress. A republican Congress produces republican government, and the republican government produces republican substantive principles. The process, it may be hoped, can endure for a long time.

Chapter Ten

REPUBLICAN SOCIETY

*The preservation of the sacred fire of liberty
and the destiny of the republican model of
government are justly considered, perhaps,
as deeply, as finally, staked on the experiment intrusted to the hands of the American people.*

George Washington,
First Inaugural Address, 1789

THE LAST CHAPTER recalls the beginning—and the promises that were made at that time. Congress was to be
described root and branch. And so it was, with its numerous
constituencies and its highly original ways of work.

The Executive Force then appeared as a threat to the
place of Congress in American society. The trends in modern life that promote the Executive Force at the expense of
the Republican Force were traced. Doubts were raised
concerning the strength of the legislature's social support.

However, a set of reforms were proposed which would
ward off the advances of executive power. At the same time,
methods of tapping the high potential of representative government were presented. A congressional metamorphosis is
possible.

Still many must doubt that this new republican society,
based even upon the transformed Congress, would be better
than an executive society. Their doubt is to be considered.

Furthermore there occurs the question whether republicanism must stop at the water's edge and have no further application in space and time. To these two matters this last chapter is devoted.

LESSONS OF THE PAST

> *Let them be left without a government, every body of Americans is able to improvise one and to carry on that or any other public business with a sufficient amount of intelligence, order, and decision. This is what every free people ought to be; and a people capable of this is certain to be free . . . But where everything is done through the bureaucracy, nothing to which the bureaucracy is really adverse can be done at all.*
>
> J. S. Mill, *On Liberty* (1859)

The American republican system originated in part in the Middle Ages. It was then—in the ninth to eleventh centuries, accelerated in the twelfth and thirteenth—that representative assemblies began to be formed. As the disunited and feudal elements of various areas were merged and managed by kings, legislatures functioned to reduce the stresses and strains between localism and nationalism. That these assemblies inherited doctrines from the Romans was commonly understood. "What affects everyone should be approved by all." So proclaims the Code of Justinian of the sixth century, and the Middle Ages used the slogan liberally. The monastic orders of the Christian Church grew strong then and created representative institutions. These were carried to a high state by the thirteenth century. Thereupon representative government was handed over from Church to State.

From the fourteenth to the eighteenth century, except to a degree in England, representative government was submerged in the tides of monarchical absolutism. Then with the American and French revolutions and the great reforms of the English government, a period of legislative supremacy emerged in the Western World. Soon the principles of republicanism spread throughout the world.

However, before the victory of parliamentarism could be complete, a great reaction set in. Communism and Fascism destroyed parliamentary regimes in some of the leading countries of the world. Many other countries with authoritarian regimes of the past set up walls of hard reality against theories of republican government that had been imposed upon them; most of South and Central America, Japan, Spain, and other parts of the world resisted the victory.

When, following World War II, a new set of colonial peoples achieved freedom, they too adopted republican forms. But they did not possess the spirit and accept the conditions that would realize the form in fact. In 1963 Professors Banks and Textor discovered only 28 fully effective legislatures in the 100 on which they had adequate information. In contrast to these legislatures, which were reasonably co-equal with the executive branch in law-making, stood 23 that were partially dominated by the executive or other group, 21 that were completely dominated by the executive or a single party machine, and 28 that were wholly ineffective hulks. It must be concluded that the political world has become generally hostile to the true operations of representative government, even while accepting it *pro forma*.

The conditions that have caused the weakness of republican government in the past are not unknown to American history. Every significant episode in the history of representative government is recapitulated in the less universal and shorter legislative history of the United States. The decline of independent local elites, such as has occurred in

England in the last two centuries, has tended to weaken representative government in other countries. The same tendency may be observed in the United States.

The rise of bureaucracies based upon a merit system, career service, permanence, secrecy, elaborate rules, and a special way of life, has undermined republics in other places and times. The effect of the same influence and development is felt within the United States.

Economic crisis has shaken the foundations of legislative institutions in America, though it has never suddenly destroyed them, as it has in other countries. The Great Depression of 1929-1939 contributed as much as any war to the bureaucratization of American society and the growth of presidential power.

Sometimes republics have failed to pass the test of social mobility. They have prevented the demands of lower classes of society to be given full citizenship from being satisfied. With the exception of the Negroes, this problem has been well handled in the United States. Indeed, the Civil War is in this respect and many others the major contradiction of American history. It was the great failure of republicanism. A classical constitutional failure, it traumatized the normal constitutional development of the nation. It laid a curse upon every republican institution.

Perhaps all discussion of law, concept, principle and behavior must, in the light of the Civil War, be prefaced by an understanding that the politics of indignation is beyond principle. The politics of indignation must be accepted or rejected outside of the normal procedures of political and constitutional life. This politics of righteous rage is constantly operative in American politics, but it cannot achieve the complete supremacy over normality that it had during its Civil War phase, between 1840 and 1964. It occurs whenever a person—one or a million—says that one of his preferences is immovable and absolute, knowing that the same value is completely in opposition to a value of others.

It is normal to have millions of such conflicting preferences, weakly diluted and unrecognized, in the social atmosphere, but they do not have a great effect upon the operations of the political system. Only rarely can they swell out to fill some area of life and displace its usual principles, seeping from there then into other critical areas. The Civil War, a veritable Hundred Years' War, only now perhaps ending, was a fully-formed peak expression of the politics of indignation in America.

The military test has been passed by the United States on a number of occasions. The first, too well-known to permit recital, had to do with George Washington's refusal of a dictatorship. Later on, given the temper of Andrew Jackson and his followers, it may be ventured that the United States was preserved from a species of despotism only by the highly decentralized and vigorous federalism of the country. Lincoln's administration posed another test and the negative effects of the experience are still felt. Every generation faces the problem anew. In all such crises can be detected signs of the republican disorder that in other times and other countries invited assumption of power by the military.

The United States has suffered from a succession of foreign relations problems too. Sometimes they were coupled with military problems and sometimes not. The Alien and Sedition Acts of 1799 made citizenship difficult and suppressed actions and ideas favorable to radical or foreign-born movements and ideas. They were a classical case, to be repeated with each major war, of the damaging of free institutions by suspicious and terrorized factions.

The problems of secrecy and denial of access are still with the country and mount in importance as more and more tasks are bureaucratized in the land. Increasingly, material about what is going on in government is withheld from public knowledge, even though the particular public in question may consist largely of experts in the subjects whose discussion is forbidden. Representative government has never been able to operate under conditions of secrecy or where conspiracies are alleged to be threatening the safety and security of the land. When these conditions occur, the executive, the military, and/or the bureaucracy take over the government, and only with the greatest of difficulty is republicanism restored.

It would seem, in reviewing the history of the failures of republicanism, that the survival of republican institutions in America has been partly the effect of good fortune, and partly of visible advantages of the American system. The American republic is based upon wise initial planning. That planning, embodied particularly in the American Constitution, was done in a fairly calm and objective atmosphere by men perusing carefully experience at home and abroad.

The American Congress has been tied in with federalism. It has been tied in with active and influential sets of publics. It has been tied in too with a free enterprise system creating a great many supporting elements which all together lend independence to the characters of the representatives. In these respects and others, the American system of government has had a measure of planned superiority which, together with good luck, has preserved it to this day.

REPUBLICAN AND EXECUTIVE SOCIETIES

Is it not the chief disgrace in the world, not to be an unit—not to be reckoned one character—not to yield that peculiar fruit which each man was created to bear, but to be reckoned in the gross, in the hundred, or the thousand, of the party, the section, to which we belong; and our opinion predicted geographically, as the north, or the south?

R. W. Emerson (1837)

Yet the Republican Force is in decline. The Executive Force is moving toward conquest of American society. For various reasons, most Americans cannot be counted in opposition to the bureaucratic society. There are various reasons for enduring the prospect of a bureaucratic future (or any likely future). It may seem less bad than it will be. It may not seem bad by the time it happens. It may not be very bad. The alternative may be just as bad or worse. The alternative may not be very good. And the alternative may involve too many intervening hardships.

That the executive society seems less bad than it will prove to be is probable. It is necessary to speak in riddles to say why. The bad of the future seems less bad when the future appears to contain less mystery and chance. The future of bureaucratic society is easier to map than that of republican society.

It is furthermore easier to give assurances on matters that have not been tried than on a tested way of life. Large portions of the people, regardless of right or wrong, feel that the republican system is indissolubly connected with vicious practices in human relations, particularly ethnic persecution and discrimination. To them the alternative to the bureaucratic society has little appeal; it seems as bad or worse. The Executive Force in America, speaking through a totally favorable intelligentsia, has in the past generation taken credit for all improvements in the situation of those groups who have to a greater or lesser degree felt such discrimination.

It will bear much study to learn whether the social mobility upwards of ethnic and racial groups in America has been more rapid when pursued by means of the apparatus of society that can be called republican, in contrast with that called executive. But whatever the answer for the past, one can feel more certain that the answer of the future will be that republican society has to promote social mobility more rapidly than bureaucratic society. The reason, again paradoxical, is that under a bureaucratic society, where promotions are by "merit" and done in an "orderly" manner by rules, individual idiosyncracies are penalized, whatever their source, and group norms are more general, while group preferences are limited to whatever the gross plan of the society deems good.

Now all of this may not seem bad to most people by the time that it arrives. A gradual reduction of living standards and freedom of choice and behavior can be put into a sufficiently positive light to make it appear not only acceptable, but desirable. Even if the great majority is to be hurt by the coming of a new society, the voices that speak for the majority will be, as they are now, singing the Hallelujah over its advent.

Why do they do so? Why do so many professors, social work experts, politicians, businessmen, educators, journalists, and others herald a future that is most likely not to be? In the first place, they hail the short-run effects of the changes; at first, Mississippi will be chastised; more money will go to big-city budgets, shining new schools will be built in many suburbs, and social scientists will be hired by the thousands, like engineers in aircraft factories, to work in Washington and elsewhere. Money will flow, big money, from big government. The euphoria will lift up men's souls for a few years. Only much later will the nasty side-effects and basic shortcomings begin to reveal themselves. The society will only then tighten up and begin to close. But by that time the situation of man can be rationalized as coming from future causes—the loss of international trade, war, foreign aid, the balance of payments, social irresponsibility of remaining segments of republican society, and such other arguments as gain currency.

Concerning the question whether it will be very bad, who can say whether *choice* causes more pain than *acceptance?* The Republican Force promises freedom, the Executive Force certainty, security. We have weighted our study on the side of free men, from the first chapter onwards, and must say that the possibilities of a secure society providing freedom are less than of a free society providing security. So it has been in history and therefore freedom is to be preferred for itself and for the probability that, when it will occur, security will be provided as the by-product.

With such prospects, who can believe that the alternative, which we are limiting to the Republican Force, could be just as bad or worse? The answer is simple: all those who do not believe that there will occur such long range effects of the Executive Force, or who believe out of misplaced patriotism that our society must inevitably, owing to the inbred intelligence of the people, settle into a happy golden mean, where the best of both worlds is achieved; they will mentally erase all that they do not like about both the Republican and Executive Forces and substitute dreamed-of virtues in their place.

There remains to fortify the future prospects of the Executive Force those who are persuaded of the virtues of republicanism but lack the will to make the necessary sacrifices on its behalf. A common belief about a way of life that is supposedly declining is that its support is an easy matter for an individual. On the contrary, liberalism—that is, the acceptance of allegedly progressive trends in society —is much the easier political position, socially and psychologically. When, to the essentially conservative position, is added a program of reforms that are not popular, little but misunderstanding and opposition can be expected.

It is not surprising therefore that in America today, no informed and united republican movement exists. The mass media do not see the issue and if some aspect of it strikes them occasionally they do not dwell upon it. The publics of the country are as we have described them, shifting to the views of the presidency.

The Supreme Court has no longer any shame about reading the Constitution as if its words meant nothing. Most business leaders of the country are without ideology and political discipline. They can be swayed from one position to another by a tax, a subsidy, blackmail, and "sweet talk."

The older and middle-aged generations of scholars and scientists of the country are almost entirely committed to the Executive Force. Over the period of a generation they have taken with dead seriousness the revelations of "political realism," whereupon, even while mechanically dealing out old texts about law, freedom, opportunity, and religion, they are belying such traditional messages by action and word.

Examine, for a moment, the major sub-cultures of America. (Granted there may be fewer, or more. Granted their names may be too inclusive or exclusive. Granted they may overlap.) There may be said to be nine major groupings of

Americans by manners, thought, and wish. What position do they take in respect to the republican-executive conflict?

1. *The managerial and clerical class.* Insofar as their way of life is becoming bureaucratized, managers and clerks become somewhat like civil servants. Yet there is a pluralism of modes of work, of kinds of leadership, and of types of incomes, which would be heavily affected by a closer integration and centralization of the economy. They need freedom from their own bureaucratizing process, not incorporation in an even larger one. Still little leadership comes from this sector. Where it emerges it speaks the language of rugged individualism, which, though romantically attractive, is no substitute for the real-life language of pluralistic power.

2. *The urban workers.* Urban workers nowadays are born in and tied to the executive state. Whenever and wherever they move politically, they end up in support of the bureaucracy. All of the personal ambitions they may have are bound to drown in successive waves of regulation. Yet they must support their union leaders or be impotent mavericks. The leaders themselves, try as they may to avoid it, must end up in support of the road to the executive state.

3. *Negroes.* Most Negroes are impelled by their history to support the centralized bureaucratic State. Glimmers of consciousness that this may not be to their benefit strike some localistic leaders, middle class businessmen, and proud introspective intellectuals from time to time. The contest can be given a sharp definition: will the Negroes be completely integrated before the nation is completely bureaucratized? The answer must be no. Therefore, the chances are seriously high that the coming of the bureau-

cratic state will suppress and relegate to inferior status the
Negroes once again, for the instrumentation of the executive is perfectly suited to that end. A generation after
women were granted the suffrage, a Civil Service Commission study reported that 94% of the requests the commission received from U.S. national government agencies for
top management jobs specified *men*.

4. *The intelligentsia and Jews*. Intellectuals are recruited from all strata of society, and many are in rebellion
against narrow horizons and projected towards a great centralism. Perhaps a quarter of American intellectuals are of
Jewish background, and Jews, more than any other grouping, are oriented towards an intellectual outlook, regardless
of education and occupation.

The correlation between provincial or back-country
prejudices and republicanism is high, though perhaps not
so high as the dominant urban intellectuals make them out
to be. A social conflict is therefore invited. Again a defeat
of an old social enemy will bring temporary advantages.

But republican society, in all its confusion, prejudice,
and localism, breeds greater thinkers and artists than bureaucratic society. The centralized state is no friend of dis-
sidents or the minority, whatever its lofty position in a
nation's culture. For to create new classes in a centralized
bureaucracy is easy: it can even be done with honor and
medals—one set of medals for the intellectual hero, another
set for the state heroes. So the native and wonderful integration of the intelligentsia and Jews in American life, so
appropriate in one sense, so hard-bought in another, would
be replaced by their division off into an estate—watched,
admired, and discriminated against both positively and negatively by the executive.

5. *The rural folk.* The holders of small farms and the village dwellers from Maine to California belong to what might be called the rural folk. Their orientation is highly republican but their numbers are declining. They will soon be deprived of much of their representation in state and national legislatures too. The centralized state can do them little good that has not already been provided through the U. S. Department of Agriculture. They will not feel at home in it.

6. *The small businessman and Church Protestant.* These are the mainstay of the Republican Force historically. Their numbers are diminishing, however, since single businessmen are being merged into big business and the Church Protestants are becoming non-sectarian and unreligious. Furthermore, Catholics and Jews are increasingly numerous in their ambiance and diminish their ideological and social solidarity. The intelligentsia also is growing in numbers and powers and governs many of the decisions made in their work.

7. *The Church Catholics.* Historically pluralist of viewpoint and anti-socialist, the Catholic hierarchy and associated laymen have been nevertheless turned towards Washington by the discrimination lodged against them in traditional American society, which has been dominated in most places by the political and cultural groupings centered around the Protestant businessman. Since actual social pressures influence most people more strongly than abstract principles, Catholics have tended merely to verbalize their republicanism and actually to support the Executive Force.

8. *The Olden Southerner.* Differing from the new urbanized Southerner and only partly composed of rural folk, the Olden Southerner is a traditional, classical, urbane type

in whom pride and a sense of weakness contend mightily.
Even more than the small businessman and Church Protestant, the Southerners espouse republicanism and have a
balanced and intelligent theory of that idea. But they are
prevented from exercising full leadership nationally by being tied to the resistance against new Negro rights and by
prejudices against them among the intelligentsia.

9. *The Bureaucrat.* Increasingly, the American people
are bureaucratic in occupation and way of life and thought.
Recruits come in from all groups. Only the managerial
and clerical group of the nation succeeds in enlisting more
adherents, and the managerial group, as was stated earlier,
is slipping by sidewise motion into the orbit of collectivism.
All scarce values—power, wealth, education, prestige—are
flowing at an increased rate into the domain of national
officials and trickling throughout the bureaucratic hierarchy
and its "independent" associates.

* * * * *

The rule of law, equal opportunity, free association,
and religiousness: *Not one* of these basic social principles
would be better served under the administrative state than
under a true republic. Yet the conclusion must be that the
major social groupings of America are understandably in
favor of the Executive Force. Those which have been republican historically are declining. Those which should be,
but are not republican, will apparently be pro-executive
until too late to reverse the trend. Only the government
administrators themselves can be considered to have *both* a
short-range and long-range profit to derive from the probable course that the future will take.

Already, the defense of the republican position in any
serious way, that is, any way that drives home clearly its

points, is unpopular and can arouse a censorship and large-scale prejudice. For one has to espouse a cause against his natural friends. He has to refuse benefits to groups that seem on the surface to be long overdue to them. He has to drink every day from the bitter cup of anti-liberalism, knowing that only thereby can he postpone a final more complete disaster to liberalism following upon its triumph.

Still, American republicanism is stronger than any other in the world today. It may carry along, it may be temporarily submerged, it may even surge forward. It has, after all, survived a number of different types of threats in the past. To succeed, it must pursue a set strategy:

First: Find support among scientists and intellectuals. An increase of from a level of 20% to a new level of 40% support of republican principles here would bring a total change in the over-all situation. Also persuade Catholic leaders of the need to hold to their own social theories despite short-run advantages of supporting the Executive Force.

Second: Delay as much as possible the Executive Force program to permit the classical social mobility of America to erase as many stupid social, economic, ethnic, and cultural prejudices as possible before the gates of individual movement are closed and all movement is required (or forbidden) by collectivist law.

Third: Seek the republican reforms of the national government presented in the last chapter.

Fourth: Extend the ideology of this book beyond the legislative system, so as to apply to the executive system, the economic system, the educational system, and the social system, and into the systems of local government and federalism. For each a careful plan is needed.

CONGRESS AS A UNIVERSAL EXAMPLE

We have recognized in representative government the ideal type of the most perfect polity, for which, in consequence, any portion of mankind are better adapted in proportion to their degree of general improvement.

J. S. Mill, *Representative Government* (1861)

When a force is weakening, it appears rash to suggest that it may serve as an example elsewhere. Furthermore, it is often asserted and readily believed that no nation's institutions can serve to inspire another's. This, like most such statements, is true when true, false when false. Roman law works well in dozens of countries. America functions on many a borrowed organ.

Yet the science of grafting political institutions is no further advanced than that of grafting animal organs. The exuberance with which a number of South American countries, newly independent, adopted literally the American legislative system, was soon followed by difficulty, then despair, and finally a kind of chronic invalidism that accepted the non-functioning organ without further experimentation and invention. Similar analogies might be drawn in Eastern Europe and the Far East after World War I and in Africa and Asia after World War II.

Even in those countries where parliaments are strong and integrated into the society, the experience is recent and the consciousness of its full meanings not general. The British, who have had the longest recent experience with a strong Parliament, have permitted in the past half century various developments whose contribution to the weakening of republicanism has been detailed in these pages already: bureaucratism, decline of local autonomy, exalting of the party chief, socialism.

Two accidents have thus far saved the British parliament from the fate of many another: the smallness in size of the country (artificially diminished in fact by the decline of Empire and Commonwealth) and the presence of the Monarchy, which has prevented the rise of magical leadership in the executive. Certain highly favorable attitudes supporting parliamentarism are, of course, found among the older elements of the British elite. These help the situation, but would not otherwise prevail.

Countries of less experience have less confidence. There it is often asserted, after some brief experience with a legislature, sometimes modelled directly upon the American Congress, that the legislature is failing and the "country is not ready for it," "it is a block to national planning," "it is a nest of self-seekers," etc. The epithets are carried in a hundred newspapers every day in many countries.

The fact is that the country is failing the legislature. Cut out localism, eliminate the various publics by socialism, give great powers of legislative decision to the bureaucracy, and exalt the chief executive: there is nothing the legislature can do save to expire peaceably, without troubling anybody.

Especially were it to be reformed, Congress can serve as a universal example. Perhaps it will be as part of the total body of experience with republics that is brought before the inventive human mind. Perhaps more as an inspiration, if only it were to be better understood. Or perhaps only as a convenient historical tag, while the conditions that create government by legislature in the United States are replicated elsewhere.

The idea of Congress can be rephrased in current scientific language. In this generalized, abstract, and modern form, it can move across international boundaries. Though foreign to the many historical personages who created that system, such language is more meaningful to the contemporary vocabulary of politics around the world and among the intelligentsia: *Men aspiring to a cooperative and equal state will seek to be ruled in accord with their dignity. Such rule is rule by law and rule by consultation. A controlled collective decision-making body—freed from major superstitions and magical interventions—is the highest form of government that man has yet devised. It can express itself in the family, in the school, in business, in the church, and in the state. So long as men wish a voice about their social destiny, they will seek to be ruled by congresses. They may change the system in many respects: practically no component need retain its particular form and manner. But in the end, it must still be the congressional system in substance that will prevail among a self-respecting citizenry.*

CONCLUSION: CONGRESS A MODERN INVENTION

On the ingenuity and skill with which the social inventiveness of our time develops and the readiness with which inventive suggestions are received and made effective depend in large measure the future of our civilization.

C. E. Merriam
The Role of Politics in Social Change

Congress, that is to say, can be viewed as an instrument not only of historical and traditional government, but of the future. It is modernistic beyond the presidency and executive establishment, quite beyond the Courts. Of course, it should be made clear that Congress is not the perfect instrument of a democratic republic as it stands. No such instrument is available, or is even to be found. Man is not destined to build a heavenly contraption that will free him from human problems. What has been said about the past and present and what we endeavor to say here about the future is that Congress is a better and more perfectable institution than any other, except the educational system itself, to achieve the democratic republic.

The legislature, not the executive, is the pinnacle of rational achievement in government. The strong executive is an inefficient idea. It has been improved in particulars, usually under the justification of introducing consultative and control elements into the institution. But this is only to say that the institution has been in some way made into a legislature.

Many another so-called improvement in the institution of the executive goes back to an ancient desire to have a long arm that could reach everywhere instantaneously. It was a mad Roman emperor who said "I wish the Roman people had but one head, so that I might cut it off with a single stroke of my sword."

The more difficult tasks of redesigning an enduring government by legislature can engross the best minds for a great many years. Still, the new development of Congress and government by legislature does not have to be cut out of whole cloth. America leads the world in the social and behavioral sciences, that is, in those forms of knowledge and practice that enable man to control human relations and direct them towards agreed-upon goals.

One of the best developed and highly respected branches of the new sciences is administrative analysis and its applied form, administrative management. In the last generation, the great achievement of administrative analysis and management has been to developed a kind of democratic leadership whereby autonomous executives, in full consultation and communication with the employees they supervise, arrive at group decisions concerning the welfare of a company. The same theory and some practice towards its goals can be found in educational science, in hospital administration, and in the new army.

Yet while this has been going on, Congress, which is the paragon of group decision-making, is being banished from the minds of a great many people, some of whom, as scholars and administrators, were contributors to the very development just recited. Political controversy and contradictory ideologies have trapped them into making false distinctions between their own familiar fields and the field of federal government. What has been consistently espoused all along is a scientific approach to the conduct of legislative government.

The history of legislative institutions can be rewritten from a behavioral standpoint. The functions of the legislative system would be re-analyzed and redescribed in the language of the latest administrative science and science of group behavior. The theory of group dynamics, the theory of business government, the latest ideas of educational administration, the new ideas of behavioral political science—in short, the armament of the fastest developing sciences would be brought to bear upon the central problem of the organization of the American republic.

A future of progress toward a republican society, rather than of decay and decline, has to contain a greater role for a Congress. Those who say that Congress is old-fashioned and a throwback, outmoded, far from liberal, and insist upon this view, dismissing the permanent and improvable functions of representation incarnated in such a body, make themselves part of the degenerative and ideologically unfree movement that itself is a relapse into the primeval. Ultimately, if civilization is to become more creative and comfortable, representative government, both old and new, would have to rule all over the world.

———— END ————

APPENDIX A: PROPOSALS TO REFORM CONGRESS

Summary of the Conglomerate of Recommendations Received in One Month of Hearings, 1962, from All Sources.

(Note: These are *NOT* the recommendations of the author. They are a mere collection to show the variety and focus of reform ideas. See p. 194 for the author's comment on them. The recommendations of the author are contained in Chapter Nine and elsewhere; they are listed in the Index on page 298 under the heading "Congressional reforms promoting the Republican Force."

Committee Structure and Operation

1. Create a standing Senate Committee on Veterans' Affairs.

2. Create standing Committees on Civil Rights in both Houses.

3. Establish a Joint Select Committee on the Organization of Congress.

4. Provide machinery for coordination and evaluation of legislative policy on fiscal affairs.

5. Perfect the parallelism of the committee structure of the two Houses.

6. Reduce size of minor Senate committees and increase size of major committees.

7. Increase 5 Senate standing committees from 13 to 15 members each, and the Appropriations Committee from 21 to 23 members.

8. Increase size of Committee on Foreign Relations.

9. Make the Committees on Foreign Relations and Appropriations exclusive in their membership.

10. Give each first-term Senator one major committee assignment before any first-term Senator receives two major committee seats.

11. Clarify definitions of committee jurisdiction.

12. Realine the congressional committee structure.

13. Central scheduling of committee meetings to avoid conflicts.

14(15). Allow subcommittees to hold executive sessions without obtaining approval of full committee (sec. 133f).

16. Increase staff of Senate Minority Policy Committee.

17. Relax the conflict-of-interest statute to permit committees to employ persons on a temporary basis.

18. Clearance of official committee stenographers by the FBI.

19. Amend House rule to provide for admission of professional committee staffs to House floor when their committee bills are under consideration.

20. Proportion allowances for staff of Senators' offices to the population of the States they represent.

21. Fix clerk hire allowance of Representatives at $12,500 a year.

22. Permit Representatives to employ administrative assistants.

23. Classify positions in legislative service and compensate each grade uniformly.

24. Establish a salary scale for congressional employees on a par with salaries paid for comparable work in executive branch.

25. Make the base salary of congressional employees their actual salary (S. 633).

26. Raise ceiling on salary payable temporary committee personnel.

27. Condition compensation of borrowed personnel upon prior approval of Administration Committees.

28. Adjust retirement benefits for legislative employees, by amending title VI of the Legislative Reorganization Act.

29. Add the fields of national defense, recreation, public health, immigration, forestry, fisheries, insurance, crime, and atomic energy to those in which senior specialists may be appointed in the Legislative Reference Service (sec. 203b).

30. Change "price economics" to "marketing" (sec. 203b).

31. Amend rules of both Houses so as to allow standing committees to reimburse Legislative Reference Service for services rendered.

32. Authorize the Legislative Reference Service to (a) index printed hearings; (b) prepare analyses of lobby data; (c) digest pending amendments of major bills.

33. Restore funds for the publication staff of the Legislative Reference Service.

34. Permit House and Senate Legislative Counsel to make staff appointments without the necessity of clearing with the Speaker of the House or the President protempore of the Senate.

Work Load on Congress

1. Ban the introduction of all private bills and delegate all private legislation to appropriate administrative agencies.

2. Create a new Joint Standing Committee on Private Legislation of all types, with an adequate staff.

3. Grant home rule to the District of Columbia.

4. Create a Congressional Commission to Study the Devolution of Governmental Functions.

5. Reduce workload on Congress by—

   (a) Avoidance of special investigating committees.

   (b) Fewer committee assignments per Member.

   (c) Systematic personnel arrangements.

   (d) Addition of more staff where needed.

Oversight of Administration

1. Increase oversight of administration by congressional committees (sec. 136).

2. Conduct a televised "report and question period" fortnightly in both Houses.

3. Require committees to review administrative legislation and recommend to Congress disapproval of regulations contrary to legislative intent.

4. Use the Subcommittee on Senate Investigations as a central investigating body for the Senate.

5. Establish a Joint Legislative Council.

Strengthening Fiscal Controls

1. Create a Joint Committee on the Budget, with an expert staff (S. 913).

2. Let the Joint Budget Committee furnish estimates of probable cost of proposed authorizations.

3. Let the Joint Budget Committee make a study of existing authorizations to see if any could be repealed.

4. Consolidate all the general appropriation bills.

5. Require a record vote on all appropriation bills, and on all committee amendments offered thereto.

6. Include cost estimates in committee reports.

7. Authorize President to veto individual items in general appropriation bills.

8. Establish a permanent Congressional Commission on Government Efficiency and Economy.

9. Increase expert staffs of Appropriations Committees.

10. Make greater use of the facilities of the General Accounting Office.

11. Require amendments offered to appropriation bills to specify where the money shall come from.

12. Reduce the number of appropriations; break each appropriation down into subheads; and empower Budget Bureau to sanction transfers between subheads.

13. Appoint a single accountable officer in each department to prepare and defend the appropriation accounts.

14. Let the appropriation accounts be audited for Congress by an audit department completely independent of the Executive.

15. Establish a Public Accounts Committee to receive and review the Auditor General's report.

16. Start the fiscal year October 1 instead of July 1.

Registration of Lobbyists

1. Clarify scope of application of lobby law.

2. Delete the words "principal" and "principally" in section 307 of title III.

3. Require lobbyists before executive agencies to register and report.

4. Require groups engaged in "indirect lobbying" to register and report.

5. Authorize withdrawal of registrations of persons who have stopped lobbying.

6. Extend exemption granted under section 308 of the lobby law to include radio, television, and facsimile.

7. Exempt organizations receiving and spending less than $1,000 a year, directly or indirectly, from lobby law.

8. Amend section 305 to require reporting of contributions of $100 or more.

9. Require lobbyists to gives names and addresses of contributors of $500 or more.

10. Require lobbyists to report campaign contributions.

11. Amend the lobby law to require an allocation of payments into lobbying and nonlobbying categories.

12. Require a statement of total expenditures of organizations engaged in influencing legislation, broken down into broad categories, with legislative expenditures itemized.

13. Require quarterly listing of name and address of each recipient of an expenditure of $50 or more (sec. 305, a4).

14. Prohibit payment of contingent fees to lobbyists.

15. Require lobbying organizations to file statement of their bona fide total membership.

16. Require lobbying organizations to state how their legislative policy was determined and to indicate the responsibility of their agents.

17. Deny the privilege of the floor to ex-Members who are engaged in lobbying.

18. Create a Joint Committee on the Legislative Process to supervise administration of the lobby law and the Corrupt Practices Act.

19. File lobby statements in triplicate with Department of Justice, Clerk of House, and supervisory committee.

20. Require registrations and reports under lobby law to be filed either with Clerk of House or Secretary of Senate, not with both.

21. Simplify the information published quarterly in the Congressional Record under the lobby law, and use one form for filing.

22. Do not require notarized oath on registration forms under lobby law.

Compensation and Retirement of Members

1. Increase congressional salaries.

2. Increase compensation of Members of Congress to $15,0000 a year (S. 1290).

3. Increase congressional salaries to a minimum of $25,000 a year.

4. Establish a Commission on Congressional Salaries (S. 1117).

5. Refer the question of adequate salaries for Congressmen and fair retirement allowances to the Chief Justice of the Supreme Court and the Chairman of the Federal Reserve Board.

6. Let the President name a commission to study congressional salaries and pensions.

7. Repeal tax exemptions allowed Members of Congress and high executive officers (S. 1290).

8. Permit Members of Congress to deduct official expenses in computing their income taxes.

9. Grant expense allowances to Members of Congress.

10. Grant more adequate allowances for travel.

11. Grant allowances to enable Senators to travel abroad.

12. Increase retirement allowances for Members.

13. Amend section 602 to base retirement allowances on length of service in Congress rather than on age, with 12 years' service a minimum condition.

14. Provide an alternative option of retirement under title VI at age 55, with appropriate reduction in annuity.

15. Permit former Members of Congress to participate in the Federal retirement system.

Composition and Tenure of Congress

1. Amend Constitution to provide that term of office of Representatives shall be 4 years, with half the House selected each biennium.

2. Four-year term for Representatives.

3. Limit first term of Senators to 2 years.

4. Consider methods of fixing a future age limit on service in Congress.

5. Equalize the size of constituencies in the House of Representatives.

Congressional Ethics and Immunity

1. Repeal congressional immunity section of the Constitution (Article I, section 6).

2. Amend title 28 of United States Code to allow damage suits by persons defamed by Members of Congress.

3. Provide that no Senator or Representative shall be immune from civil liability for any defamatory statement inserted in the Congressional Record.

4. Make it unlawful for any Member of Congress to receive or accept any part of the salary of his employees.

5. Amend the Corrupt Practices Act to cover receipts and expenditures in primary campaigns, and to check smear methods of campaigning.

6. Require certain members of the legislative, judicial, and executive branches of the Government to disclose the amounts and sources of their income.

7. Forbid persons registered under the Lobby Law to distribute literature under congressional franks.

8. Limit distribution of franked matter to a Member's district or State.

9. Limit distribution of franked matter in proportion to the population of a congressional district or State.

10. Assign a monthly quota for free distribution of franked matter.

11. Find a formula for maintaining confidential character of Congressional documents (sec. 202d).

12. Regulate nepotism.

Party Government in Congress

1. Consolidate the several leadership groups in each House into one truly effective and responsible leadership committee for each party.

2. Make the party leadership committees in each House responsible for:

   (a) Regular meetings of party membership.

   (b) Submitting policy proposals to party membership.

   (c) Selection of committee chairmen.

   (d) Assignment of members to committees.

   (e) Planning the legislative schedule.

3. Establish party policy committees in the House of Representatives.

4. Place more responsibility upon the party caucus and party steering committees.

5. As regards seniority:

(a) Abandon or modify seniority rule in committee appointments.

(b) Let party caucuses elect chairmen of standing committees.

(c) Provide for the democratic selection of chairmen and members of committees.

(d) Appoint standing committee chairmen on some other basis than seniority.

6. Translate party platform pledges into legislation action.

7. Give priority in legislative scheduling to implementation of party platform promises.

Public Relations of Congress

1. Have the Library of Congress make a study of the public relations of Congress, under auspices of Joint Committee on the Library.

2. Televise public hearings of congressional committees.

3. Make committee hearings available to American people through radio and television.

4. Broadcast and televise important House sessions, via commercial broadcasting companies, subject to a code of ethics.

5. Experiment with broadcasting and televising important debates.

6. Adopt a planned program of televising selected committee hearings, with a code of fair practices.

7. Broadcast and televise all sessions of both Houses and selected committee hearings, via Nation-wide networks owned and operated by Congress.

8. Provide facilities for making motion-picture films for use in television stations in home States.

9. Arrange the sessions of Congress so as to have more frequent recesses.

10. Arrange for a regular congressional recess, during first session of each Congress, from July 1 to September 15.

11. Provide for adjournment of Congress during April, August, and September in odd-numbered years.

12. Make the Daily Digest section of the Congressional Record separately available for public sale.

13. Phrase the titles of bills and resolutions so as to summarize their objectives and contents.

14. Include at end of each printed edition of a bill a digest of its objectives and contents.

15. Print periodically a full history of legislation pending before both Houses.

Congressional Procedures

1. Arrange for a general revision of the standing rules of the Senate.

2. Adopt a rule of relevancy in Senate debate.

3. Adopt an improved cloture rule in the Senate.

4. Provide for majority cloture on all matters before the Senate.

5. Amend the Senate cloture rule.

6. Amend rule XII of the Senate standing rules (re disorder in debate) so as to permit the Chair or the Senate to rule upon its violation.

7. Hold committee meetings and Senate sessions on alternate days.

8. Vote by electricity in the House.

9. Vote by electricity in both Houses.

10. Limit power of House Rules Committee over legislation which may be considered from the calendar.

11. Restore the "21-day rule" in the House of Representatives.

12. Liberalize the present House rule concerning the discharge of committees from further consideration of bills.

13. Reduce required number of signatures on House discharge petitions from 218 to 150.

14. Require House Appropriations Committee to hold open hearings.

15. Hold joint hearings on identical or similar bills.

16. Hold joint hearings on departmental appropriation bills.

17. Abolish riders on appropriation and other bills.

18. Abolish or limit the practice of pairing.

19. Add the following sentence to the rule limiting the power of conferees (sec. 135): "It is hereby expressly provided that this paragraph shall be deemed to include reports on measures where one House has struck out all after the enacting or resolving clause and inserted a substitute."

Administration of Congress

1. Establish an Office of Congressional Services to coordinate the housekeeping facilities of Congress and modernize methods of personnel administration.

2. Modernize methods of office management.

3. Appoint a business manager to rationalize housekeeping services of Congress.

4. Abandon antiquated patronage system on Capitol Hill.

5. Improve facilities of Senate Office Building for radio and television.

6. Provide more adequate office space for Senate Committees.

7. Improve labor-saving devices, mimeograph facilities, and restaurant services in the Capitol and Senate Office Building.

8. Survey the facilities and needs of the Service and Duplicating Department of the Senate.

9. Increase telephone and stationery allowances for Senators.

APPENDIX B

NOTE ON METHODS AND SOURCES OF "REPUBLIC IN CRISIS"

A note and comment on the methods used and the sources for the materials of this book may be in order. Since the author aimed to open up a large area of American government to new forms of thought and action, certain valuable rules of scholarship had to be treated lightly. Full documentation and citations in footnotes were passed over so as to make the general argument more clear and to allow it to be stated in brief compass. At the same time it must be admitted that many of the most important theories and facts about the Congressional system and American society have not entered the realm of full empirical proof or disproof. Some of these may never do so because of the inapplicability of known techniques of observation and analysis to them, but a good many others have not entered the realm of empirical investigation simply because researchers have not had a sufficiently broad overview of the important problems to include them.

The book follows a plan of development that seems scientifically unexceptionable whatever its internal problems may be. At the beginning it is said that the problem of American democracy centers about a large conflict of two sets of social forces. These forces are given names. The center of activity occurs in connection with the Congress, which is described as a system operative within the larger system of the political society. It is stated that a system and its functions cannot be described or evaluated without a determination in advance of what values (i.e. positively evaluated behaviors) are expected as output. Therefore certain large values—local autonomy, equal opportunity, etc.—were postulated, without elaboration, asking only that those who could be expected to agree with them should follow the line of recommendations in the end. A defense of the values, it is understood, would have occupied a work twice this size. Nor has social science, especially political science, granted the pioneering work of Harold Lasswell, Clyde Kluckhohn and Wayne Leys in this area, been able to specify such values as are postulated. What is said here can be defended on grounds

that it is at least as specific a statement of values as most others
that are put forward in works such as the Rockefeller Brothers
Fund reports, the Lasswell-Rogow book, *Power, Corruption &
Rectitude,* and sundry highly acclaimed "scientoid manifestoes"
(as I have called them elsewhere), without mentioning those
more numerous works on Congress and the presidency pretend-
ing to empiricism but loaded with values that are apparently
not realized by the author in the secret recesses of his mind.

The work goes on to examine the mechanisms available in
the existing large Congressional system for putting into effect
the goal values postulated and discovers some serious, indeed
fatal, incapacities. The incapacities are growing to an unsup-
portable extent, and the work must engage therefore in some
trend analysis to show that this is the case. However, it does
not base its conclusions upon historical trends so much as upon
an always existing state of things, that is, general principles of
human behavior. Those who drafted the American Constitution
were as much aware of the central theme and problem of this
book as we are today, or more so. There was no trend yet
established, but they knew the problem was ever-present.

Whereupon this book proceeded to evaluate those measures
that had already been proposed to remedy the problems of
the existing system, and it was discovered that such remedies
in many cases were contradictory to the purposes postulated for
the system and were often trivial nostrums as well. There was
also an inadequacy of larger reform proposals; hence a number
of new plans were put forward. These were applied to the
system and it was projected that the system would function differently if the new plan were implemented. At the same time
it was indicated that large changes in the attitudes of the publics and the postures of scientists had to be obtained if the
reforms were to be put into effect.

As the author worked on the early stages of his theories, it
became apparent to him that he was in need of a theoretical
model. Model development has come to be a favored technique of the social sciences, though by other words the logical
process has many ancestors in the history of science. When a
vastly complex phenomenon of little understood forces is being exposed, it is often useful to sketch out the total system in
all of its manifestations and set up all the expected relations
and interactions taking place within the system. That has been
done here even though the mathematics that would denote a

thoroughgoing model are quite beyond reach. There is naturally some confusion between a programmatic statement and a model, and some early readers of the manuscript insisted that the attempt at fashioning an Executive Force and a Republican Force had no more validity than the magical slogans employed in any political diatribe. That is for the readers to judge. The author would only suggest to those who are quite unfamiliar with the practices of social theory and of model construction that they learn a little about the subject before condemning the logic of the work.

Early critics also seemed to confuse the fairly simple style of the work both with the model and then with the ideas involved. The style, such as it is, has nothing to do with the underlying method. The author, who has been known to use his share of jargon, merely chose to control that jargon in the interest of an audience beyond his small band of associated political scientists. He realizes that in some quarters a simple style of writing is considered a professional offense. Unfortunately, many a bad theoretical structure and absence of meaningful fact are also covered in the literature of political science, sociology, and psychology beneath the snowy mantle of jargon.

The use of the model in the present work is associated with a great deal of analysis of myth and ideology. Again a distinction is needed. There can be models of economic transactions of a most material kind, without economic psychology, or of the ways in which votes are cast in time and space, without reference to the psychology of voting. Here, however, the model is used to expose ideologies and myths. It merely states that persons who subscribe to one or the other force will believe in distinctly different institutions and reforms; they will not fully realize so, but they will contribute to a process of change in society nevertheless.

A "myth" as used in this work is used in its scientific sense as a belief that occupies the position of a fact in the mind of the believer but which is essentially a representation of the world loaded with values that are unprovable and only partially realized as being values by the possessor. An ideology is a collection of related myths giving the possessor a set view of the world. It too has conscious and unconscious components and affects a large realm of behavior which only the most diligent empirical and theoretically-guided probing will reveal—first to the observer and then only finally to the possessor of the ide-

ology. Furthermore, and this is a fact that must contribute to
pessimism about the outcome of large-scale social reform, an
ideologue can only rarely be retrained and then only by thoroughgoing measures of education. Often verbal relearning takes
place without affecting real basic beliefs on the subject of those
verbal relearnings.

The several methodological theories put forth in the preced-
ing paragraphs are contained in works such as Hans Vaihinger,
The Philosophy of "As If," Max Weber's *Theory of Social and
Economic Organization* and *The Methodology of the Social
Sciences,* Sorel's *The Myth of Revolution,* Pareto's *Mind and
Society,* Mannheim's *Ideology and Utopia,* Harold Lasswell's
and Dorothy Blumenstock's *World Revolutionary Propaganda,*
Benjamin Nelson's study, *Of the History of the Idea of Usury;
From Universal Brotherhood to Universal Otherhood,* Harold
Lasswell's and Robert Lane's studies of political personalities
and the MIT studies of businessmen and their attitudes to-
wards tariff policies. But the literature of this field has greatly
increased and dozens of citations could be garnered from the
ABS guide, the *International Affairs CODEX,* and other con-
ceptually indexed bibliographies.

A number of early reactions to a mimeographed version of
the draft manuscript indicated that some tender spots were
being touched by the theories of the work. It is difficult to believe that several rage reactions which occurred were normal
rejections of the hypotheses stated. Personal insults, projected
in a couple of cases via identification with the largest values of
science and society, confirmed to the author that an ideology
was being probed. One man wrote that he could never recommend the work, despite its merits, to his "gullible undergrad-
uates." He and others heaped scorn upon the work because it
did not represent the (largely mythical) monograph and compared it unfavorably with a non-existent political science freed
from all prejudice and documented to the hilt. They quarreled
over picayune points and reproached the author for the lack
of evidence. Persons who from personal knowledge of the author had not grown famous for their devotion to empiricism,
suddenly became vastly and absolutely empirical, denouncing
any attempts at larger middle theory, much less total system-
theory.

One professor accused the author of Hegelianism, and though
not in those words, of un-American continentalism. The au-

thor has not been psychoanalyzed, but can trace his intellectual origins clearly back to the Chicago school of political science where prominent influences in his learning of social psychology were John Dewey, Bentley, Cooley, Charles Merriam, Mary Parker Follett, Harold Lasswell, Louis Wirth, Nathan Leites and T. V. Smith. But going back of the last generation, it was the author's naive belief that the seventeenth and eighteenth century English revolutions and the American Revolution and eighteenth century Enlightenment focused very sharply upon the type of problem the author has chosen for his major theme. But neither Hegel nor even Karl Marx should be excluded, for they contributed much to the study of political ideologies as did Vico, Locke, Pareto, Max Weber, R. Michels, Karl Mannheim, Jeremy Bentham, John Stuart Mill, Ernst Cassirer, and others. All trumpet loudly on the main concerns of this work.

Granted that the model is stated imperfectly. It is a first attempt. Much more can be done with it. The last dissertation in political science, particularly in political theory, has not been written, and there is many a subject exposed in the work for such research. In part, the difficulties of setting up the model are owing to the fact that the submodels are stated badly. For example, the model itself depends upon a submodel of representation. Up until the last couple of years, little happened in this area besides the author's work, alone and with Harold Gosnell, two decades ago. Given the recent studies by Eulau-Wahlke-Buchanan-Ferguson, which are both theoretical and empirical, a similar work soon to be published by Miller and Stokes on legislative relations with the constituencies, and works in progress which the Universal Reference System soon will be reporting in a CODEX on decision-making and deliberative processes, we should soon have better models which can be related to a total system of a republic.

The author is highly critical of the old simplistic executive theory of government that was put forward, understandably, by political scientists and administrative theorists beginning perhaps in America with Woodrow Wilson and extending down to the present through writers such as L. D. White and Charles E. Merriam (who, incidentally, was too sophisticated a theorist and writer to be classified absolutely as an executive apologist of the old school). Their endeavor to set up a rationalized "old army" pyramid as their model for all organizations has had a devastating effect upon the classical theory of democracy as centered in complicated relations among the many publics, the legislatures and the executive branch of government. One cannot dismiss the older writers on legislative systems, particularly the expansive Robert Luce. And certainly Woodrow Wilson, like Merriam, had a good sense of legislative behavior even while contributing mightily to the mainstream of executive domination of society. But Locke, Bentham, Mill, and others who, in general theory had much to offer to the construction of a viable republic, ignored important internal systemic problems of government by legislature. So we come up to the present with remarkably little to offer, and then suddenly we discover that in the last several years more middle and low level theoretical work and empirical investigation of first quality have been performed than in all the history of the study of representative government. A generation of scholars just beginning to make substantive contributions to the discipline has settled upon legislative systems. This is remarkable considering that they have received no impetus from conventional political science. And their training de-emphasized the classics, which did deal with these subjects.

By another decade, we should have elaborated enough materials on the many complicated and subtle relations that constitute representative government to propose highly persuasive models and submodels going beyond the simple ones put forward in this work. Political scientists should be enabled to advise much more competently and correctly their political cohorts on how to achieve certain goals of a plural society. It is to be hoped that the fuller knowledge and its applicability will come before the demand for it diminishes to the vanishing point. Sometimes a new science becomes outmoded by the facts of life before it has a chance to display its capabilities.

So as better to display the new and valuable literature on the study of the congressional system and its ramifications within the society of the republic, the author has placed a number of titles in relation to the present work. Topics treated in the text are mentioned together with studies that bear upon them.

For a general view of the legislative system one can begin with John Locke, J. S. Mill, Alexis de Tocqueville, Jeremy Bentham, and Gaetano Mosca. We owe much also to R. Luce, *Congress: An Explanation* (1926), *Legislative Procedure* (1922), *Legislative Assemblies* (1924), *Legislative Principles* (1930), and *Legislative Problems* (1935), and A. F. Bentley's *The Process of Government*. D. B. Truman's *The Governmental Process:*

Political Interests and Public Opinion (1951); T. V. Smith, *The Legislative Way of Life* (1940); J. Burnham, *Congress and the American Tradition* (1959); J. C. Wahlke, H. Eulau, W. Buchanan and L. Ferguson, *The Legislative System: Explorations in Legislative Behavior* (1962); and J. C. Wahlke, "Behavioral Analyses of Representative Bodies," in A. Ranney, ed., *Essays on the Behavioral Study of Politics* (1962), 173-90, are more recent and important works of general purview.

On the image of Congress and its self-image, see the papers edited by Michael O'Leary entitled *Congressional Reorganization: Problems and Prospects* (Dartmouth College, 1964). The concept of the nuclear constituency can be studied *via* H. F. Gosnell, *Machine Politics: Chicago Model* (1937), and *Democracy, Threshold of Freedom* (1948); E. C. Banfield, *Political Influence* (1961); R. A. Dahl, *Who Governs? Democracy and Power in an American City* (1961); and M. Janowitz, ed., *Community Political Systems* (1961).

Various works have examined the nature of the participating and apathetic public including: the pioneering study by C. E. Merriam and H. F. Gosnell, *Non-voting: Causes and Methods of Control* (1924); W. Kornhauser, *The Politics of Mass Society* (1959); L. W. Milbrath, *Political Participation: How and Why Do People Get Involved in Politics* (1965); R. E. Lane, *Political Life: Why People Get Involved in Politics* (1959); H. F. Gosnell, *Getting Out the Vote* (1928); M. Rosenberg, "Some Determinants of Political Apathy," *Public Opinion Quarterly*, 18 (1954-1955), 353-54; S. Rokkan, ed., "Citizen Participation in Political Life," *International Social Science Journal*, 12 (1960); and J. L. Woodward and E. Roper, "Political Activity of American Citizens," *Am Pol Sci Rev*, 44 (December 1950), 872-75.

The major studies of voting behavior have elaborated on the electoral system from the viewpoint of the individual voter and his actions and perceptions. See P. Lazarsfeld, *et al.*, *The People's Choice* (1948); B. Berelson, *et al.*, *The Voter Decides* (1954) and *Human Behavior* (1964). Other works include: A. de Grazia, *The Western Public: 1952 and Beyond* (1954); V. O. Key, Jr., *American State Politics: An Introduction* (1956) and *Southern Politics* (1949); W. N. McPhee and W. A. Glaser, eds., *Public Opinion and Congressional Elections* (1962); and for a review of the literature one can examine A. Campbell, "Voters and Elections: Past and Present," *Journal of Politics*, 25 (November 1964), 745-57. G. A. Almond and S. Verba's study,

Democracy in Five Nations (1963) describes political beliefs, emotions, and participation in politics of citizens in Germany, Italy, Mexico, Great Britain and the United States. R. E. Lane's *Political Ideology: Why the American Common Man Believes What He Does* (1962) and S. J. Eldersveld's *Political Parties: a Behavioral Analysis* (1964) are also significant studies. H. Hyman's *Political Socialization* (1959); E. Katz and P. F. Lazarsfeld's *Personal Influence* (1955); C. Merriam's *The Making of Citizens* (1931) and *Civic Education in the United States* (1934); S. de Grazia's *Political Community* (1948), and F. Greenstein's *Children and Politics* (1965) should all be consulted for data on the initial formation of political attitudes.

On the subject of interest group representation see A. Leiserson, *Administrative Regulation: a Study in Representation of Interests* (1942) A. de Grazia, "Nature and Prospects of Political Interest Groups," *Annals* 319 (September 1958), 113-22; C. M. Hardin, *The Politics of Agriculture* (1952); R. Engler, *The Politics of Oil* (1961); C. D. Jones, "Representation in Congress: The Case of the House Agriculture Committee," *American Political Science Review*, 55 (1961), 358-67; E. P. Herring, *Group Representation Before Congress* (1929); E. E. Schattschneider, *Politics, Pressures, and the Tariff* (1935); B. C. Cohen, *The Influence of Non-Governmental Groups on Foreign Policy-Making* (1959); A. Wildavsky, "TVA and Power Politics," *American Political Science Review*, 55 (September 1961), 576-90; V. O. Key, Jr., *Public Opinion and American Democracy* (1961); Chapter VIII, "American Pluralism" in A. de Grazia, *Public and Republic: Political Representation in America* (1951); E. Latham, *The Group Basis of Politics: A Study in Basing-Point Legislation* (1952); and B. E. Gross, *The Legislative Struggle, A Study in Social Combat* (1953).

Concepts of the public interest have been developed in W. Lippmann, *Public Opinion* (1922); J. Dewey, *The Public and Its Problems* (1927); W. A. R. Leys, "Philosophy and the Public Interest," *Political Research Organization and Design*, 2 (September 1958), 12-13, and *Ethics for Policy Decisions: The Art of Asking Deliberative Questions* (1952); R. A. Dahl, *A Preface to Democratic Theory* (1956); G. A. Schubert, *The Public Interest: A Critique of the Theory of a Political Concept* (1960); and H. D. Lasswell, "The Public Interest: Proposing Principles of Content and Procedure," 54-79 and other essays in C. J. Friedrich, ed., *Nemos V, The Public Interest* (1962).

Numerous bloc and party voting studies have recently appeared. See D. B. Truman, *The Congressional Party, a Case Study* (1959); W. H. Riker and D. Niemi, "The Stability of Coalitions on Roll Calls in the House of Representatives," *American Political Science Review,* 56 (1962), 58-65; D. MacRae, Jr., *Dimensions of Congressional Voting: A Statistical Study of the House of Representatives in the Eighty-First Congress* (1958); G. M. Belknap, "A Method for Analyzing Legislative Behavior," *Midwest Journal of Political Science,* 2 (1958), 277-402; C. D. Farris, "A Method of Determining Ideological Groups in Congress," *Journal of Politics,* 20 (1958), 308-38; K. Kofmehl, "The Institutionalization of a Voting Bloc," *Western Political Quarterly,* 17 (June 1964), 256-72; S. I. Greenstein and A. F. Jackson, "A Second Look at the Validity of Roll Call Analysis," *Midwest Journal of Political Science,* 7 (May 1963), 156-66.

The motives of Congressmen and state legislators for voting and the meaning of parties have been examined by J. C. Wahlke, *et al.,* cited above; L. Dexter, "The Representative and His District," *Human Organization,* 16 (1947), 2-13, also in R. L. Peabody and N. W. Polsby, eds., *New Perspectives on the House of Representatives* (1963); W. E. Miller and D. E. Stokes, "Constituency Influence in Congress," *American Political Science Review,* 57 (1963), 45-56; L. A. Froman, Jr., *Congressmen and their Constituencies* (1963); J. Turner, *Party and Constituency: Pressures on Congress* (1951); E. E. Schattschneider, *The Struggle for Party Government* (1948); C. A. Berdahl, "Some Notes on Party Membership in Congress, I, II and III," *American Political Science Review,* 43 (April 1949), 303-21, and (June 1949), 492-508, and (August 1949), 721-34. One should recall, too, the work of L. A. Lowell, "The Influence of Party upon Legislation in England and America," *Annual Report of the American Historical Association,* 1 (1901), 321-542.

Psychological, economic, geographic, organizational, and legal causes of political behavior are discussed in a vast literature. Several works which have to do with legislatures and Congress include: J. C. Wahlke and H. Eulau, eds., *Legislative Behavior: A Reader in Theory and Research* (1959); J. D. Barber, *The Lawmakers: Recruitment and Adaptation to Legislative Life* (1965); C. L. Clapp, *The Congressman: His Work as He Sees It* (1963); D. R. Matthews, *U.S. Senators and Their World* (1960); G. L. Grassmuck, *Sectional Biases in Congress on Foreign Policy* (1951); H. P. Green and A. Rosenthal, *Government of the Atom:*

The Integration of Powers (1963); G. Goodwin, Jr., "The Seniority System in Congress," *American Political Science Review,* 53 (1959), 412-36; H. D. Price, "Race, Religion, and the Rules Committee: The Kennedy Aid-to-Education Bills," in A. F. Westin, ed., *The Uses of Power: 7 Cases in American Politics* (1962); and J. H. Kessel, "The Washington Congressional Delegation," *Midwest Journal of Political Science,* 8 (February 1964), 1-21.

No works have developed directly the concept of successive majorities. Indirectly, the rationalization of the legislative process is dealt with in the works of Lindsay Rogers *(The Senate),* and of R. Luce and T. V. Smith, cited elsewhere. Many case studies, also cited in this note, provide useful material; *cf.* the writings of Saloma, Wildavsky, *et al.*

On the problems of scientists in government and organizations and their ideas, see the files of *Science* magazine of the past few years and the special issue of the *American Behavioral Scientist,* 6 (December 1962) called "Science, Scientists and Society"; A. de Grazia, "The Scientific Reception System and Dr. Velikovsky," *ABS,* Sept., 1963, and the special May, 1964 issue of the *American Behavioral Scientist* entitled "The Federal Government in Behavioral Science," W. Ellis, ed. Other works on these and related subjects include: A. de Grazia, "The Science and Values of Administration," *Administrative Science Quarterly,* 5, Part I (December 1960), 363-98 and Part II (March 1961), 557-83; T. S. Kuhn, *The Structure of Scientific Revolutions* (1962); C. Stover and L. Hatch, eds., *Science and Democratic Government: Report of a Conference on the Role and Responsibilities of Science Executives in the Federal Service* (Santa Barbara, Calif.: Center for the Study of Democratic Institutions, 1963); R. Gilpin and C. Wright, eds., *Scientists and National Policy-Making* (1964); C. W. Taylor and F. Barron, eds., *Scientific Creativity: Its Recognition and Development* (1963); and J. Bronowski, *Science and Human Values* (1965).

The study of officials quoted extensively in the text is W. L. Warner, Paul Van Riper, *et al., The American Federal Executive* (1963). Permission to quote by The Yale University Press is acknowledged, with thanks. See also H. A. Simon, *Administrative Behavior* (1947); F. A. von Hayak, *Road to Serfdom* (1944); and D. Waldo, *The Administrative State* (1948).

A large amount of material has appeared on apportionment, mostly from an equal-population-district point of view. One can consult C. E. Baker, *The Politics of Reapportionment in Washington* (1960); A. de Grazia, *Essay on Apportionment and Representative Government* (1963); W. C. Havard and L. P. Beth, *The Politics of Mis-Representation* (Florida) (1962); M. E. Jewell, *et al., The Politics of Reapportionment* (1962); D. Lamb, *et al., Apportionment and Representative Institutions, the Michigan Experience* (1963); J. E. Larson, *Reapportionment and the Courts* (1962); G. Steiner and S. Gove, *Legislative Politics in Illinois* (1960); the special section on apportionment reform in *State Government* (Spring 1965); A. L. Clem, "Measuring Legislative Malapportionment: In Search of a Better Yardstick," *Midwest Journal of Political Science*, 7 (May 1963), 125-44; C. C. Harris, Jr., "A Scientific Method of Districting," *Behavioral Science*, 9 (July 1964), 219-25; H. R. Alker, Jr., and B. M. Russett, "On Measuring Inequality," *Behavioral Science*, 9 (July 1964), 207-18; G. Schubert and C. Press, "Measuring Malapportionment," *American Political Science Review*, 58 (June 1964), 302-27 and (December 1964), 966-70; J. B. Weaver and S. W. Hess, "A Procedure for Nonpartisan Districting: Development of Computer Techniques," *Yale Law Journal*, 73 (No. 2, 1963), 288-308; E. Forrest, "Apportionment by Computer," *American Behavioral Scientist*, 8 (December 1964), 23, 35; J. S. Appel, "A Note Concerning Apportionment by Computer," *American Behavioral Scientist*, 8 (March 1965), 36; S. S. Nagel, "Simplified Computer Redistricting," University of Illinois (Mimeographed, 1965); National Municipal League, *Court Decisions on Legislative Apportionment*, 15 vols. (1962-65); A. L. Goldberg, "The Statistics of Malapportionment," *Yale Law Journal* (November 1962), 90-106; H. D. Hamilton, *Legislative Apportionment: Key to Power* (1964); A. Hacker, *Congressional Districting: The Issue of Equal Representation* (1963); and J. B. Weinstein, "The Effect of the Federal Reapportionment Decisions on Counties and Other Forms of Municipal Government," *Columbia Law Review*, 65 (January 1965), 21-54.

On Negro politics and racial voting: relevant works include P. Lewinson, *Race, Class, and Party: A History of Negro Suffrage and White Politics in the South* (1932, new edition 1965); A. de Grazia, "The Limits of External Leadership Over a Minority Electorate," *Public Opinion Q.*, 20 (Spring 1956), 113-28; W. Brink and L. Harris, *The Negro Revolution in America* (1964); A. M. Rose, ed., "The Negro Protest," *The Annals* (January 1965), whole issue; D. R. Mathews and J. W. Prothro, "Negro

Voter Registration in the South," in A. P. Sindler, ed., *Change in the Contemporary South* (1963), 119-149 and "Southern Images of Political Parties: An Analysis of White and Negro Attitudes," *The Journal of Politics,* 26 (February 1964), 82-111; and A. Clubok, *et al.,* "The Manipulated Negro Vote: Preconditions and Consequences," *The Journal of Politics,* 26 (February 1964), 112-129.

The subject of socio-religion and politics is infrequently treated in the context of government by legislature, but can be approached via M. S. Stedman, Jr., *Religion and Politics in America* (1964); J. C. Bennett, *Christians and the State* (1958); L. E. Ebersole, *Church Lobbying in the Nation's Capital* (1951); P. H. Odegard, *Religion and Politics* (1960); R. R. Lord, *Communism and the Churches* (1960); L. Fuchs, *The Political Behavior of American Jews* (1956); L. S. Dawidowicz and L. J. Goldstein, *Politics in a Pluralist Democracy: Studies of Voting in the 1960 Election* (1963), which emphasizes the role of the religious and ethnic characteristics of voters; E. Raab, *Religious Conflict in America* (1964), which contains essays by S. M. Lipset, J. S. Coleman and others; and J. M. Yinger, *Sociology Looks at Religion* (1963). The case study by F. J. Munger and R. F. Fenno, *National Politics in Federal Aid to Education* (1962), also contains much of interest.

Several works by authors who are exponents of the Executive Model are: J. M. Burns, *Congress on Trial: The Legislative Process and the Administrative State* (1949) and *The Deadlock of Democracy: Four-Party Politics in America* (1963); L. Brownlow, *The President and the Presidency* (1949); J. P. Harris, *The Advice and Consent of the Senate* (1953); the Supreme Court decision in the case of *United States v. Curtiss-Wright Export Corp.,* 299 U.S. 304 (1936); Commission on Organization of the Executive Branch of the Government (Hoover Commission), *Reports* (Washington, 1949 and 1953); President's Committee on Administrative Management (Brownlow Committee), *Report with Special Studies* (Washington 1937); Committee on Economic Development, *Improving Executive Management in the Federal Government* (1965); L. W. Koenig, *The Chief Executive* (1964); L. D. White, *Introduction to the Study of Public Administration* (1926 *et seq.*); J. P. Harris, *Congressional Control of Administration* (1964); D. M. Berman, *In Congress Assembled* (1964); J. S. Clark, *Congress* (1964), and ed., *Congressional Reform* (1965); E. P. Herring, *Public Administration and the*

Public Interest (1936). But a great many works cited elsewhere here represent the executive's perspectives.

For works which deal with the world as a constituency see J. L. Dunning, "The Kennedy Assassination as Viewed by Communist Media," *Journalism Quarterly*, 41 (Spring 1964), 163-69; B. C. Cohen, *The Press and Foreign Policy* (1963); D. D. Nimmo, *Newsgathering in Washington: A Study in Political Communication* (1964); and J. E. Pollard, *The President and the Press* (1947).

The Presidency during a crisis is viewed in C. P. Cotter and J. M. Smith, *Powers of the President During National Crises* (1961); E. R. May, ed., *The Ultimate Decision: The President as Commander in Chief* (1961); R. E. Neustadt, *Presidential Power: The Politics of Leadership* (1960); H. Feis, *Japan Subdued: The Atomic Bomb and the End of the War in the Pacific* (1961); R. C. Snyder and G. D. Paige, "The United States Decision to Resist Aggression in Korea: The Application of an Analytical Scheme," *Administrative Science Quarterly*, 3 (1958), 342-78; American Enterprise Association, *The Berlin Crisis;* and R. Wohlstetter, "Cuba and Pearl Harbor: Hindsight and Foresight," *Foreign Affairs*, 43 (July 1965), 691-707. Also of interest are J. K. Galbraith, *The Great Crash, 1929* (1961) and A. M. Schlesinger, Jr., *The Age of Roosevelt: The Crisis of the Old Order, 1919-1933* (1957) and *The Age of Roosevelt: The Coming of the New Deal* (1959).

The relationship of the Chief Executive and the Congress is discussed in many studies: R. Egger and J. P. Harris, *The President and Congress* (1963); N. W. Polsby, *Congress and the Presidency* (1964); C. P. Cotter and M. J. Smith, "Administrative Accountability: Reporting to Congress," *Western Political Quarterly*, 10 (1957) 405-15; H. N. Carroll, *The House of Representatives and Foreign Affairs* (1958); R. A. Dahl, *Congress and Foreign Policy* (1950); J. A. Robinson, *Congress and Foreign Policy-Making: A Study in Legislative Influence and Initiative* (1962); L. H. Chamberlain, *The President, Congress, and Legislation* (1946); C. S. Hyneman, *Bureaucracy in a Democracy* (1950) uses a republican model within the executive branch; E. P. Herring, *Presidential Leadership: The Political Relations of Congress and the Chief Executive* (1940); W. E. Rhode, *Committee Clearance of Administrative Decisions* (1959); E. M. Byrd, *Treaties and Executive Agreements in the United States* (The Hague: Nijhoff, 1960); Henry Hazlitt, *Instead of Dictatorship*

(1933); J. W. Anderson, *Eisenhower, Brownell and the Congress* (1964); J. L. Freeman, *The Political Process: Executive Bureau-Legislative Committee Relations* (1955); S. Scher, "Congressional Committee Members as Independent Agency Overseers: A Case Study," *American Political Science Review*, 54 (December 1960), 911-20; M. Kesselman, "Presidential Leadership in Congress on Foreign Policy," *Midwest Journal of Political Science*, 5 (August 1961), 284-89; R. H. Dawson, "Congressional Innovation and Intervention in Defense Policy: Legislative Authorization of Weapons Systems," *American Political Science Review*, 56 (March 1962), 42-57; E. Huzar, *The Purse and the Sword: Control of the Army by Congress through Military Appropriations* (1950); A. W. Macmahon, "Congressional Oversight of Administration: The Power of the Purse," *Political Science Quarterly*, 58 (Nos. 2 and 3, 1943), 161-190, 380-414 and also in R. L. Peabody and N. W. Polsby, *New Perspectives on the House of Representatives* (1963), 305-24; H. L. Nieburg, "The Eisenhower AEC and Congress: A Study in Executive-Legislative Relations," *Midwest Journal of Political Science*, 6 (May 1962), 115-48; H. P. Green and A. Rosenthal, *Government of the Atom: The Integration of Powers* (1963); E. S. Corwin, *The President, Office and Powers 1787-1957* (fourth revised edition, 1957); R. E. Neustadt, "Presidency and Legislation: The Growth of Central Clearance," *American Political Science Review*, 48 (September 1954), 641-71 and "Presidency and Legislation: Planning the President's Program," *American Political Science Review*, 49 (December 1955), 980-1021; W. E. Binkley, *President and Congress* (1947); C. Rossiter, *The American Presidency* (1956); R. F. Fenno, *The President's Cabinet* (1959); and S. Horn, *The Cabinet and Congress* (1960).

Among the few works that can be cited which examine trends in governmental intervention in the lives of the people: The President's Committee on Recent Social Trends, *Recent Social Trends* (1933); A. de Grazia and T. Gurr, *American Welfare* (1960), and in *Hearings*, USC, HR, CEd and Labor, Subcomm. on Poverty, HR10400, 1964, Pt. III, 1276-99; W. B. Boyer, "Policy Making by Government Agencies," *Midwest Journal of Political Science* (August 1960); and U.S. Sen., Comm. on Gov. Operations, *Organization of Federal Executive Departments and Agencies* (continuous); Max Lerner, *America as a Civilization* (1957); F. Dewhurst *et al.*, *America's Needs and Resources* (1955).

On the technical equipment of Congress to carry on its work see: U.S. Congress, Joint Committee on Organization of the Congress, *Organization of Congress*, Senate Report 2022 (79 Cong., 2 Sess., 1946); U.S. Senate, Committee on Rules and Administration, Subcommittee on Standing Rules of the Senate, *Hearing, June 16, 1961, on Senate Resolution 10 and Senate Resolution 14, Proposed Amendments to the Reorganization Act of 1946* (Washington, 1961); E. Griffith, *Congress: Its Contemporary Role* (1961); T. Taylor, *Grand Inquest* (1954), a critical study of Congressional investigations; R. Heller, *Strengthening the Congress* (1945); J. A. Robinson, *The House Rules Committee* (1963); G. Goodwin, Jr., "Subcommittees: The Miniature Legislatures of Congress," *American Political Science Review,* 56 (1962), 596-604; W. H. Riker, "The Paradox of Voting and Congressional Rules for Voting on Amendments," *American Political Science Review,* 52 (1958), 349-66; I. Hinderaker, "From the 86th to the 87th Congress: Controversy over 'Majority Rule,'" *American Government Annual, 1961-1962* (1961); N. A. Masters, "Committee Assignments in the House of Representatives," *American Political Science Review,* 55 (1961), 345-57; R. L. Peabody, "The Enlarged Committee on Rules," in R. L. Peabody and N. W. Polsby, *New Perspectives on the House of Representatives* (1963), 129-64; G. A. Schubert, Jr., "The Twenty-One Day Rule: The Politics of Legislative Procedure," *Political Science,* 5 (1953), 16-29; K. Kofmehl, *Professional Staffs of Congress* (1962); A. C. McCown, *The Congressional Conference Committee* (1927); G. Y. Steiner, *The Congressional Conference Committee: Seventieth to Eightieth Congress* (1951); J. S. Clark, *Congress: The Sapless Branch* (1964) and ed., *Congressional Reform: Problems and Prospects* (1965); and F. L. Burdette, *Filibustering in the Senate* (1940); J. Cochrane, "Partisan Aspects of Congressional Committee staffing," *Western Political Quarterly,* 17 (June 1964), 338-48; E. Kefauver and J. Levin, *A 20th Century Congress* (1947); L. W. Milbrath, *The Washington Lobbyists* (1963); H. H. Lowell and S. Hofheimer, "The Legislators' Source of Expert Information," *Public Opinion Quarterly,* 18 (Fall 1954), 300; R. K. Huitt, "The Congressional Committee," *American Political Science Review,* 48 (June 1954), 340-65; Congressional Quarterly Service, *Congressional Reform* (April 1964); W. Buchanan, *et al.,* "The Legislator as Specialist," *Western Political Quarterly,* 13 (September 1960), 636-51; F. M. Riddick, *The United States Congress: Organization and*

Procedure (1949); N. Meller, "The Policy Position of [State] Legislative Service Agencies," *Western Political Quarterly,* 5 (March 1952); M. M. Kampelman, "The Legislative Bureaucracy: Its Response to Political Change, 1953," *Journal of Politics,* 16 (August 1954), 539-50; T. F. Broden, Jr., "Congressional Committee Reports: Their Role and History," *Notre Dame Lawyer,* 33 (1958), 209-38; C. D. Jones, *Party and Policy-Making; The House Republican Policy Committee* (1965); and D. H. Riddle, *The Truman Committee: A Study in Congressional Responsibility* (1964).

The subject of Congressional leadership or the oligarchy is within the scope of the following works: R. K. Huitt, "Democratic Party Leadership in the Senate," *American Political Science Review,* 55 (June 1961), 333-44; L. A. Froman, Jr., and R. B. Ripley, "Conditions for Party Leadership: The Case of the House Democrats," *American Political Science Review,* 59 (March 1965), 52-63; H. B. Fuller, *The Speakers of the House* (1909); J. S. Clark, *The Senate Establishment* (1963); P. D. Hasbrouck, *Party Government in the House of Representatives* (1927); R. B. Ripley, "The Party Whip Organizations in the United States House of Representatives," *American Political Science Review,* 58 (September 1964), 561-76; N. W. Polsby, "Two Strategies of Influence: Choosing a Majority Leader, 1962," in R. L. Peabody and N. W. Polsby, eds., *New Perspectives on the House of Representatives* (1963), 237-70; M. C. Cummings, Jr., and R. L. Peabody, "The Decision to Enlarge the Committee on Rules: An Analysis of the 1961 Vote," in Peabody and Polsby cited above, 167-194; D. Marvick, *Political Decision-Makers* (1961); G. R. Brown, *The Leadership of Congress* (1922); D. MacRae, "Roll Call Votes and Leadership," *Public Opinion Quarterly* (Fall 1956); and B. Bolles, *Tyrant from Illinois: Uncle Joe Cannon's Experiment with Personal Power* (1951). A forthcoming study by R. E. Wolfinger and Joan Heifetz (1965) in the *American Political Science Review* is valuable; it is called "Safe Seats, Seniority, and Power in Congress."

When considering theories and ideas related to Congressional leadership, the concepts and methods employed in the following works may prove to be of value: R. A. Dahl, "The Concept of Power," *Behavioral Science,* 2 (July 1957), 201-215; D. MacRae, Jr., and H. D. Price, "Scale Positions and 'Power' in the Senate," *Behavioral Science,* 4 (July 1959), 212-18; J. G. March, "An Introduction to the Theory and Measurement of Influence,"

American Political Science Review, 49 (June 1955), 431-51 and "Measurement Concepts in the Theory of Influence," *The Journal of Politics,* 19 (1957), 202-26; H. Goldhamer and E. A. Shils, "Types of Power and Status," *The American Journal of Sociology,* 45 (September 1939), 171-82; F. L. Neuman, "Approaches to the Study of Political Power," *Political Science Quarterly,* 65 (June 1950), 161-80; W. H. Riker, *The Theory of Political Coalitions* (1962); Anthony Downs, *An Economic Theory of Democracy* (1957); C. E. Merriam, *Political Power* (1934); H. D. Lasswell, *Psychopathology and Politics* (1930), *Politics: Who Gets What, When, How* (1936), and *Power and Personality* (1948); and H. D. Lasswell and A. Kaplan, *Power and Society: A Framework for Political Inquiry* (1950).

The budgetary process is an area of growing interest to behavioral scientists: M. L. Weidenbaum, "Federal Budgeting: The Choice of Government Programs," in *Congress and the Federal Budget* (American Enterprise Institute for Public Policy Research: Washington, 1965); J. S. Saloma III, "The Responsible Use of Power: A Critical Analysis of the Congressional Budget Process," in *Congress and the Federal Budget* cited above; O. A. Davis, M. A. H. Dempster, and A. Wildavsky, *On the Process of Budgeting: An Empirical Study of Congressional Appropriation* (unpublished paper, Carnegie Institute of Technology, Graduate School of Industrial Administration); A. Wildavsky, "Political Implications of Budgetary Reform," *Public Administration Review,* 21 (Autumn 1961) and *The Politics of the Budgetary Process* (1964); R. F. Fenno, Jr., "The House Appropriations Committee as a Political System: The Problem of Integration," *American Political Science Review,* 56 (June 1962), 310-24; B. K. Gordon, "The Military Budget: Congressional Phase," *Journal of Politics,* 23 (November 1961), 689-710; J. Burkhead, *Government Budgeting* (1956); E. Huzar, *The Purse and the Sword: Control of the Army by Congress through Military Appropriations* (1950); A. Smithies, *The Budgetary Process in the United States* (1955); R. A. Wallace, *Congressional Control of Federal Spending* (1960); and L. Wilmerding, Jr., *The Spending Power: A History of the Efforts of Congress to Control Expenditures* (1943). Also consult the hearings before the Subcommittee on National Policy Machinery of the Senate Committee on Government Operations, "Organizing for National Security," Part 8, "The Budget and the Policy Process" (Washington, 1961); the Commission on the Organization of the

Executive Branch of the Government (Second Hoover Commis-
sion, 1955), "Budget and Accounting" (1955); and R. K. Huitt,
"Congressional Organization and Operations on the Field of
Money and Credit" in the Commission on Money and Credit,
Fiscal and Debt Management Policies (1963), a review of the
working of Congress on financial matters.

A valuable source of information and understanding of the
Congressional system is the legislative case study: S. K. Bailey,
*Congress Makes a Law: The Story Behind the Employment Act
of 1946* (1950); F. W. Riggs, *Pressures on Congress: A Study of
the Repeal of Chinese Exclusion* (1950); T. L. McDonald, *The
Wagner Housing Act: A Case Study of the Legislative Process*
(1957); D. M. Berman, *A Bill Becomes a Law: The Civil Rights
Act of 1960* (1962); A. K. McAdams, *Power and Politics in Labor
Legislation* (1964), a case study of the development and passage
of the Landrum-Griffin Act of 1964; R. A. Bauer, I. De Sola Pool,
and L. A. Dexter, *American Business and Public Policy: The
Politics of Foreign Trade* (1963), a study of the politics of for-
eign trade from the renewal of the Reciprocal Trade Act of 1953
to the passage of Kennedy's Trade Expansion Act; M. E. Ridge-
way, *The Missouri Basin's Pick-Sloan Plan: A Case Study in
Congressional Policy Determination* (1955); J. A. Robinson, *The
Monroney Resolution: Congressional Initiative in Foreign Policy*
(1959); H. Stein, "The Foreign Service Act of 1946," in H.
Stein, ed., *Public Administration and Policy Development: A
Case Book* (1952), 661-737; W. R. MacKaye, *A New Coalition
Takes Control: The House Rules Committee Fight of 1961*
(1963); Congressional Quarterly Service, *Revolution in Civil
Rights* (1965), a Congressional history of the 1964 Civil Rights
Act with background material on the acts of 1957 and 1960;
C. Zinn, *How Our Laws are Made* (Washington, 1956); and
Congressional Quarterly Service, *The Trade Expansion Act of
1962* (1962).

The relevant literature on the Supreme Court can barely be
sampled here: R. G. McClosky, ed., *Essays in Constitutional Law*
(1957); C. H. Pritchett, *Congress Versus the Supreme Court,
1957-1960* (1961) and *The Roosevelt Court: A Study in Judicial
Politics, 1937-1947* (1948); W. F. Murphy, *Congress and the
Court: A Case Study in the American Political Process* (1962);
C. S. Hyneman, *The Supreme Court on Trial* (1963); A. F.
Westin, *The Anatomy of a Constitutional Law Case: Youngstown
Sheet and Tube Co. v. Sawyer, the Steel Seizure Decision*

(1958); C. Rossiter, *The Supreme Court and the Commander-in-Chief* (1951); G. A. Schubert, Jr., *The Presidency in the Courts* (1957); F. V. Cahill, *Judicial Legislation: A Study of American Legal Theory* (1952); E. S. Corwin, *The Doctrine of Judicial Review* (1914); C. G. Haines, *The American Doctrine of Judicial Supremacy* (1914); W. F. Murphy and C. H. Pritchett, *Courts, Judges, and Politics: An Introduction to the Judicial Process* (1961); V. Rosenblum, *Law as a Political Instrument* (1955); J. R. Schmidhauser, *The Supreme Court: Its Politics, Personalities, and Procedures* (1960); G. A. Schubert, Jr., *Constitutional Politics: the Political Behavior of Supreme Court Justices and the Constitutional Policies That They Make* (1960), *Quantitative Analysis of Judicial Behavior* (1959), and as ed., *Judicial Decision Making* (1963), "Bibliographic Essay: Behavioral Research in Public Law," *American Political Science Review*, 57 (June 1963), 433-45; "A Psychometric Model of the Supreme Court," *American Behavioral Scientist*, 5 (November 1961), 14-18, and "The 1960 Term of the Supreme Court: A Psychological Analysis," *American Political Science Review*, 56 (March 1962), 90-107; L. Loevinger, *et al.*, "Jurimetrics," *Law and Contemporary Problems*, 28 (Winter 1963), 1-270, a symposium; T. A. Cowan, "Decision Theory in Law, Science and Technology," *Rutgers Law Review* 17 (Spring 1963), 499-530; J. B. Grossman, "Role Playing and the Analysis of Judicial Behavior: The Case of Mr. Justice Frankfurter," *Journal of Public Law*, 11 (1962), 285-309; R. Arens and H. D. Lasswell, *In Defense of Public Order: The Emerging Field of Sanction Law* (1961); H. D. Lasswell, "The Impact of Psychiatry Upon Jurisprudence," *Ohio State Law Journal*, 21 (Winter 1960), 17-27, and "Interplay of Economic, Political and Social Criteria in Legal Policy," *Vanderbilt Law Review*, 14 (March 1961), 451-71; R. C. Lawlor, "What Computers Can Do: Analysis and Prediction of Judicial Decisions," *American Bar Association Journal*, 49 (April 1963), 337-44, reviews the current status of studies and applies the method to right-to-counsel cases; A. S. Miller and R. F. Howell, "The Myth of Neutrality in Constitutional Adjudication," *University of Chicago Law Review*, 27 (Summer 1960), 661-95; S. S. Ulmer, "Analysis of Behavior Patterns in the United States Supreme Court," *Journal of Politics*, 22 (November 1960), 629-53 and "Scaling Judicial Cases: A Methodological Note," *American Behavioral Scientist*, 4 (April 1961), 31-34; C. L. Ruttenberg, ed., "Frontiers of Legal Research," special issue of the *American Behavioral Scientist*, 7 (December 1963), 1-55; and

"Congressional Reversal of Supreme Court Decisions: 1945-1957," *Harvard Law Review*, 71 (May 1958), 1324-37. In addition one should examine some of the brilliant dissenting opinions in the recent apportionment cases: *Baker v. Carr*, 369 U.S. 186 (1962) dissent of Mr. Justice Frankfurter, joined by Mr. Justice Harlan, 266-330 and dissent of Mr. Justice Harlan whom Mr. Justice Frankfurter joined, 330-48; *Wesberry v. Sanders*, 376 U.S. 1, 20 (1964), involving Congressional districting by the states; and *Reynolds v. Sims*, 377 U.S. 533 (1964), involving the apportionment of state legislative seats.

On the history of Congress see: G. B. Galloway, *History of the House of Representatives* (1961); M. Farrand, *The Framing of the Constitution of the United States* (1913); R. V. Harlow, *The History of Legislative Methods Before 1825* (1917); D. A. S. Alexander, *History and Procedure of the House of Representatives* (1916); G. H. Haynes, *The Senate of the United States* (1938); E. J. Eberling, *Congressional Investigations: A Study of the Origin and Development of the Power of Congress to Investigate and Punish for Contempt* (1928); L. G. McConachie, *Congressional Committees: A Study of the Origin and Development of our National and Local Legislative Methods* (1898); M. N. McGeary, *The Development of Congressional Investigative Power* (1940); E. C. Mason, *The Veto Power: Its Origin, Development, and Function in the Government of the United States, 1789-1889* (1890); A. N. Holcombe, *Our More Perfect Union: From Eighteenth Century Principles to Twentieth Century Practice* (1950); A. de Grazia, *Public and Republic: Political Representation in America* (1951); and W. W. Crosskey, *Politics and the Constitution in the History of the United States* (1953).

For the history of the legislative idea in the world, the quotations at the beginning of each chapter and section of the book represent the kinds of material available. They do not of course include the valuable histories of special periods of a single legislature. *Cf.* the *Revue Francaise de Science Politique* (Paris, 9 March 1959), entitled "La Constitution de la Cinquième Republique," which is also the title of a special printing of this issue in book form (Paris, 1959). One should also see P. Williams and M. Harrison *De Gaulle's Republic* (London, 2nd ed., 1961) and D. W. S. Lidderdale, *The Parliament of France* (London, 1951). For the British legislature see *Parliamentary Reform, 1933-1958*, published by the Hansard Society (London, 1959); Sir Ivor Jennings, *Parliament* (1960); K. Mackenzie, *The English Parliament* (1950); R. Young, *The British Parliament*

(1962); and H. Laski, *Parliamentary Government in England* (1938). Among the publications of the Inter-Parliamentary Union, one should note *Parliaments: A Comparative Study on the Structure and Functioning of Representative Institutions in Forty-One Countries* (1961). In addition, the following works on politics deserve to be studied: R. Michels, *Political Parties* (1949); M. Duverger, *Political Parties* (1954); R. McKenzie, *British Political Parties* (1955); R. Rose, *Politics in England* (1964); S. M. Lipset, *Political Man: The Social Bases of Politics* (1960); and K. C. Wheare, *Legislatures* (1963) and *Modern Constitutions* (1951). Statistical interrelations of types of legislatures and social conditions are carried in the remarkable work of A. S. Banks and R. B. Textor, called *A Cross-Polity Survey* (1963).

Because several suggestions have been made regarding the use of modern computer techniques to aid Congress, it may be well to cite certain titles: C. P. Bourne, *Methods of Information Handling* (1963); J. Becker, *Introduction to Information Storage and Retrieval: Tools, Elements, Theories* (1963); F. P. Brooks, Jr., *Automatic Data Processing* (1963); H. Borko, ed., *Computer Applications in the Behavioral Sciences* (1962); K. Janda, *Data Processing: Applications to Political Research* (1965); T. Gurr and H. Panofsky, eds., "Information Retrieval in the Social Sciences: Problems, Programs, and Proposals," a special issue of the *American Behavioral Scientist*, 7 (June 1964), 1-70; A. de Grazia, "The Universal Reference System," *American Behavioral Scientist*, 8 (April 1965), 3-14; C. L. Ruttenberg, "Report on Data Archives in the Social Sciences," *American Behavioral Scientist*, 8 (April 1965), 33-4; the special issue "Social Research with the Computer," *American Behavioral Scientist*, 8 (May 1965), 1-44; The Council on Library Resources, Inc., *Automation and the Library of Congress* (Washington, 1963); B. E. Markuson, ed., *Libraries and Automation: Proceedings of the Conference on Libraries and Automation* (Washington, 1964); L. E. Allen, *Automatic Retrieval of Legal Literature: Why and How* (1962); J. Diebold, "The Application of Information Technology," *The Annals*, 340 (March 1962), 38-45; US Sen. Comm. on Gov. Operations, 86th Cong., 2nd Sess., *Documentation, Indexing, and Retrieval of Scientific Information* (1960). On current, quantifiable models, there may be specially cited H. Guetzkow, ed. *Simulation in Social Science* (1962); the ABS May 1965 issue (cited above); and K. Deutsch, "On Communication Models in the Social Sciences," *Pub. Opin. Q.*, 16 (1952), 360.

INDEX

ACKNOWLEDGMENTS

The author acknowledges with thanks the permissions granted to quote passages from Ezra Pound, *The Classic Anthology Defined by Confucius*, Cambridge, Mass.: Harvard University Press, Copyright 1954, by the President and Fellows of Harvard College; and W. Lloyd Warner, Paul P. Van Riper, Norman H. Martin, and Orvis F. Collins, *The American Federal Executive*, Yale University Press, Copyright 1964 by Yale University. He also thanks Columbia University for permission to reproduce the chart appearing on pages 81 and 82, taken from Lawrence Chamberlain's *The President, Congress and Legislation*, Columbia University Press, Copyright 1946.

70
71
72
74
75
76
77
79
81
83
85
88